EVERY LITTLE THING
GONNA BE ALRIGHT

D1069312

EVERY LITTLE THING GONNA BE ALRIGHT

THE Bob Marley READER

Edited by

Hank Bordowitz

DA CAPO PRESS
A Member of the Perseus Books Group

A list of credits for individual articles appears on page 299

Cataloging-in-Publication data for this book is available from the Library of Congress

First Da Capo Press edition 2004
ISBN 0–306–81340–8

Published by Da Capo Press
A Member of the Perseus Books Group
http://www.dacapopress.com

Da Capo Press books are available at special discounts for bulk purchases in the U.S. by corporations, institutions, and other organizations. For more information, please contact the Special
Markets Department at the Perseus Books Group, 11 Cambridge Center, Cambridge, MA
02142, or call (800) 255–1514 or (617) 252–5298, or e-mail special.markets@perseusbooks.com.

2 3 4 5 6 7 8 9——07 06 05 04

CONTENTS

Give Thanks and Praises: Acknowledgments   xi
Marley: Cultural Icon   xiii
Foreword by Roger Steffens   xvii

I

WAKE UP AND LIVE
The Life and Times of Robert Nesta Marley   I

**1 Waiting in Vain: Oral History/Past Tense,
1962–1972**   2

Remembering Bob Marley   3
Rita Marley, *Essence*, February 1995

Bob Marley at Studio One   6
Hank Bordowitz, previously unpublished

Bob Marley: The Story Behind *Chances Are*   12
Atlantic Records Biography, October 1981

2 Stir It Up: International Attention, 1972–1976   18

I Was a Wailers   19
**Lee Jaffe, excerpt from *One Love, Life with Bob Marley and
the Wailers* (W. W. Norton)**

Bob Marley Is the Jagger of Reggae   36
Patrick Carr, *The Village Voice*, June 30, 1975

Musicmakers: Bob Marley and the Wailers   43
Vernon Gibbs, *Essence*, January 1976

Innocents in Babylon: A Search for Jamaica Featuring   46
Bob Marley and a Cast of Thousands
Lester Bangs, *Creem Magazine*, June and July 1976

3   Top Rankin': The First Great "Third
    World" Star, 1976-1981   89
    The Rasta Prophet of Reggae Music Speaks   90
    Tom Terrell, MCY.com, January 2001

    The Reggae Way to "Salvation"   96
    J. Bradshaw, *New York Times Magazine*, August 14, 1977

    Bob Marley: Movement of Jah People   110
    Vivien Goldman, *Sounds*, May 28, 1977

    Tuff Gong: Bob Marley's Unsung Story   123
    Carol Cooper, *The Village Voice*, September 10, 1980

4   Blackman Redemption: The Death of Bob
    Marley and His "Second Coming," 1981-2002   136
    The Chapel of Love: Bob Marley's Last Resting Place   137
    Chris Salewicz, *The Face*, June 1983

    So Much Things to Say: The Journey of Bob Marley   144
    Isaac Fergusson, *The Village Voice*, May 18, 1982

    One Love   160
    Robert Palmer, *Rolling Stone*, February 24, 1994

    Chanting Down Babylon: The CIA & the Death of   171
    Bob Marley
    Alex Constantine, *High Times*, February 2002

    Bob Marley's Star Finally Rises in Jamaica   176
    Howard Campbell, *The Michigan Citizen*, February 27–March 4, 2000

5 Judge Not: The Marley Estate and
   Other Legalities, 1982–2004   180

   Marley's Ghost in Babylon: A $30 Million Wrangle   181
   over a Tangled Estate
   Jerry Adler with Howard Manly, *Newsweek*, April 8, 1991

   Talkin' Over: Marley Estate Case Ends; Island Logic,   184
   Family Can Purchase Assets
   Maureen Sheridan, *Billboard*, December 21, 1991

   Let's Get Together and Deal All Right   187
   Kirk Semple, *Miami New Times* (Florida), March 18, 1992

   Early Wailers: Fussing & Fighting; Ska Compilation   193
   Generates Intrigue
   Don Jeffrey, *Billboard*, June 18, 1994

   Marley Deal Prompts Lawsuit; Producer Sues Family,   197
   Universal
   Eileen Fitzpatrick, *Billboard*, June 28, 1997

II

MUSIC GONNA TEACH THEM A LESSON
The Meaning of Bob Marley   199

1 Zion Train: Religion, Rasta, and Revelation   200

   Bob Marley—Rastaman, Reggae Musician   201
   Rose Blount, *Black Book Bulletin*

   Bob Marley Live: Reggae, Rasta, and Jamaica Fourteen   205
   Years after Marley's Death
   Mark Jacobson, *Natural History*, November 1995

2 Babylon System: Politics in Jamaica and Beyond 216

Reggae and the Revolutionary Faith . . . The Role of 217
Bob Marley
Michael Manley, *The Rising Sun* (People's National Party
newspaper), May 1982

Bob Marley in Zimbabwe: The Untold Story 225
Adapted by Ree Ngwenya from *Bob Marley: Songs of Freedom*
by Adrian Boot and Chris Salewicz, Zimbabwe Standard/African
News Service, June 12, 2001

3 Children Playing in the Street:
Bob Marley, Family Man 231

Marley Boys Set to Popularize Reggae 232
Anya McCoy, *Variety*, June 8, 1998

Only Natural: The Marleys Carry on Their Father's 234
Mission—As They See It
Celeste Fraser Delgado, *Miami New Times* (Florida),
May 2, 2002

Cedella Marley Launches a Distinctive Line of 236
Customized Denim and Leather Reminiscent of
Her Father's Rude Boy Style
Tuff Gong press release, 2001

4 So Much Trouble in the World Today:
"Third World" Hero 239

Redemption Day 240
Alice Walker, *Mother Jones*, December 1986

Marley: Tale of the Tuff Gong (excerpt) 245
Written by Charles Hall (from a treatment by Mort Todd);
Art: pencils by Gene Colan, painted by Tennyson Smith,
lettering by John Costanza; Marvel Comics, September 1994

5 Work: Recording Bob Marley   254

Bob Marley: In the Studio with the Wailers   255
Richard Williams, *Melody Maker*, June 23, 1973

Chris Blackwell: An Interview with the Founding Father   259
of the Reggae Music Industry
Timothy White, *Billboard*, July 13, 1991

6 Wailing: The Musicians He Left Behind   271

A Good Smoke with Peter Tosh   272
Stephen Davis, *Oui*, 1979

Bunny Wailer, Reggae Survivor: Last of Wailers Returns   279
to Reggae Road
Mitch Potter, *The Toronto Star*, August 24, 1990

Still Wailing; Aston "Family Man" Barrett of the   285
Wailers Is Keeping a Reggae Tradition Alive
Joshua Green, *Denver Westword*, February 19, 1998

The Wailers' Al Anderson   291
Klaus Ludes, *Classical Reggae Interviews*, May 29, 1998

The Wailers' Earl "Wia" Lindo   294
Klaus Ludes, *Classical Reggae Interviews*, May 29, 1998

Wailers Keep Spreading Marley's Message   296
Craig MacInnes, *Toronto Star*, February 20, 1987

Credits   299
Index   303

GIVE THANKS AND PRAISES: ACKNOWLEDGMENTS

Ben Schafer, my editor at Da Capo and one of the most erudite people dealing with words on music that I know.

James Fitzgerald, as always—the entertainment writer's agent par excellence. I'm lucky to have him in my corner.

The cast and crew at the Suffern Free Public Library who went above and beyond on this project. Excelsior!

Nancy Jeffries and Tori Johnson at Bob Marley Music.

The minions of the Lincoln Center Library for Music and the Performing Arts, home of the most astounding collection of information about music that there is.

The good folks at the Schomburg Center, the heart of the modern Harlem renaissance.

Melissa Barlow, the document-sharing supervisor at the Perry Castañeda Library at the University of Texas in Austin.

Larry Stephan and Jon Moorehead for some ideas on how to make the book "more commercial."

Stephen Davis, Roger Stephens, Molly Kleinman, Barbara Grieninger, Eric Rubenstein, CC Smith, Martin Paul, Jerome Rankine, Jim DeRogatis, Greg Kot, Mike Mullis, Jonathan Daniel, Ted Cowan, Daniel Nelson, Barney Hoskyns, Zoe Gemelli, "Ras" Roger

Acknowledgments

Steffens, Barbara Slavin, Linda Verigan, Charlie Koones, Klaus Ludes, Robert Matheu, Debra Weydert, Patti Conte, Paula Balzer, Dave Marsh, Sasha Carr, Patrick Carr, Jennifer Snow, Jim Mullin, Danielle Robinson, Ginny Lohle, Gwen Mitchell, Steve Bloom, Roberto Rionda, Julian Anderson, and Katherine Cluverious for help in the arduous rights process.

MARLEY:
CULTURAL ICON

Throughout Africa, the Caribbean, London, America, and among people of all races, the image of Bob Marley has become fraught with deeper meanings than just that of a musician who put his spiritual and political beliefs into hypnotic, rhythmic, direct, hard-hitting songs. He has turned into a touchstone of the possibilities inherent in the "third world," the developing nations of the world.

Part of what made him an icon was the high-profile nature of his career. He moved anyone who enjoyed good, soulful music, often in spite of the message rather than because of it. He became a one-man marketing force for a genre of music once heard only in the ghettos of Trenchtown, Brixton, Brooklyn Heights, in Jamaica, and where Jamaican expatriates gathered.

Another factor of his status could have to do with his tragic death from cancer at thirty-six years old, at the pinnacle of his career. He is a musical and cultural martyr who suffered for the sins of his audience, a Jesus (or Selassie) figure for the twenty-first century.

Part of the appeal may well have centered in the ever-present spliff. It is not coincidental that the pinnacle of Marley's career came at the height of marijuana's worldwide popularity as a cultural aperitif. For Marley, it was a sacrament. For many of his fans, it was fun.

Marley's steadfast faith also plays a part in this. While he always considered himself simply a follower and messenger of Rastafarianism, to many he became the religion's high priest, the person that fellow Rastas looked to for insight, information, and inspiration. Even to non-Rastafarians, his faith and his resolute following of it served as a route back to the spiritual. Say what you will about Rastafarianism, the followers of the religion are among the most devout and highly spiritual people you will ever meet.

But mostly, through the power of his personality and his music, Bob Marley took an isolated, indigenous music and turned it into an international phenomenon. He took reggae, with its "one-drop" off beat, and brought it to the attention of the world through his own recordings and concerts, as well through hit cover versions by artists ranging from Texas middle-of-the-road crooner Johnny Nash (the first to bring Marley's music to a wider audience) to guitar god Eric Clapton.

Reggae as proselytized and promoted by Marley fueled entire movements in music and helped spawn English groups like Steel Pulse (one of Marley's favorites) and UB40, not to mention informing the music of groups like The Police, the whole 2-Tone ska movement in England that featured groups like the Specials and Madness, and the American ska movement that continues to this day with groups like No Doubt and The Mighty Mighty Bosstones. As much as contemporary folk singers call themselves "Woody's Children," these artists are Marley's Children.

That over twenty years after his death his music survives intact and is covered by artists ranging from Public Enemy to Aerosmith speaks to his enduring influence.

He is also one of the most written-about artists, especially in the years after his death. The fascination with his career, with the inherent spirituality of his music and his message, with his aggressively political stance even as he denied interest in "politricks"—"Me no sing politics, me sing freedom"—all speak to fans from the '70s through next week and beyond. It has led writers ranging from *The Color Purple* author Alice Walker to academics to nearly every music journalist to take their shot at figuring out what makes Marley a nearly sacred name in popular culture.

I hope this book manages to synthesize some of these viewpoints into a cohesive reading experience. My goal is to inform, entertain, and allow the reader to form an image of this remarkable man.

As such, the book takes a fragmented approach. It will deal with Marley as a political force, a spiritual force, a musical force, and most of all as a human force. By shining a light through the many facets of what Marley accomplished in his short life, his even shorter career, and even briefer time in the limelight, I hope to make the energy and puissance of his music and his accomplishments that much easier to grasp.

FOREWORD
Bob Marley: Artist of the Century

Music raises the soul of man even higher than the so-called external form of religion.... That is why in ancient times the greatest prophets were great musicians.

HAZRAT INAYAT KHAN,
THE MYSTICISM OF SOUND AND MUSIC

Without doubt, Bob Marley can now be recognized as the most important figure in twentieth-century music.

It's not just my opinion, but also, judging by all the mainstream accolades hurled Bob's way lately, the feeling of a great many others too. Prediction is the murky province of fools. But in the two decades that Bob Marley has been gone, it is clear that he is without question one of the most transcendent figures of the past hundred years. The ripples of his unparalleled achievements radiate outward through the river of his music into an ocean of politics, ethics, fashion, philosophy, and religion. His story is a timeless myth made manifest in this *iwah*, right before our disbelieving eyes.

"There will come a day when music and its philosophy will become the religion of humanity.... If there remains any magic it is music."

Unlike mere pop stars, Bob was a moral and religious figure as well as a major record seller internationally. To whom does one compare him? In a Sunday *New York Times* Arts and Leisure lead story, Stanley Crouch makes a compelling case for Louis Armstrong as the century's "unequaled performer," excelling not just in his instrumental inventiveness but in his vocal style as well, transforming the way music was made and listened to, and influencing performers of all stripes right down to this very day. But you don't see thousands of Maori and Tongans and Fijians gathering annually to pay honor to Louis Armstrong; you don't witness phalanxes of youth wandering the world sporting Louis Armstrong t-shirts. In fact, big as the Beatles were, you hardly see any Beatles shirts around anymore, except for those few featuring John Lennon's sorrow-inducing visage. Can you imagine an image of Elvis sewn onto the sleeve of an armed guerilla? When was the last time you saw a Michael Jackson flag or a Bob Dylan sarong or Madonna rolling papers? All of these exist in Marleyite forms, his iconography well nigh a new universal language, the symbol, as Jack Healey of Amnesty International continues to tell people, of freedom throughout the world.

"That music alone can be called real which comes from the harmony of the soul, its true source, and when it comes from there it must appeal to all souls ... Music alone can be the means by which the souls of races, nations and families, which are today so apart, may one day be united ... The more the musician is conscious of his mission in life, the greater service he can render to humanity."

Most of the pop stars thrown up over the past hundred years had entertainment as their first and foremost goal. Not so Marley. He was conscious of his role as the bringer of the message of Rastafari to the consciousness of the outside world. He cared nothing for earthly trappings, and loved nothing better than lying on Jah's cool earth at night watching the heavens revolve above him, rock stone as his pillow. He was here to call people to God.

So we can't compare Marley to other well-known musical figures. As for politics, he eschewed them, although his actions caused him to be perceived (and sometimes feared) as a profoundly radical political leader too. But his were the anti-politics of salvation through love and love alone, an unshakeable knowledge of the oneness of all humankind.

"Music is behind the working of the whole universe. Music is not only life's greatest object, but music is life itself.... Music being the most exalted of the arts, the work of the composer is no less than the work of a saint."

As for innovation, Marley was a multi-talented synthesizer of new ideas and rhythms, beginning with his precocious "Judge Not" solo debut at the dawn of the ska era, right up through his ongoing experiments with gospel, r&b, rock, folk, jazz, Latin, punk, scat, disco, and even (in unpublished form) bossa nova. Bob understood that reggae had the magnificent capriciousness to absorb all other influences and anchor them solidly to the drum and bass underpinning that is its essential element, the sweet seductive secret of its success.

Actually the real secret is that Marley's music is about something. It has value. Bob's art is life-transforming, answering our highest needs. It answers in a positive way the question that Carlos Santana says we must always ask before we begin any activity in life: How is this going to make the world a better place? Although Bob became a commercial artist, he was not making commercial art. His art transcended pop fluffery. Many are there who swear that his music literally saved their lives.

"The use of music for spiritual attainment and healing of the soul, which was prevalent in ancient times, is not found to the same extent now. Music

has been made a pastime, the means of forgetting God instead of realizing God. It is the use one makes of things which constitutes their fault or their virtue."

It is in the vast amount of adherents that Bob's work continues to lure, that we begin to sense his obvious immortality, even from this early point of focus. Elvis Presley may have been the biggest single rock icon of all time, but are his songs (none, incidentally, penned by him) really saying anything beyond mere pop cliche? Bob Dylan may be the most respected poet of his generation, but his often deliberately obfuscatory lyrics stand in the way of clear translation, and limit his appeal to the non–English speaking audience. Marley, on the other hand, refined his lyric art to a steely perfection, using the language of the streets to attain the stars. His words were so perfectly simple that they achieved eloquence. Today, his elemental stories can be related to and understood by people anywhere who suffer and love and long for salvation. In other words, just about every one of us.

Marley's ready embrace of herb, and the flaunting of his startling mane of locks that grew more ferocious as the '70s wound down, contributed to his image as a rebel for all reasons, treated like a deity among defiant youth and seasoned revolutionaries alike, who recognized him as one of their own, embracing him in Harare during Zimbabwe's independence, and sending him messages of solidarity from Peruvian jungles and Himalayan hideaways.

So it appears, at least to this writer, that Bob Marley has the clearest shot at being recognized as the Artist of the Twentieth Century, at least as far as music is concerned, and probably a lot more. I hereby predict with reckless confidence that hundreds of years into the future, Marley's melodies will be as prevalent as those of any songwriter who has ever lived.

"No Woman No Cry" will still wipe away the tears from a widow's face;

"Exodus" will still arouse the warrior; "Redemption Song" will still be a rallying cry for emancipation from all tyrannies, physical and spiritual;

"Waiting in Vain" will still seduce;

and "One Love" will be the international anthem of a coffee-colored humanity living in unity, in a world beyond borders, beyond beliefs, where everyone has learned at last to get together and feel all right.

"(Man) loves music more than anything else. Music is his nature; it has come from vibrations, and he himself is vibration ... There is nothing in this world that can help one spiritually more than music."

In his true heart of hearts, Bob Marley heard the harmony of the heavens, and shared that celestial sound with the god-seeker in each of us. Thus it is not surprising that the *New York Times*, seeking one video to epitomize the past century, preserved in a time capsule to be opened a thousand years hence, chose *Bob Marley Live at the Rainbow, London, 1977.* Or that the same "newspaper of record" called Marley "the most influential artist of the second half of the twentieth century."

We are all ennobled by our proximity to Marley and his art, his eternal songs of freedom.

—Roger Steffens

Roger Steffens is the founding editor of *The Beat* magazine, and edits its annual Bob Marley edition. He lectures internationally on the life of Bob Marley at venues such as the Smithsonian, the Rock and Roll Hall of Fame, universities, and clubs. Chairman of the Reggae Grammy Committee since its inception in 1985, he is the co-author of *Bob Marley: Spirit Dancer, Bob Marley and the Wailers: the Definitive Discography*, and *One Love: Life with Bob Marley and the Wailers*, and is author of *The World of Reggae Featuring Bob Marley: Treasures from Roger Steffens' Reggae Archives*, the catalog for his eight-month-long exhibit at the Queen Mary in 2001. As co-host of the award-winning *Reggae Beat* show on NPR's L.A. outlet, his first guest was Bob Marley in 1979. He has served as music consultant for several major Marley documentary films for PBS, VH1, and Britain's Channel Four, and co-produced the 12-disc JAD series *The Complete Bob Marley and the Wailers, 1967–1972.*

I

WAKE UP AND LIVE

The Life and Times of

Robert Nesta Marley

1

When the Wailers had their first hit, "Simmer Down" in 1964, the Anglo-centric Jamaican daily newspaper, *The Gleaner*, was more interested in covering the world's reaction to the Beatles and Jamaican popular success abroad (such as Millie Small, who scored a stateside hit in 1964 with "My Boy Lollipop") than any local recording act, no matter how in tune they were with *The Gleaner*'s coverage at that time. "Simmer Down" was an anti-"hooliganism" song, just as *The Gleaner* frequently decried the growth of hooliganism (and the rise in the use of ganja) at the time the single hit.

Therefore, pretty much anything about the Wailers during this period will have the benefit of hindsight. After all, without any on-the-spot, first-hand coverage of the events in Marley's life from 1962 until the early '70s, the only information in print comes from interviews and research conducted after the Wailers started making inroads into the international consciousness, largely courtesy of the Island Records media machine. This also gives some license to revisionist history and some *Rashomon* effects from people with different viewpoints on how the band came together and what caused members to leave. Notice, for example, how producer and DJ Coxsone Dodd conveniently forgets that Rita Anderson already had a daughter before she hooked up with Bob Marley. Or how even an ostensibly well researched bio puts Rita in the original Wailers line-up instead of Cherry Green.

Remembering Bob Marley

by Rita Marley
(Source: **Essence,** *February 1995)*

O N first impression, you wouldn't imagine Bob to be a show-business personality. He was quite reserved. I believe he had a lot of complexes, being the son of a White man. I would see him suffer a lot just trying to be himself. We met in the mid-sixties in Trench Town, Jamaica, when I was 18 and he was 19. 1 think he was attracted to me, in part, because I am dark, and also because I bear a close resemblance to his mother, Cedilla Booker. But at first I didn't like him, the seriousness about him, the standoffishness. Besides, every girl my age wanted a tall, dark-skinned boyfriend, so Peter Tosh was the one who originally caught my eye.

Then Bob and I started to sing together. He would be the one to work with my group, the Soulettes. He rehearsed us every day, and I liked the way he carried himself, his high level of consciousness. I had a little daughter, Sharon, and I thought to myself, *This man looks like he would be a good father*. I started to see he *was* the person I should like.

I had sympathy for Bob. He didn't know his father, his mother had moved to America, and he was living in a recording studio, sleeping on the floor. Life was rough for him. Remember that song that said, "Cold ground was my bed last night"? That was real for Bob. Over time I grew and grew in respect for him. It was a sisterly love. I said to myself, *Okay, Bob, I'm going to take care of you.* I took him food, bed linens. It was natural that we started loving each other.

I felt we were meant to be together. But in February 1966 his mother got a visa for him to join her in Delaware. She wanted a better life for him. He was very upset and said he wasn't going. Then he said the only way he would go is if "Rita marry to me, so I know she mine." It was crazy because we didn't have any money, didn't have anything. But my aunt said, "If you got love for each other, that's enough." So we got all "dolly-dooleyed" up, and we got married.

When Bob went to America, I wrote him every day. He was very sad. He would not eat. He had a job in housekeeping at a Delaware hotel. One day when he was vacuuming, the machine exploded and dust went everywhere. That was it. So after about eight months, he decided to come back to Jamaica, little Sharon and me. Deep down he always knew he was a singer and that he would not spend his life in America doing odd jobs.

Our daughter, Cedella, was born in August 1967, less than a year after he returned home. Bob gave her the pet name "Nice Time." It was inspired by his homecoming. You may know his song that says, "Long time we no have no nice time." Ziggy came in October 1968, Stephen in April 1972 and Stephanie in August 1974. Bob would take us driving, and we would jam together in the evening. We would sing and he would play his guitar. He was very serious about his music, always serious about it. It was the reality of his life, but also of the lives of millions. Like "Get Up, Stand Up." This was an encouragement to be strong, be faithful. "One love, one heart, let's get together and feel all right"—freedom fighters in Zimbabwe say that song got them going when they were seeking their independence from Britain.

One of the first times we performed in America, we were at Madison Square Garden in New York City opening for a major U.S. group. After we finished, everybody got up and left. Bob Marley outdid this popular American group. That was something—to see an American audience accept us. Another time we were in London, and where we were singing there was a pool in front of the stage. It was full of muddy water, but everybody jumped in just to get closer to us.

We worked hard. I remember being in the studio back in Jamaica, eight going on nine months pregnant, thinking, *I can't take this.* I just knew I was going to have this baby in the studio. But Bob said, "This album must finish." Sometimes when I was sleeping, he would shake me. "Listen to this," he would say. And he would play his guitar and sing and I would take down the lyrics.

Our harmony was tested when word would come that another woman had had a baby for him. At first I said to him, "Are you crazy? Is this something I'm going to have to live with?" But I asked God to give me the understanding, 'cause our love was more than for flesh or looks, it was something so deep. I found tolerance. I grew to love what he loved. Now I have a relationship with the children's mothers. We were never enemies. And I made sure the children got to school, got to the dentist. Today I say I have 11 children, a bunch of grands, a village in Africa and a world of people. I have acquired a perfect love, which helps me to this day.

When our five were little, I knew they would be somebody. They would beg their father to let them sing a song in the studio. He said to let them go to music school first and learn to read and write music, something he had never done. Poor Ziggy, he was so disappointed. He was always eager to show Daddy. When Bob would go on the road, Ziggy would stand on the side of the stage begging to perform.

Today Ziggy Marley and the Melody Makers are headliners. Ziggy is similar to Bob in dedication to his work and in his positiveness. And what a thing! I've seen father and son look alike but never such a step-out-of-you-into-me–type likeness. But Stephen—he's Bob, too, in his reserve, the shape of his hands, the way he walks.

I miss Bob. When I feel things are too much to bear—particularly with the legal battles [over the Marley estate]—I especially wish he were here. It was cancer that took him. It started in his foot and spread up through his body. As a Rasta though, you'd never hear him saying "If I die . . ." or "When I die . . ." To Rastafarians life is an everlasting gift. But one day in the hospital Bob was ready to go. I heard him say, "God, take me please." I held him in my arms and started singing to him. Then I started to cry. Bob looked up at me. "Don't cry," he said softly, "keep singing."

Bob Marley at Studio One

by Hank Bordowitz
(Previously Unpublished)

BEFORE Bob Marley became an international hero, before he even became an icon at home in Jamaica, he paid his dues. Like so many other Jamaican artists, he paid them to Studio One Records.

Started by mobile sound system DJ Clement "Sir Coxsone" Dodd to ensure that he had music no other DJ on the circuit had (others did the same), Studio One became a major force in Jamaican music. Dodd had an excellent ear for what his listeners wanted and the artists he recorded at Studio One filled that bill. The studio and label became the breeding ground for nearly every major Jamaican star, and just about anyone who is or was anyone in reggae and ska passed through Studio One at one time or another. Dodd says that he didn't even have to go looking for the artists he signed.

"I used to have a sound system, what they now call a discotheque, playing all over," he explains. "It started from the rhythm and blues, and we played a little jazz, until we started recording our own music in Jamaica. I used to visit a lot of live dances. That sound was what we emphasized when we started recording. So I had my fans and when we started recording locally, I had guys rooting for me. Whenever they would hear a good artist, they would bring them."

One of these fans was Secco Patterson. "This chap, Secco, he was the one who brought them," Dodd recalls of how Bob Marley and the Wailers came to Studio One. "He said, 'Boss, I have a good group here.' He was a close friend of mine. He loved the music that I played on my sound system. Every weekend, he'd be where we had our session. Secco knew these guys and brought them for an audition. They were four boys and two girls. All singing. He was with them until Bob died. He played conga for them."

The six singing sensations Secco secured at Studio One were Marley, Peter McIntosh (who later lost the "McIn" and went by the name of Tosh), Bunny Livingston (who took the band's name and called himself Bunny Wailer), Junior Brathwaite, Beverly Kelso, and Cherry Green. They sang around Kingston as The Teenagers (which they certainly were at the time), the Wailing Rudeboys, and the Wailing Wailers, which they ultimately shortened to just the Wailers. When they came to Studio One, they were very young and unformed. Marley was barely eighteen.

"I was the only producer out there building the artists up from the ground floor," Dodd says. "The other producers wanted somebody who was strong already and in the limelight. I would take a no-name guy by just auditioning and hearing his voice. I understood what it took to put it together. I took a little time putting it together. The more artists hear themselves playing back, the more confident they become. And when they sing a certain way and it sounds good, they know to stick to that method. It just came naturally."

As one of the first people to record and release ska in Jamaica during the early '60s, Coxsone Dodd was instrumental in establishing ska and the rock steady, blue beat, nyahbinghi, and other subcategories of reggae that followed. As opposed to the calypso sound produced at Federal Records, the only other studio in Jamaica when Dodd started recording, Dodd's music emphasized a strong off-beat, an exaggeration of the strong "one" that characterized R&B, especially from New Orleans, a city close enough that the radio would waft over the Caribbean to Jamaica. "It goes with the way that the West Indians dance," Dodd explains. "When Bob came up with the 'one drop' he really meant that off-beat. That's the 'one drop' he was referring to."

In addition to recording their early music, he claims to have bought Marley and Tosh their first guitars. As with so many things Dodd did, the motivation was pragmatic rather than generous. "After a couple of months," he says, "I realized that giving them a guitar would allow them to build their harmony and rehearse by themselves. Peter was more inclined to be a musician than even Bob was. He could play before Bob. He was able to strum on it."

While the Wailers, like most Studio One artists—and to be fair, most recording artists *anywhere* during the early '60s—never saw much in the way of royalties, the studio helped hone their style and abilities. The house band at Studio One was the legendary ska band The Skatallites, featuring such revered players as Roland Alphonso, Tommy McCook, and Don Drummond. Dodd set up something of a mentoring program at Studio One, and as Heartbeat Records president Chris Wilson points out, "When Bob was first learning to sing in the studio, most of these horn players were like his daddy."

"He worked with people like Roland Alphonso," Dodd concurs. "They helped him a lot."

The Wailers' early repertoire, as heard on Studio One reissues and compilations (through Wilson's Heartbeat Records in the U.S.), reflected a great deal of the music in Jamaica at the time. For years, they did covers of American and English pop and R&B hits. "American music had an influence on us all the way through," Dodd remarks. "That's why, in the early days, we recorded 'Teenager In Love' and songs like that. Even then, they didn't have the right knack or approach to writing original lyrics. As time went by, they picked up on the approach to writing songs and stuff like that."

By this time, the band essentially lived in the studio. "They were at the back of the studio," he recalls. "They occupied a three-bedroom flat back there, so near to the studio. It's where the water tower is in back of the studio. I had a building behind it. Being that close to the studio all the time helps the artist. What really happened was the freedom that they had in the studio, hearing themselves over time, they got that confidence to say, 'Well, this is working,' and they stuck with it."

While Dodd may have been the first producer to approach making records like that, he certainly wasn't the last. For example, one floor of the late, lamented Power Station studio in New York City was basically living space, including beds for musicians and engineers, along with owner Tony Bongiovi's own office/apartment—complete with waterbed and hot tub.

Still, the Wailers presented their own set of problems. Certainly one of the working names for the group, The Rudeboys, said a lot for both the nature of the group and their environment. "At one point the behavior of the youth," he remembers, "we call it the rude boy era, it was hard to control them. That was during rock steady. It was a trip. What made it difficult with the Wailers was the company they kept. It was a rough kind. But being with the sound system from the early days, most of the people who came around had that kind of respect. It kept them from getting out of line."

The Wailers also kept on getting better. While Tosh, initially, might have been the better musician, the early seeds of Marley as a pre-eminent songwriter were sown at Studio One. His very early song—and the Wailers' first hit single—"Simmer Down" points to the direction he would take as a writer and performer in the future. It spoke directly to the audience about one of their chief concerns, what Dodd described as "getting out of line." It also featured the group's distinctive harmonies, a sound that would characterize Marley's music, albeit with different voices.

Within a few years the Wailers changed in many ways. As Marley became more adept as a musician and songwriter, he took more control of the group. Over the course of the mid-'60s, the group dwindled from a sextet to a trio. "When they started," says Dodd, "it was Junior the lead singer on 'It Hurts to Be Alone' and a couple of more songs, he was definitely the leader, because he had that beautiful, strong voice, that high-pitched tenor. Then he left Jamaica and joined his family abroad. By then I knew that Bob was the right person to really take his place and be the leader of the group."

Beyond that, Marley had fallen in with another of Studio One's young stars. Rita Anderson sang with another Studio One vocal group called the Soulettes. Dodd had assigned Marley to mentor them. "They met each other by my studios," Dodd smiles fondly at the memory. "When I found out she was pregnant, being old-fashioned, I said, 'You've really got to get married.' I didn't want the people outside to think I was a careless man, letting the kids get together and have kids. So I said they should get married. At that time, there was no other means of income for either of them. Their only means of income was by me. They weren't working otherwise."

Nor was it always an ideal marriage. While the union produced four children, unions between Marley and other women produced seven more offspring that Marley acknowledged. And while he recognized these children from outside his marriage with Rita, sometimes he would even deny being married. While both the Wailers and Rita had long ago left Studio One behind for other labels and producers, Dodd says that he was the one Rita would run to for help. "This is when he caught with the Rasta scene," says Dodd. "He would say stuff like, 'We're not married, she's just my little sister.' Then Rita got scared, and she came by saying, 'Would you have our marriage picture?' I always had one, and I'd loan it to her and she could bring it by and straighten him out."

One of Rita's better qualities, it would seem, was being very organized, a trait she continues to display in maximizing the exposure of her late husband's music as well as her own and her children's. For example, when Bob could no longer find harmony with Tosh and Wailer, musically or otherwise, she put together the I-Threes, a backing harmony trio for the new Wailers that debuted with *Natty Dread* in 1974.

Although the Wailers had moved through the ministrations of Lee "Scratch" Perry and into the star-making machinery of Island Records, long after their days at Studio One and the watchful eyes of Coxsone Dodd, Dodd theorizes the battles that followed Marley's death as a possible reaction to how much influence Rita had come to exert on the business of being Bob Marley. It may well have been sheer orneriness over these familial and professional power struggles, Dodd postulates, that left Marley to die intestate, even though he knew he had a lot of estate to leave and he certainly knew he was dying. "That was a shame and a pity," Dodd says over the ensuing legalities that would stretch on over a decade after Marley's death. "It was a needless thing. He knew he was going to die. It was more out of spite. Rita was becoming too strong at that point."

What Marley's Studio One output proves is that even before Rita, Bob Marley was strong musically. Songs like "One Love" date back to initial recordings on Studio One. Wilson believes that an even earlier song, the Wailers' first Jamaican hit "Simmer Down," informed every song Marley wrote thereafter. "When you hear stuff like 'Simmer Down,'" he contends, "the message of 'Simmer Down' he went back to his whole career. He never deviated from his first hit. It really captured the feeling of Kingston in the 1960s, that undercurrent of violence. That was never far from any music he made after."

Bob Marley: The Story Behind *Chances Are*
(Source: Atlantic Records Biography, October 1981)

IT is the rare artist indeed who possesses the talent, vision and force to transcend barriers between nations and cultures. The late Bob Marley was such an artist. He was, of course, primarily responsible for bringing the Jamaican sound of reggae to the rest of the globe—both as a performer and as a writer. On that count alone, his place in musical/cultural history would have been assured. But Bob Marley was far more than reggae's prime ambassador. He was a supremely gifted man, a brilliant musician and lyricist, a charismatic and sensual personality who used his art to convey a deeply felt message of love, peace, freedom and unity among all people. Dubbed a "soul rebel," a "natural mystic," Bob Marley remains one of the few truly original voices of this or any other age.

The final decade of Bob Marley's life, from his signing to Island Records in the fall of 1972 to his death this past May, has been well-documented and analyzed. However, Marley's musical career extended back for another full decade—a period that remains largely unexposed to the world. *Chances Are* is a new album of previously unreleased tracks by the king of reggae, and is being released in the U.S. by Cotillion Records through an agreement with WEA International. Recorded between 1968 and 1972, the eight songs on the album provide a fresh perspective on the *complete* music of Bob Marley. In order to understand how this music came to be recorded, it is necessary to place it in the context of Marley's developing career.

Robert Nesta Marley was born in the countryside parish of St. Ann's, Jamaica on February 6, 1945. His father, a white British naval officer, left before Bob was born. As a teenager, Marley began to work as a welder. One of his co-workers was Desmond Dekker, who soon began to achieve success as a singer and encouraged Bob to audition for the Beverleys label. With the help of Jimmy Cliff, Bob recorded his first song, "Judge Not," at the age of 15. During the same period, Marley met Mortimo Planno, the presiding force in Jamaica's Rastafarian movement. Planno became Bob's life-long mentor, and Marley's music became infused with a highly spiritual quality that emanated from his Rastafarian beliefs.

In 1964, the Wailers came together in Trenchtown, the ghetto area of Kingston, Jamaica's capital. The group initially consisted of Marley, Peter McIntosh (Tosh), Bunny Livingston (now Wailer), Junior Braithwaite, Beverly Kelso and Bob's future wife, Rita. The Wailers began to record for producer Clement Dodd's Studio One/Coxsone label and enjoyed a remarkable series of Caribbean chart-toppers: "Simmer Down" (their first hit, penned by Bob), "Put It On," "Rude Boy," "I'm Still Waiting," "Rule Them Rudie" and many others.

Meanwhile, by 1966 the Wailers had been reduced to the trio that is now commonly referred to as "the original Wailers": Marley, Tosh and Livingston (Rita would later rejoin the group as one of the I-Threes, Bob's female backing singers). Unfortunately, as with most performers in the early years of reggae, the Wailers saw little monetary reward for their efforts. Frustrated, Marley left Jamaica for America, where he lived with his mother, Cedella Booker, in Delaware and worked in several factories.

Marley stayed in the U.S. less than a year, returning to Jamaica reportedly to avoid the military draft. The Wailers were reunited and began to record again. Then, in 1967, Bob met American soul singer Johnny Nash and his business partner Danny Sims. And it is here that the story behind *Chances Are* begins. Sims and Nash attended a Rasta festival in the Jamaican mountains with disc jockey Neville Willoughby who, according to Sims, "told Johnny and me that there was an artist that was so fantastic that he thought this kid had international potential and could be the biggest Caribbean act ever." Sims and Nash were immediately intrigued and went with Willoughby to meet Mortimo Planno. As Marley's mentor, Planno was supervising his career and screening all those who wished to meet with Bob. After first talking with Danny and Johnny, Planno then brought Marley to them.

"I listened to maybe fifty of Bob's songs," Sims recalls of his first meeting with Marley, "because he played one song after another after another. All he did when he came to visit me was play his guitar and sing." Danny and Bob became close friends and, with the blessing of Mortimo Planno, Sims began to oversee his career as a combined publisher/manager/executive producer. This period of Bob's life is discussed in the recently-published biography by Adrian Boot and Vivien Goldman: "At a time when Marley's musical career had seemed very shaky after a series of rip-offs, it was Johnny Nash

(Sims's partner in the JAD record company) who stepped in, involving Bob in all manner of excitement . . . "

So it was that Bob Marley (along with another young Jamaican musician, Paul Khouri) showed Johnny Nash how to play reggae music; and Nash in turn began to record some of Bob's songs. In 1970, Marley traveled with Danny and Johnny to Sweden to work on a film project. The following year, the trio went to England, where both Marley and Nash were signed by CBS International via Sims and JAD Records. Among their activities in the U.K., Bob and Johnny did an unorthodox tour of secondary schools, combining duo and solo performances with question-and-answer sessions. Near the close of the tour, CBS released Nash's version of the Marley song "Stir It Up," which topped U.K. charts in 1972 and U.S. listings in 1973. Among the many other Marley tunes recorded by Nash were "Guava Jelly," "Bend Down Low," "Nice Time," "Comma, Comma" and "You Poured Sugar On Me." Thus, in an interesting turn of circumstances, it was Nash who gave Bob Marley his first non-Jamaican hits, at least as a writer; but it was ultimately Marley who, at first through the medium of Nash, gave reggae to the world.

Between 1968 and 1972, while working with Nash and Sims, Marley recorded in the neighborhood of 72 songs on his own. In addition to his own material, Bob also recorded a series of songs by the R&B writing team of Jimmy Norman & Al Pyfrom (two of which are included on *Chances Are*). The idea was, quite simply, as Sims notes, "to cut Bob Marley in a rhythm and blues, Top 40 style so we could try to gain acceptance for him in America. For the truth of the matter was that it was to be many years before American radio would become receptive to genuine Jamaican reggae, a situation which has only very recently begun to change. Even in Jamaica, because of his Rastafarian beliefs, Marley's early records sold without benefit of airplay, through the underground market.

According to Danny Sims, Marley eventually came to feel that the success of Johnny Nash, an American interpreting the reggae feel, was overshadowing his own work. Sims, in turn, had come to realize that Marley and Nash would only be competing with each other for a single record company's attention, as reggae was still in its infancy. Therefore, at this point, JAD and CBS made arrangements to allow Marley to record for Island Records, while retaining a financial interest in his career. Danny, clearly not wishing to hold up his friend's career, released Bob from the recording and management portions of their agreement, while continuing to serve as his publisher.

Bob and Danny came in regular contact throughout the ensuing decade, and Sims continued to be involved in Marley's career. In fact, in 1983 Mortimo Planno, still serving as Bob's adviser, met with Danny in Jamaica and asked him to return as Bob's manager. Sims coordinated Marley's final U.S. concert tour, promoted his biggest U.S. single to date, "Could You Be Loved" (from his last album, *Uprising*), and was his close companion during his final days.

The songs selected for inclusion on the *Chances Are* album (a compilation already planned prior to Marley's untimely death) are described by Danny Sims as "love songs, inspirational songs. Island Records received more controversial or revolutionary type of material from Bob; but the material we recorded is more romantic. It came at a point in Bob's life when he was seeking emotional release following a series of disheartening recording experiences. The songs that I picked were personal to me and to Bob. I chose songs that really told the story of Bob Marley. I think you really have to get into the words in these songs. This album is a purely lyrical explanation of who Bob Marley really was, because Bob only wrote about life—his life and things around him."

With the emergence of *Chances Are*, we are able to hear a marvelous side of Bob Marley largely unexplored on his more recent albums. The songs on the LP were produced by Marley and noted producer/arranger/composer Larry Fallon, and they have been thoughtfully chosen by Danny Sims and remixed under his careful supervision. *Chances Are* now takes its long overdue, much-deserved place in the brilliant catalog of Bob Marley's work. As Sims notes, the material on the album is dominated by infectious songs of love and moving songs of life, from the full-bodied "Dance Do The Reggae" to the autobiographical classic "Soul Rebel" to the touching, concluding "(I'm) Hurting Inside." "He had a definite vision," Sims notes. "He always acted like a superstar. He never behaved like he was just an act trying to make it. He always felt that he had it; he always felt that he was much further along."

Two songs in particular rank as landmarks in Marley's prolific career. The opening "Reggae On Broadway" is described by Sims as "the first rock song Bob Marley ever did, the song that distinguished Bob, with his predilection for rock'n'roll, from other reggae artists." A decade after it was recorded, the song stands among Marley's most joyous and powerful tunes. Then there is the album's title track, the hauntingly beautiful ballad "Chances Are." As Sims relates, "This was a vision he had of the future." While Bob regularly denied that he was a prophet ("God is the prophet," he would say), the words of this song remain as a fitting epitaph for this singular man of remarkable beauty, spirit, energy and talent.

Chances are we're gonna leave now/
Sorry for the victim now/
Though my days are filled with sorrow/
I see years of bright tomorrows.

2

Stir It Up:
International Attention,
1972–1976

For close to a decade, Bob, Peter, and Bunny—the last of the remaining sextet that started as the Wailers—had on-again, off-
again hits. However, because of the corruption endemic in the Jamaican music business (which made the business in the United States
look like a Boy Scout jamboree) and the infrequency of the hits—not
to mention Bunny's time in jail for a ganja bust—they continued to
ply other trades. During this time, Bob notes he worked at "welding
and soldering," soldering being Jamaican slang for having sex. As Rita
says in the previous section, he did work as a welder (and also as a jan-
itor) in Delaware for much of 1967.

Then a few things happened that began the quick, precipitous
climb of Bob Marley and the Wailers:

On Bob's return to Jamaica, the group began working with legendary producer Lee "Scratch" Perry.

As the previous chapter ("The Story Behind *Chances Are*") also relates, Marley cut several hits backing Texas soul singer Johnny Nash, including his own "Stir It Up," which went top 20 toward the end of 1973.

Then, while in London during 1971, Marley walked into the Island
Records offices and walked out with an advance to record *Catch a Fire*.

Finally, Eric Clapton cut a version of "I Shot the Sheriff" that topped the U.S. and U.K. charts at the beginning of 1974.

All this built up to international acclaim, not just for the band but for the music they helped create and popularize—rock steady, a slowed down, earthier version of ska, which had brief international success via hits by Millie Small ("My Boy Lollipop"), Desmond Dekker ("Israelites"), and Jimmy Cliff ("The Harder They Come"—both the movie and the song).

For the three years between 1972 and 1975, the Wailers were a band standing on the verge of getting it on.

I Was a Wailers

by Lee Jaffe

(Source: Excerpt from **One Love, Life with Bob Marley and the Wailers** *[W. W. Norton])*

THE first time I met Bob was in January 1973, in New York City. It was at a hotel called the Windsor, on 56th Street and Sixth Avenue. I was visiting Jim Capaldi, the drummer and co-writer of songs for Traffic, whom I'd met in England through the actress Esther Anderson. They were one of the most popular bands in the world, both critically and commercially, and they had just broken up. It was a typical early Seventies rock'n'roll-type scene, with groupies running around the halls and various press and record company people.

Bob Marley was in Jim's room, sitting in a corner of this big suite, very quiet, very shy. We just started talking. He told me he had finished an album for Island Records, *Catch a Fire*. He had a cassette of it that we listened to. I had just seen *The Harder They Come* in England the week before, so I was totally prepared. It was like the movie had just walked off the screen. And I was now face to face with the voice of a group whose music was the most revolutionary I had ever heard, who were both black and white and transcended race, whose music was both spiritually and socially conscious.

That was the beginning of a week that Bob and I spent together in New York. The album was completely contagious. I was very anxious to show off what I had found to all my artist and musician friends in New York.

I was staying in a loft at 112 Greene Street, in Soho, the centre of the art world at that time. On the ground floor was a gallery. Now it's Greene Street Recording Studios, where some classic hip-hop has been recorded. The floors were all wood and corroded. In the basement, Gordon Matta-Clarke, one of the great sculptors of the 20th century, had "recycled" all these glass bottles. It was the first time I'd ever heard the word "recycle". He brought a humanistic fire to the art world in a way the Wailers brought it to popular music.

It was at that time, too, that I met Dickie Jobson, then Bob's manager. Dickie was the best friend of Chris Blackwell, the owner of Island Records, the label that had recently signed the Wailers. Dickie had come to New York with Bob to buy equipment for the band. I went with them to Manny's on 48th Street, where every musician up to the biggest rock stars would go to buy equipment. I helped them pick out their gear and deal with all the salesmen.

I took Bob around to visit my musician friends. He'd play guitar, I'd play harmonica. The only thing that came close to my friends' reaction to his album was their reaction to Jimi Hendrix's first album in 1967.

First week with Bob, New York City, winter 1973

The ice crackled under my feet. The wind taunted my breath. If I had known, really, what a Rastaman was, I would have thought this was no place for a Rastaman. We were cruel weather's toys, hunched in our coats, begging for Mother Nature's forgiveness. But we were on a mission. A mission that, for the years we sparred, was interminable, relentless, intractable—the search for the better herb.

I pierced the night air with a high-pitched wail to let Bob know I was a sufferer, too. It was all he could do not to double over laughing as we picked up the pace along Central Park West, trying not to lose our balance on the salted-slick sidewalk, coming down 85th Street, to where my friend Brew, a main distributor of the better strains of Colombian golds and reds, kept a stash house.

Normally only Brew's dispatcher, the Dile, was ever allowed there. He accepted deliveries of bales enclosed in innocuous cardboard boxes to the brownstone apartment, and in turn distributed them to half-a-dozen dealers scattered throughout the city. But I was a trusted exception.

I had met Brew through his brother The Fox in the late sixties. I went to college with him at Penn State, where I had been one of the students mainly responsible for elevating the consciousness of a significant portion of the student body by turning them on to various (what were then exotic) controlled substances. We had hung out a lot in New York during our breaks from school; he, an aspiring artist like me, stayed at his parents' swanky Upper East Side apartment, which had a leopard-skin pattern velvet couch and a perfect view of the East River and the Fifty-ninth Street Bridge. His parents were living mostly in Florida. I'd often stay over there, and we'd spend our time getting high, tripping and having sex with as many girls as possible. We did our first pot deals together. We'd scrape together enough money to buy a pound and sell ounces and half ounces. The proceeds got us into concerts at the Fillmore East and clubs like The Scene and Salvation, and helped us buy drugs, which helped us pick up more girls.

When I was done with college, I went off to Brazil, and Brew continued his life in the herb trade, eventually convincing his brother to quit his lucrative Wall Street job to come help him turn his successful pot dealing into a real business. Now we were together escorting the new signee to the label of Traffic and Cat Stevens, eager to impress this third world advocate of herbs and revolution.

The pale din of headlights bobbing, a cab scowling around a corner, a beggar in sundry rags, wheeling a shopping cart overflowing with all his worldly possessions, coughed, floated among the newly floating flakes of snow glowing in the lamplight, teetered on the verge of madness and disappeared from consciousness as we bounded up the brownstone stairs toward the ethereal cathedral of cannabis.

Was I proud. My old buddy made good. Bale upon bale of crocus-sacked mystical foliage, which in turn were clear plastic wrapped and sealed, numbered and graded A or AA, with weights 22.5, 26.3 Magic Markered on the see-through outer covering. I looked into Bob's deep, mischievous eyes. He glared in return . . . a pause like a pause between Aston "Family Man" Barrett's bass notes . . . "You t'ink you somet'in', Lee Jaffe?" Then came the laughter, volcanoing, lyrical, the sounds beading off each other, luminous. Brew shook his head and resisted a smile. He liked to think of himself as hard. He was taking kung fu and had grown a short, scruffy beard to disguise his baby face. I had turned him on to an advance copy of *Catch A Fire*, and he had all the lyrics of the songs memorized in just a few days. "Every time I hear the crack of a whip, my blood runs cold. I remember on a slave ship how they brutalized our very soul." Mimicking Bob's accent. Then, in falsetto, "Catch a fire," as he whipped a switchblade from his jeans pocket and, with the shimmering blade, motioned for us to follow him to the back room of the long, cavernous apartment.

The floor was covered with Afghan and Indian rugs and pillows and in the dim transitory light he opened a Moroccan-looking chest containing several small bricks of bud, punctiliously carving an opening in the herbal sheath with the lacerating weapon, pulled out a handful of black, well-defined sticky and, holding it up face-high for us to whiff and contemplate declared, "Cheeba."

The sound resonated clear through to the mountains and sequestered valleys of Cartagena. Peasants plying the fields, gathering the cured stalks hanging upside down in the steamy afternoon haze. I imagined hundreds of Juan Valdez hats and tiny scissors, clipping the buds off the thick, tough branches, soft pressing them into bales, meandering on donkeys down craggy hillsides to meet ancient generic trucks, the grizzled drivers with machine guns waiting for the chance to deliver the sweet and pungent cargo to a trawler of undetermined origin, parked Federale-protected in the azure glistening Caribbean harbor. . .

Then, the overlong voyage around the Caribbean into the green Atlantic to avoid DEA detection, with designated gringo on board, swinging back in toward the Florida Keys to rendezvous with Miami-Cuban cigarette boats too swift for the Coast Guard to follow, the state-of-the-art speedboats cutting razor-thin wakes in the semi-tropical moonlight, meeting waiting vans ready to scurry up the perilous one-road causeway through the Keys to a Homestead warehouse south of Miami where my other college friend, Robbie, and his harmonica playing Italian partner Johnny B., from South Plainfield, New Jersey, would come to sort through their allotment, paying extra to Stone and Jonni (ultimately a Wailers fan), their Cuban connections, for the chance to pick the best to send in car trunks and false-backed U-Hauls up the coast to the first city.

I had some zigzags and offered them around. Brew beamed, being the Man, and we broke up buds on a large, lavishly engraved silver tray. He sensed Bob's consternation and jumped in, "It's cool, mon. I rent this place from my brethren and he's the only other tenant in the building. Everything's safe." I was thinking of white Americans talking like Jamaicans. I thought, laughing to and at myself, damn, what a trendsetter I am. Bob rolled such a giant spliff that it shocked even Brew. He blurted: "This herb very, very strong, mon," as if to say, no need for such exaggeration. But what Brew didn't know was that that was just a normal-sized joint for the Rastaman.

Bob lit the spliff, and gave Brew a sly, discerning smile. He took some short, quick tokes, fanning the fire, before taking a long, deep draw, the smoke disappearing, reappearing, filling the beclouded room. Brew stopped trying to act unimpressed. We were both bug-eyed. I had taken hundreds of acid trips, peyote, psilocybin, I had been smoking since I was 15 and was now 22, but I knew as my jaw dropped that I was entering a new world. The world of The Most High. It was not just the size of the spliff, but the whole way that Bob approached it: with such reverence, such respect. For Brew, it was a path toward a new Mercedes and Rolex watches, and boosting his ego. For me, it was a way to help reveal mystical truths. But for Bob, it was something more. A way to connect and live in harmony with his Otherness. A gateway to a universe where words and music flowed in clear unpolluted celestial streams, sometimes raging, sometimes lazily weaving through the palm-tree-pillared rainbow kingdom of Jah, where sun and rain mixed in tranquil bliss and King David played his harp.

Jamaica, winter 1973

Bob was a hero in Trench Town, Ghost Town—all the hardcore ghetto places. And we'd go to the country and it seemed incredible how all the country people knew him—like a son or a brother or a nephew and I could never tell, when people would offer us their best herbs or ital food [no salt, no meat] or just best wishes, if they had nothing else to give, if they were actually related or just knew him because he was in The Wailers and loved him for the music and the joy and hope that the music would always bring. And we'd stop at the tiny roadside shops of rusted tin and wood and they'd always have a jukebox and there'd always be a few old Wailers singles and I'd want to stop at every one of these shops because there might be a Wailers' record I hadn't heard. I can remember hearing "Trench Town Rock" for the first time, at one of these places on a winding mountain road on a lazy, golden late afternoon in St Ann's Parish, on our way to Nine Mile where Bob was born. On the track, he sang, "Hit me with music, when it hits you feel no pain." No recording had ever moved me like that. I must have been shaking I was so blown away, and Bob had gone around to the back of the shop to look at some herb and roll a spliff and I just needed to hear that song over and over again, the scratchy vinyl 45 emanating from the ancient machine, and Bob came around the front of the store and said, "Whappen to you, mon?" And I opened my mouth to try to say something but it just stayed open with nothing coming out and Bob joked, "Look like a duppy get you mon!"—meaning it looked like a ghost had possessed me—and finally I said, "That's the greatest record I ever heard." And he threw his arm around my shoulder and he just started to laugh, and then we were both laughing and he handed me his spliff, which he had just lit, and he said, "Take this spliff, Lee Jah-free, you need a good draw to scare dem duppy away."

After Carnival in Trinidad, early 1973

The wind hot and crimson circling clouds streaming lavenders and lapis darkening as a near full moon burning silver rose while the last scraps of daylight dipped and dissolved sinking down through the Caribbean horizon in the lazying forlorn west. My harmonica wailed mournful blues from the back seat of Bob's Capri as Esther chatted nonstop from the shotgun side, Bob maneuvering around potholes—while listening intently—deftly and with a supreme concentration.

We weaved and stuttered our way through to Port Royal, where some three hundred years before a great earthquake had destroyed what was the most bustling town in the whole West Indies: where pirates Morgan and Cook and Bluebeard whored, where slave ships routinely dumped their human cargo, the worthwhile remains to be bartered and auctioned after the interminable voyages from West Africa, during which less than half would survive in the seasick starving galleys in chains and emerging half or three quarters dead from the ship's hull squinting, iron clanging in the searing white hot sun from their allotted positions arm to arm, head to feet, not an inch wasted, calculated, diagrammed, packaged, the proprietors knowing more or less how many would perish in the premeditated mass murder of beasts of burden needed to cut the cane to be boiled into molasses from which would be extracted and bleached white and therefore "pure"—sugar—to sweet the fancy of the white-wigged pale and powdered white-faced lords and ladies of the boundary-less queendom called the British Empire.

And what remains . . . A cannon, a fort ruined beyond ruins. A town of ghosts whistling ballads and jigs cacophonic—fleeing in and out of consciousness, turning curtly, violently to catch what was there or what is not.

We curled through a roundabout and out to the desolate, dark harbour, where women with kerosene lamps sold fried fish—snapper, jack, king and sprat—from creaky wooden tables, topped by flimsy glass cabinets glowing faintly in the hazy firelight. I could imagine these women, some maga with craggy skin, some round and oversized with fatty bum-

bums in their day jobs, pounding the cassava root with wooden mallets into quarter-inch thick cakes to be fried and sold with the fish—salted and therefore un-ital—the yellow-white chewy—called bammie.

And Esther ranting about how the Spanish and then the English came to obliterate the indigenous people, the Caribs and the Tainos, their Arawak language centuries lost, and me in my stern silence acknowledging what I knew to be true, and Bob in turn sensing the white youth so recalcitrant, implacable in his revolutionary zeal.

We chose the fish we wanted from the various ladies wishing for a sale and Esther begged me to take a piece of bammie to go with them. They served the poor man's feast in white newsprint-like paper, and we meandered out onto a dilapidated wooden pier that extended some twenty yards out into the near-still water. I could see the tangerine lights of Kingston pulsing across the bay, the sky argentous, scintillating—the breeze dreamy, warm, wistful.

"You know cassava was more than just a root to be mashed up and fried for the original people here, Lee Jaffe," Esther continued as if in some remote way in my whiteness I too might need to take on some responsibility for the iniquitous Iberian legacy.

"It was a sacred thing for the Tainos. They believed in a superior being, a life-giving force they called Yucahu and Yucahu represented sea and cassava because both were never-failing sources of sustenance. They sat here six hundred years ago and ate the same t'ing we a-naym now." She laughed. "A true, mon. . .

"And the Spanish a wicked, you see, mon? Dem would string dem poor innocents up by dem raas feet and light a fire beneet dem and laugh while dey watched dem slowly burn. Or dem would play games seeing who could chop up an Indian de fastest and then feed them to some vicious dogs they did a-bring wit' dem from Spain. They made slaves of them to dig in mines for gold, but dem never find no raas gold a Jamaica, and some of dem would run away or just hang dem-

selves, whole families, children too, rather than subjugate themselves
to de pernicious blood-claat who did call themselves Christians."

I suffered Esther's ravings which, on the one hand, seemed directed
at me, and on the other were for Bob, to show off her radical social
consciousness, but I couldn't help but smile, the fish being so succu-
lent, the bammie sweet from coconut oil. Then Bob produced three
twelve ounce bottles of a creamy white liquid and passed them around.

"What's this?" I asked of the label-less bottles.

"Irish moss and soursop juice," Bob replied with the assured confidence that this would blow my mind. "Ital, mon. No sugar, no con-
demned milk. Only honey use fe sweeten it." And yes, it was smooth
and as dreamy as the soft wind lilting through the coconut trees. Then
magically, as if scripted by Jah, some Christmas tree–like buds appeared. "Lamb's bread, mon. I and I get eet from Sledger who helped
grow eet a St. Ann's, the parish dem call Jah's parish, the parish where
I and I a born. Lamb's bread a special herb a hard for get eet, seen?"

"Can we go there? I want to see the country. I want to see where
you came from?"

"Yeah, mon. We can reach dem parts dere."

"And can we actually go to the herb field where this came from?"
Bob laughed.

"You want to see every t'ing, Lee Jaffe . . ." Esther chimed in.

"Go for me guitar, my youth," said Bob, as he rolled separate,
huge, cone-like spliffs for each of us.

I bounded to the car to get Bob's acoustic. I could sense the in-
choate stirrings of word and music brewing in a soul born of disparate
continents. In a soul wailing, tormented with the burden of the crimi-
nally poor, the indigent, the starveling, and the destitute of the shanty
towns from Kingston to Cape Town, from Bed-Stuy to the stilted
slums of Bangkok. But a soul also so free in the mellow moonlight glistening off the tropical sea mingling with the lamp lights and the open

wood fires, a soul uplifted by the gift of Jah's good herb and the intoxication of love at first sight with his Jamaican East Indian peasant-born entertaindom-royalty princess who through a simple phone call—"forget that Hollywood crap and go make a good movie"—had the power to resurrect the languishing career of her ex-boyfriend Marlon Brando and at the same time igniting the career of a budding Italian cineaste, Bernardo Bertolucci, her call being the catalyst for what would become *Last Tango in Paris*. Bob took a long, slow draw off the extravagant spliff, the fire tip glowing amber as I passed him his guitar. Then lighting my own while taking in the celestial night sky, more rich with glitter than any I'd witnessed, I began to follow the ethereal rhythm of his right hand against the steel strings with my trusty D harp, my breathing in and out caressing the metal reeds, careful to augment and not overwhelm his guitar, leaving space for his voice to be intimate without straining. And Bob began to sing:

> *So Jah say*
> *not one of my seeds shall sit in the sidewalk and beg your bread*
> *(No they can't and you know that they won't)*
> *So Jah say*
> *you are the sheep of my pasture*
> *so verily, thou shall be very well . . .*
> *and down here in the ghetto*
> *and down here we suffer*
> *I and I a-hang on in there and I and I, naw leggo . . .*
> *For So Jah Say.*

Kingston, 1973

We were just jamming, and then I remember there were these two really really fat girls dancing when Bob came out with that line. It came from Bob saying "I shot the sheriff." And then I said, "But you didn't get the deputy." 'Cause he was making this joke about him hanging out with this white guy—me. So it was like this comment about that.

It was such a funny song, the beach wasn't that crowded, but we had a whole bunch of people just dancing to that song. I remember these two huge fat girls just dancing, and all these other people dancing around them. And Bob was playing the guitar and I'm on harmonica.

I wrote down all the lyrics Bob was singing. And I was excited 'cause I knew it was a big song and I felt I was integral in its conception, and then I came up with the line "all along in Trench Town, the jeeps go round and round," 'cause the police and military drove jeeps and I was thinking of the curfews that were being called in the ghetto and what it was like for the poor people, the "sufferers," to live in a militarized zone and to have the basic freedom of walking in the street taken away and how it related to politics and the U.S. involvement in Southeast Asia and the C.I.A. pressure on the Caribbean and Latin America and I flashed on being on the beach in Rio in Ipanema, being with a girlfriend who was a radical student leader and she, pointing out a blonde, crewcut guy with his wife and two pre-teenage daughters relaxing on a Sunday morning and hipping me to the fact that he was an American sent by Nixon to train torturers, and I was thinking of what was taking place in Chile, and how the events there had resulted in me being in Jamaica, and what a genius Bob was for coming out with the line "I shot the sheriff," because, though it was funny, it was also poignant, so relevant to the global repression, and later he changed the line to "All along in my home town" and that was better, because it made the point that these violent interventions into everyday life in the shanty towns of Jamaica were intrinsically foreign-influenced. And when I said, "But you didn't get the deputy," it was ironic and slightly self-deprecating, because what it was saying was, yeah, I got the balls to shoot the sheriff, but I don't have it to-gether by myself to get all his backup and this is going to be a long, tragic struggle that's going to need a lot of everyday heroes.

New York, summer 1973

Max's Kansas City was an amazing place. It started in the Sixties as a place for painters, sculptors, visual artists to hang out, and Mickey Ruskin, the guy who owned it, would trade with artists for food. And he had great taste in art, so he wound up with this amazing collection. He died very young, but when he died he had a collection that had become worth millions of dollars. He was trading with everyone from Dan Flavin to Andy Warhol. I was in school for sculpture, so all my heroes were hanging out there. Dan Flavin had a big red fluorescent light piece which was in the far back corner, called *Cross of Fire*. Incredible.

I took the *Catch a Fire* album with the cigarette lighter cover, called up the guy at Max's who did the bookings, his name was Sam Hood, and made an appointment to see him. And I marched in there and he had this tiny little office upstairs at Max's, filled with records and posters and kind of messy. Flipped open the album cover—it opened like a cigarette lighter in the middle. He pulled out the vinyl, put it on his turntable, listened to the first track and went to the second track, listened to a few bars of the next track, and he said, "The Drifters with raised consciousness! OK. I'll do that." And he gave us this week opening for Bruce Springsteen.

It made sense, right? It was incredibly perfect for us, because the guy had so much hype and his record label, Columbia, was a New York-based record company, the biggest company in the world, and they were promoting him saying he was the next Bob Dylan, and it was Columbia and John Hammond blah-blah-blah. And there was a lot of backlash at this point, because nobody had heard of him. Now everybody's comparing him to Dylan, so a lot of people resented that. But everybody from the media had to be there to see this guy. So there was no better forum for us, coming from total obscurity, to be able to play with that intense an audience. So we had every single music journalist, plus almost anyone who wrote on culture there to see this.

It could hold a few hundred people, I guess. Long and narrow, like a long loft type of thing. Maybe 250, 300 capacity. It was tight. But when they started to run groups, the whole atmosphere at Max's started to change. It was no longer just a place for artists to go. . . You also had people like Todd Rundgren, Patti Smith and Lou Reed, all kinds of brilliant people hanging out there.

But first we had to get the band there. I had arranged things with this immigration lawyer, but the work permits didn't come in time. So this lawyer knew a person that worked at immigration in Niagara Falls. And he worked a certain shift, like four to 12 or something. And we flew to Toronto from Kingston the day before the first New York gig. The idea was to drive to Niagara Falls when this guy was on duty, because he was going to let us in. But, of course, what happens is, we arrive in Toronto and we looked like we were going to overthrow the government. And they went through every piece of luggage. They took hours and hours and hours. By the time we got to Niagara Falls it was two o'clock in the morning. So I got the lawyer's number at home and woke him up, and he woke up the immigration guy to come, and it was like four o'clock in the morning, and that's how we got into America . . .

This was another world. I mean, we were all of a sudden right in the center of the heart of rock and roll glamourdom. This was the place in the world, the hippest place in the world you could possibly play, opening for Bruce Springsteen at his first Columbia Records show. I mean everybody who was anybody was there that week. I mean more than once. We were playing two shows a night, and this was the kind of thing where people came more than once. Every writer, everybody from the fashion world, every musician that meant anything who was in New York had to go see this. And we were there and by the end of the week everybody knew who we were. . . We were blowing people's minds! People were flipping out over us. We were getting amazing respect—it started the love affair of the press with the Wailers that week. And it never ended.

Marvin Gaye concert, Jamaica, 1974

In Jamaica they are very picky about what kind of American music they like, but Marvin Gaye was special. A lot of his popularity had to do with the social and political themes of the songs on the *What's Goin' On* album. He showed up in Jamaica with a 70-piece orchestra. It was a really big event, a hot ticket. The promoter added the Wailers on to the show, but nobody really believed they would play, because they hadn't played in Jamaica in many years and several previous shows had falsely advertised The Wailers. The reason we played the show was that everyone was swept up in the vibe. There was a new Wailers single out and it was a smash and we felt we wouldn't be overshadowed by Marvin, that even with his huge crew he couldn't upstage us. And that proved to be true.

What was exciting for me, particularly, was that we had just put out "Road Block" and it was a massive hit. It was a number one record and it featured my harmonica playing, and I knew that we would have to do that song, and there was no way that The Wailers could do that song without me getting up there and playing on it, because I'm playing from the intro on. And just having the harmonica on a reggae track was such a novelty, the novelty aspect definitely contributed to the record having such immediate popularity.

Of course, most important was the lyrical content of that song, because there were road blocks anywhere, anytime, and it was particularly difficult for people like us dreadlocks, because there's no way that we would be caught in a road block and the police just saying that you could go. And since we smoked herb all the time, we were living in a world that hovered between total apprehension and a heightened state of all-encompassing fear. So I remember being very anxious that whole day. First of all, none of The Wailers were really quite sure if we were going to play. It was going to be the kind of thing where Bunny and Peter would show up at Hope Road, because it was Bob, Bunny and Peter who would have to decide. And there would be some kind of reasoning as to "Are we going to get this together?" and if the vibe was right, there was an outside chance that it just might happen.

The whole town was buzzing over Marvin Gaye's appearance. It seemed like this buzz over him in some way took some of the pressure off us, and we're paying some kind of tribute to, or acknowledgement of, Marvin by showing up there. And at the same time it was a matter of playing when the Wailers hadn't played Jamaica in a long time, and being that we were just opening for this big event that this show had become, there wouldn't be so much focus of attention on us.

I remember Peter and Bunny showing up separately in the morning, and it was just kind of the vibe of let's do it. So I was all excited, because I knew what that meant. I was going to have to get out there. We have the number one song and I'm playing on it and it's totally political about the police busting you for herb, and I'm going to be onstage with the whole consciousness of the island focused on these twenty to thirty feet.

And the show ended up mega-packed, because the Carib Theatre only held 2,500 people, and thousands of people couldn't get in. The show could have drawn 20 to 30,000 people easily. So the Wailers come out, they play five songs, and the audience is totally loving it, and I'm on the side of the stage, and I know they gotta play it, because everybody's waiting for it. I remember standing with Skill Cole and he said, "You gotta go now," and gave me a little shove, and I was out onstage with the lights blaring at me. My locks were really big by then, I had a red tam, I definitely looked like I was in the Wailers, except that I was white. And Bob says into the microphone, "This is Lee . . ." and it flashes through my mind that Bob Marley is introducing me to Jamaica and then he finishes the sentence with an instruction to the engineer, "Don't turn him up too loud." And the audience is cracking up and then the first few notes of the intro and then I come in wailing and the place goes completely crazy.

And I'm playing through the rest of the song and my nervousness is dissolving and I'm the highest I've ever been in my life, and then I have this big solo that went on and on and I'm trading riffs with lead guitarist Al Anderson through the outro and it's sounding really good and I'm starting to feel like I passed the test. And it was totally thrilling. It was a coming forward for me and it was like I had been accepted by everybody in the band already, otherwise I wouldn't have been out there at that moment, no way, and this was kind of like the band presenting me and the audience was so electric. The fact that they had just done five songs, the place was going crazy already before I came out kind of eased the pressure because I just walked into the environment that was already totally scintillating. My nervousness disappeared, dissolved.

I was kind of lost in the music, trying not to step on Bob's vocals or I knew I'd be in a lot of trouble. I would never get the chance to go out there again. But it was good. By the time it got further down the song to my solo, I was just rocking with it. And I think I did a good job on the solo. And 26 years later I finally got to hear a tape of that performance, and the solo does sound pretty good.

The great thing about it was, after that I was just in The Wailers. Although it was a few months earlier, I believe, that Bunny had pro-

nounced while he was at Hope Road, "Lee is Wailers," being on stage
was definitely an initiation. And being part of the group obviously was
more than being in a band. It meant that I was accepted into the
whole cultural, spiritual, political context which being in this band
implied. I could be on the street in downtown Kingston and I was no
longer a curiosity, I was now an accepted part of the fraternity of musicians—and more: I was Wailers.

Bob Marley Is the Jagger of Reggae

by Patrick Carr

(Source: **The Village Voice,** *June 30, 1975)*

IT was a wonderful moment of the evening in Central Park when
they came out, the real and present long awaited Wailers, tightest
band in all of Jamaica and holders of the hip reggae torch. It was in
fact a true musical love rush, nothing less—Americans and Jamaicans
going giddy with glee at the image of genuine Jamaican religious hippie revolutionaries smoked up on the best grass in the world and
ready to blow the crowd along into reggae's most exotic turn of the
rock & roll wheel, this time on a real American tour, complete with
praise from Poor Abe the mayor telling them how proud he is and
happy to welcome their fresh new reggae sound to New York. Main
Wailer Bob Marley just ignores this rather silly attempt at Babylonian
co-optation, shouts a Rastafarian credo dedicating the night to His
Imperial Majesty Haile Selassie the lion of Judah, tosses his natty
dreadlocks, and kicks the band into "Trenchtown Rock." The bass

and guitars come in first with a balance and depth and rhythm catching all the power of the classic reggae rush and Marley cavorts loosely up to the mike: "One good thing about music, when it hits, you feel no pain." Hypnosis takes hold. Marley is charismatic.

Marley is charismatic and he's stoned from dreadlocks to toes, and he's proud of it. And it's taken for granted with the Rastafarian philosophy in mind, and it's very charming when you begin to listen to his songs and catch the images of voluptuous revolution in the context of Trenchtown, the cockpit of Black pride, the lives of shit-poor people trying to scrape through, staying loose and friendly, standing up for their rights, dodging Babylon. In his lyrics Marley fuses a Caribbean class-struggle documentary with spunky images of resistance and a benign, spiritual vision of happiness through what comes naturally. And it comes out naturally so's you can dance to it. What we have here is a whole new high in politico good-time boogie music, like if Jefferson Airplane suddenly found fresh brains and started to dig their own potatoes. Marley is trying to put what matters into music but he also knows how much it's the music that matters. The best reggae is hypnotic, riding up to the pit of your stomach on massive, smoothjerk bass lines and lulling you out with exotic gospel harmonies: big lows and brilliant highs, just like the hi-fi ads. The best reggae is beautiful, and rude. And Marley works his crowd, too, moving sinuously around the mike, his face a mime with the lyrics, his pearly teeth (cleaned with natural tree bark, no toothpaste here) flashing from the smile of the permanently stoned. Brother Bob, a natural showman. Unlike Jimmy Cliff, whose show has all the sensuality of your standard R&B lounge act, pirouettes and all, Brother Bob is most definitely funky. Very sexy, too. See it now: Marley is the Jagger of reggae, without decadence, which doesn't apply.

Marley triumphed in Central Park and the Wailers (minus Bunny Livingston and Peter Mackintosh, the other founder members of the 12-year-old band, and plus their replacements and the I-Threes (three perfect women singers) laid it down just right like a good backup band should. Some images remain: Marley swinging softly to himself through the church organ intro to "No Woman No Cry," and slipping into his finest melody song . . . "Cause I remember when we used to sit / in a government yard in Trenchtown / Observing the hypocrites / Mingle with the good people we meet."

Then there was "Kinky Reggae," when he really began to dance and the women went weak; "Rebel Music," when everyone sang along with Brother Bob's latest uppity real life in joke ("And *hey Mister Cop*, ain't got no / (*What you say down there*) / Ain't got no birth certificate on me now"); then Marley, bathed in applause and stoned messages from his crowd (this was his crowd; chic and scruffy, but all of them movers), announcing "I shot the sheriff!" and proceeding to attack that great song for all its hilarious angles on the rebel life, totally outclassing Clapton's (ha!) anemic cover version while the I-Threes mimed swinging six-guns and the band just moved along like a monster, the Barrett brothers' rhythm section living up to its reputation as the official standard for all those who wish to play reggae.

And the revelation of Marley's tricks—dreadlock-tossing now a spectacular aquatic event, what with the hot lights and all that sweat; skillful use of a towel for said dreadlocks during "I Shot the Sheriff", the guitar held firm while Marley works his loose ganja-dance around it. There's also Marley's stage singing, which incorporates all manner of eclectic quirks not heard on the Wailers' records. No matter that he wasn't close enough to the mike to be heard for significant portions of the show—sloppy mike technique and ganja dancing go hand in hand. He's a superb singer. It was dusk by the time of the grand finale, and the grand finale was, of course, "Get Up. Stand Up," with Marley's urgent vocal hammering the message home: a kind of frenzied proletarian battle cry and prayer meeting all in one—"Get up, stand up, stand up for your rights. Get up, stand up, don't give up the fight!" At this point it became impossible to discern what was Jamaican and what was American. The crowd took it to heart, and was delighted when Marley went straight to the nuts of many a person's problem with "Excuse me while I light my spliff . . . But don't give up the fight!"

It was on that note—truly funky, truly righteous—that the event came to a close. Marley had proved that he can still mesmerize, even without Bunny and Peter, whose songwriting and vocal talent contributed heavily to the Wailers' work for more than a decade, and he had proved—no small thing, this, in light of the Will Reggae Make It? question—that he can move an American audience quite seriously. And two cultures—two at the very least—had met to boogie.

We are now at a silly press conference, an event in which everybody needs an interpreter quite badly, but nobody asks for one. We have personally ascertained at least two facts about Brother Bob. He is 30 ("I am now," he says when asked) and he is the father of seven children by three women.

Here at the silly press conference, however, nothing quite so concrete is destined to result. The press is attempting to communicate with Brother Bob, who may or may not be trying to reciprocate, but who knows? Besides being a practicing Rastafarian (turn of mind) and a street-talking Jamaican (turn of lip), Marley is far more stoned than any member of the press can afford to be, given the aforementioned obstacles in the path of the old question-and-answer. Consequently, the event begins to take on a markedly tangential quality, like so:

> *Lady reporter, already identified as knowledgeable in Rasta lore:* "Are you going to take a trip across the water soon?"
> *Marley, backing away from the reporters' mikes:* "Acraaas the?" (laughs, rubs his belly)
> *Lady reporter:* "Across the water."

Marley: "Like fram?"
Lady reporter: "Oh, let's say to Europe."
Marley: "Yeewhamgup t'Europe ta. Hyiiiu." (chortles)

The subject, originally broached in what our lady reporter takes as Rasta lingo (trip across the water means return to Ethiopia) is abandoned. We now know that Marley will be in Europe at some undetermined point in the future.

This form of communication may seem confusing, but at least it is happening and like the man from *Oui* is doing, you can always make arrangements for an interpreter after the fact through the miracle of tape. The last time through New York, two years ago, Marley and the Wailers (who still numbered Bunny and Peter amongst them) holed themselves up in the Hotel Chelsea and spent their time cooking an all-inclusive soup of Rastafarian extraction and smoking massive doses of ganja nonstop, leaving their sanctum only to buy the ingredients for the soup and go to work at Max's. Those who made it into their room were faced with a knotty problem: In order for communication to happen at all, the stranger would have to smoke the ganja. Once on their level of intoxication, of course, detailed chitchat and personal histories, your usual journalistic ploys, would be preempted by more suitably stoned excursions along the Rastafarian Way. And as the rap becomes more elevated, the accents thicken. . . But this time, Marley and the Wailers seem more accessible. With Marley the obvious Jamaican contender for American success, a certain amount of exposure is more mandatory than simply prudent.

Marley fills in holes here and there during this silly press conference, and we do learn: Marley enjoyed the concert, and when he played Cleveland it was good, too. A Rasta is not something you can become; Rastas come from Creation. Grass is an herb, grows in the ground. It is for the healing of the nation because when people smoke grass, they communicate better (ironic titters from the unstoned press). Yes, the Wailers were offered spots on the Stones tour, but they couldn't make it because of schedule conflicts. Too bad: It would have been interesting to see Jagger and the Stones handle a boogie band just as professional as they are, and maybe even more interesting. And man must be free, music must be free. All this time, Marley is smiling that huge grin and chortling heartily after each response. He likes this game.

Yes, and Babylon travels on one line, free men travel on another. There's no need to collide. And reggae is a music that has plenty, plenty fight. And Toots is a Rasta, too; Jimmy Cliff is "just a man" and still making music on the Island. And white men really can't play or produce reggae music. Marley says he never heard of Eric Clapton until he heard Clapton's "Sheriff."

His uncle and granduncle, "all dose type o' people," played blues, but not American blues—more like gospel, more funky, more a country kind of music. Then Clyde McPhatter's "What Am I Living For?" was a big song with Marley, and there was Otis Redding and Sam Cooke and James Brown later in life. Now he'll go to parties in Jamaica and dance all night to "every'tin, every'tin at all." There's a man in Jamaica who plays a bamboo saxophone that is "aaaah dangerous!" Marley's manager, a man who seems to suffer from that peculiar kind of hyperthyroid condition of the mind common to his trade loosens up here to confirm Bob's assessment of the man with the bamboo saxophone.

And then maybe—yes, definitely maybe—the Wailers will play a "Midnight Special."

The conference ends with Marley, laid back in his chair, vastly amused. As we depart, he is dancing a soccer ball on his toes.

It is now Saturday night, and the Wailers are waiting in the wings of Manhattan Center while your standard Caribbean dirty comic throws a little schtick to the winds. "Take my wife, man," says Marley's press man by way of comment. This Manhattan Center is very odd: It looks like it's filled with Black accountants, really clean. When Marley begins his act—second exposure confirms that it is an act in the accepted showbiz variety of the term, and not quite a spontaneous burst of Rastafarian exuberance—there is in fact an active degree of boredom at large, as if this is something cooked up by the Tourist Board. There is definitely something wrong. The sound is totally screwed. Klieg lights bathe the multitude in brilliant white light at the most inappropriate moments.

Applause follows each number, nice and sedate. It's like everyone has a cold. Marley gives up and leaves the stage without so much as a war cry. You remember that he is an outlaw in Jamaica, not exactly your Mantovani of the Island-Paradise. Not polite, not harmless, not even entertaining.

But then, after he's gone, something else begins to happen. There is, to begin with, a rapid exodus of well-clothed human turkeys, slowly followed by a huge rumble of shouts for more from what is left of the audience: dreadfolk. All of a sudden they're there, and Marley, vindicated, comes back again for a three-song encore. The joint commences to jump and it's strange: It's almost a private party here now, almost like the old Stones or the New York Dolls or a damn good high school dance. It's a question of a thousand people swaying in unison, far away from home and even further away from talkin' to the boss. It's kinky reggae, and it's hypnotic once again. Marley stretches out his arms and hovers in the flat white light like a crucified bird, feeling the bass notes buzz up through his legs and moving softly to their rhythm as the music thunders on and on.

Musicmakers:
Bob Marley and the Wailers

by Vernon Gibbs

(Source: **Essence,** *January 1976)*

WITHIN the past year Bob Marley has led his band, the Wailers, from relative obscurity to international acclaim. Marley's volatile personal image and the ragged lope of the Wailers' music have made them the most exciting exponents of the Jamaican popular music known as reggae. It seemed only logical that they be chosen as the Jamaican headliners for the first international "dream" concert held recently in Kingston, Jamaica.

The concert, which featured Stevie Wonder, came to a tumultuous conclusion as Wonder and Marley joined each other in performing their respective hits, "Superstition" and "I Shot the Sheriff." And long after Marley had left the stage, people shouted his name.

To many Jamaicans Marley's Rastafarian involvement makes him far more than just another entertainer. Rastafarian "philosophy" and imagery have in the last five years gained more than a toehold among the nation's poor. Once the most despised segment in the Jamaican social structure, the sect today is credited with bringing about a new pride in indigenous Jamaican culture and speech patterns. Rastas are proud people who may beg for work but never for money. The only obvious sign that a man's a Rasta is his hair, which is never combed nor cut but braided into long strands and waxed. These masses of knotted curls are called "dreadlocks."

What has made Rastas seem visionary to Jamaican youth has been their alienation from Babylonian (Western) society, their refusal to pay taxes, their muddled mysticism that sees the late Haile Selassie as the personification of Jah-Jehovah-God and their spectacular success in spreading Jamaican music across the globe.

Reggae was initially an imitation of American rhythm and blues—circa 1950—and was known as blue beat, ska and rock steady before becoming popularized as reggae. From the very beginning it was characterized by a uniquely identifiable rhythmic pattern unlike anything in the world. Even though much reggae continues to imitate R&B phrasing and vocal technique, some of the best is delivered in Rastafarian transformations of English, which are totally incomprehensible to people unfamiliar with the West African rhythms of their dialect.

Some of the most popular records on the island get the least airplay because of the controversial subject matter: sex, marijuana, the dozens traded between enemy camps of musicians and a coming police state that some Jamaicans see as inevitable. Bob Marley emerged from the underground through the constant use of these themes in his music. He started writing hits 15 years ago, and aside from Jimmy Cliff he is the most consistent songwriter on the island. Like most exponents of authentic root music, it is impossible to separate Marley from his music.

"People come down ya and them ask why I turn Rasta and why I wear me hair like this. Even me own mother didn't want talk to me when she first hear that I turn Rasta. But is no me turn Rasta, is *you* turn something else. Every Black man is born a Rasta, is just that most of them don't realize it. The way I wear me hair is the natural way, the way that Jah meant for the black man to wear his hair. If I was anything else, I could explain to you. We not think that one set of people should hoard up everything, we want share what we have with everybody. Them still don't like Rasta even though there is a whole heap of Rasta. And sometimes if two policemen catch you 'round the corner, them might still want beat you. But the wicked shall perish because they deny the truth. The Black man shall run the earth again."

In Kingston the crushing levels of poverty stand in bold contrast to the sumptuous houses in the hills. The minimum wage is $20 a week, but the cost of living is twice as high for the basics and three to four times as high for a "luxury" item such as an American automobile. Rastafarian philosophy and reggae speak to this. And the music and the message have found a ready and enthusiastic audience for such criticism and social commentary.

This phenomenon has not been completely lost on the Jamaican government, which has initiated a policy of Democratic Socialism with vague hints of eventually distributing the wealth. So far bauxite, the nation's prime industry, has been nationalized, and the tourist business, which ranks second, is next on the agenda. Marley, who makes it his business to stay out of politics, is highly amused by all this.

"Maybe them go nationalize reggae next. Them didn't use to like it, but reggae is the people's music, and if them no like it, them no like the people. Them going have to do something, or the people going burn this place down in the next few years. Me no take no part in the government because me no interested in power. If me was, me would try to become a politician. But me is a Rasta man, and me talk bout things the way me see them."

Bob Marley has made being a Rasta a form of acceptance and recognition. Jamaican music has found a rallying point. And in the Kingston nights the streets throb with the looming bass shuffle and more reggae bands singing about "Rastaman" and "natty dread."

Innocents in Babylon: A Search for Jamaica Featuring Bob Marley and a Cast of Thousands

by Lester Bangs

(Source: Creem Magazine, *June and July 1976)*

THE FIRST thing that should be established is that I was only in Jamaica for a week, and there is no way to compress Jamaica or its music scene into one week, or one article. So what you are about to get is just the surface, the shell. But I hope that if you look beneath this surface you may begin, as I am, to figure out a lot of what is going on in Jamaican music, and a little of the turmoil currently besetting Jamaican society.

I can't say that this piece is really representative of that society, even from an outsider's viewpoint, because I never got out of Kingston, a bullet-pocked industrial metropolis not dissimilar to Detroit. Even though Jamaica is a country where 2 percent of the population has 80 percent of the money and the rest suffer some of the worst poverty in the world, it's also true that in Jamaica at its least urban the poor can live more comfortably than most other places in the world: build a simple house in the country, start a garden, grow food and herb, pick fruit off the trees or go to the ocean and catch fish. The trouble begins when country people come into Kingston, lured by promises of a better life in the big city. They end up in slums like Trenchtown and Jones Town, living in shacks and incredible squalor. The result, of course, is crime and violence both "random" and "political."

Out of all this, however, like oppressed black people in other places before them, they have created a vital indigenous musical form called reggae. I'm not going to argue the merits of reggae here: it's still an acquired taste for the vast majority of U.S. listeners, white or black, so if you respond to it at all you will probably love it and if not you may find it an intolerably boring form of protracted ricky-ticky rhythm. Reggae has been intimately linked with the growing awareness on the part of western Caucasians of Rastafarianism, a primitive mystical-religious sect which has been around Jamaica for several decades now. The Rastafarians believe that Marcus Garvey, father of the Back to Africa movement, was a prophet who foresaw the coming of Jah, the Savior also promised in the Bible, a Savior who would lead all oppressed black people to their Promised Land. Garvey said the Savior was coming in 1927, and in 1930 Haile Selassie was crowned Emperor of Ethiopia, becoming the first black head of a 20th Century African state. Ergo, the Rastas believe that Selassie, who was born Ras Tafari and ruled Ethiopia till his death in the Seventies, was (is) Jah; and that soon he will return to bring the Rastas, who believe themselves to be the lost tribe of Israel, home to Ethiopia a.k.a. Zion. In the meantime, while they await Armageddon as prophesied in the Bibles they read daily, they'll have nothing to do with Babylon, the present system of things— they do not vote, instead espousing pacifism, anti-materialism, growing their hair out in long, wild, bushy patches called dreadlocks, and the smoking of lots of herb a.k.a. ganja a.k.a. weed/tokes/dope to us, which they believe to be a mystical sacrament of Jah. Soon, through the combined forces of Jah and higher herb consciousness, Armageddon will come in the form of a mystical revolution which will topple Babylon and set all Jah's children free to return to Paradise.

In other words, kind of a Third World cross between John Sinclair and Jehovah's Witnesses.

Out of all this has risen one major musical figure, who represents to Jamaicans approximately what Bob Dylan represented to white American college students ten years ago: Bob Marley. Marley and his group the Wailers have thus far released four albums (plus two earlier ones in England and several more in Jamaica) which have made him a star among white youth in England, but is just beginning to break through in America, where reggae is still regarded as a bit of a curiosity by most white listeners and outright disdained by blacks. Which is why I, along with a raft of other white journalists and photographers, was flown down by Island Records for a sort of Cook's Tour of Jamaican music and the somewhat obligatory interview with Bob Marley.

I am on the phone with an L.A. rep for Island, who shall henceforth be referred to as Wooly, because of the cap this white lad wore, in imitation of the Rastas, throughout his stay in Jamaica. I tell him that, even though I love reggae with a passion that is threatening to cost me some friends, I have always considered Bob Marley's records rather cold and he is in fact my least favorite reggae artist.

He laughs. "Shhh—you're not supposed to *say* things like that!"

"Okay, then, where's this guy Marley at?"

"Well, Bob's philosophy can be summed up in one word: 'righteous.'"

"Do you mean like righteous weed, or the righteous wrath of Jehovah, or righteous brothers and sisters living off the land . . . "

"Well, kind of a combination of all three."

"I see—he's a hippie."

"Right."

Jamaica is still undergoing what might be termed a colonial hangover. It has no real indigenous population, not even a few scattered enclaves like the American Indians, because the original Jamaicans, the Arawaks, were all slaughtered by Christopher Columbus and the Spaniards. The island was for centuries but one protectorate in the British Empire, and in fact only gained its independence in 1962. Since then it has made very little progress toward autonomy, and there is a lack of motivation among most of the people that can be ascribed to more than the tropical climate. All the most negative connotations of "laid back" can be found in Kingston—people are slow, lackadaisical, facts get lost in the haze of ganja and time barely exists. "I'll be back in 45 minutes" can mean three to six hours, "We'll get it together this afternoon" may mean tomorrow night or never at all. One writer on this trip claimed that every horoscope in the *Daily Gleaner* counseled "patience," and there is an expression that you hear constantly which perfectly sums up the lazy, whenever-we-get-around-to-it tempo of Jamaican life: "Soon come." I think the discernible lack of motivation on the part of many Jamaicans can be ascribed to a rather complex combination of ganja, lack of education, and having little to no idea what to do with themselves as a people in the absence of colonialism. A lot of people (especially Americans) feel that legalization of herb would be the answer to the island's economic problems; I think that the situation in Jamaica is the most persuasive argument I've ever seen for its non-legalization, and the fact that everybody smokes it anyway does nothing to contradict that. Of course, the argument could be raised that the people resort so extensively to this dope, which is not nearly as strong as legend would have it and has the most tranquilizing effect of any I've ever smoked, to blot out their feeling of helplessness in the face of such realities as that Michael Manley, the current Prime Minister who came in on a liberal reform ticket, is now taking on some of the earmarks of a dictator. As for the Rastas, it makes sense that they should dream of a pilgrimage back to the cradle of Ethiopia since all black people in Jamaica are descended from people originally brought here as slaves, except for one hitch: the current government of Ethiopia is almost virulently anti-Selassie, and would hardly welcome an influx of Jah knows how many thousand dreadlocked dopers with almost no skills or education. I seriously doubt most of the Rastas know this, just as I doubt that most Jamaicans would know or care that their "freedom" has made the island perhaps more wide-open than ever for colonialist carpetbaggers.

What all this has to do with reggae is that for most reggae connoisseurs the old-time Jamaican music scene is rabble-rousingly epitomized in *The Harder They Come*, the Perry Henzell film about a youth who records a song he wrote himself for an unscrupulous (and archetypal) producer who pays him twenty bucks and tells him to scram. He is forced to resort to selling herb for money, the producer rips him off for all royalties, his dealings lead him to a shoot-out, and the great twist upon which this intentionally amateurish film hangs is that the kid is Public Enemy Number One and has the Number One hit single at the same time: a Bob Dylan wet dream.

Understandably, this film is banned in Jamaica. But conventional wisdom has it that the music-biz situation depicted in it has been rendered a thing of the past, principally by the founder-president of Island Records, Chris Blackwell. When reggae first became a popular export, in England in the late Sixties and early Seventies, the big English reggae label was Trojan, where boxes of tapes with nothing but artists' names and song titles printed by hand used to arrive to be waxed and sold with the artists in most cases receiving no royalties at all. It must be remembered that most of the people making this music come from poverty and illiteracy so extreme that they can have little to no idea of the amounts of money to be made from it; undoubtedly many have been satisfied merely to have a record released with their name on the label and voice in the grooves. In such a situation many vital performers and groups, such as the Pioneers and even Desmond Dekker (who had a U.S. hit in '69 with "Israelites") were allowed to die on the vine, and Chris Blackwell is the first exception to this—the first person to try to build the careers of individual reggae artists and an international market for them.

Many people, however, feel that conditions for Jamaican musicians are much the same today as in *The Harder They Come*, even if most don't actually resort to picking up the gun. The content of the records being released has become increasingly geared to visions of Rasta revolution of the mind and heart, although it is difficult to see how Babylon could fall and leave the record companies standing, a

paradox that your average Rasta musician is cosmically adroit at skirt-
ing. With all their talk of "Jah will provide," the Rastafarians may yet
prove the first people in history to actively (if innocently) collaborate
in their own exploitation by the music industry. Robert Johnson got
ripped off too, but I doubt that it was a tenet of his religion. Then
again, it may be that the Rastas are merely the logical extension of the
sad lethargy, punctuated by random blasts of berserk gunfire, which
permeates Jamaica like the smog steadily building over Kingston.

Then again, that lethargy may be as illusory as many other things
in Jamaica. The rude boys (Jamaican street punks of the early Sixties)
were not lethargic, Marley has sung that "a hungry mob is an angry
mob," and there is certainly no lethargy in a white person going to a
black country, or shouldn't be if he values his skin. There is something almost obscenely ironic in the need to find exotic strokes in
folks so far removed from you, who are not, at all, exotic to themselves; in the way white longs to lose itself in black.

Monday. Flying over Cuba, I first realized that I was heading for
the celebrated Third World. All that means for us is poor people,
poorer than you or I could probably ever conceive. There's no way
they're not gonna hate our guts, there's no way you're not gonna be
slumming no matter who you are—I had been told that they hate
black Americans as well as white (a certain odd comfort in that), and
when I got there I was to discover that the hatred you feel emanating
from many Jamaicans has far more to do with class and economic
status than race, and that many of them would display a genuine
warmth that had nothing to do with fawning with seething guts for
bwana's silver. So you might as well enjoy yourself, rubberneck, and
try not to get killed. It ain't no tropical paradise to the natives; seem
to remember a guy singing a song about tables turning, begin to see
what it means.

Flying from Montego Bay to Kingston, impressions of California; green hillsides dotted with elegant swimming pool split-levels below, but the music reverberating in my head bespoke only Trenchtown and was at such variance with what I saw down there that I could only wonder how long till they tear this place apart, burning and looting non-metaphorically with no metaphysical ganja above-it-all possible. You wonder if you'll be able to visit this country at all in a few years, and your wonder increases during your stay as you read in the daily papers how Manley is chumming up with Castro, supposedly all because of a cane thresher developed by the Cubans whose blueprints could revolutionize the sugarcane business in Jamaica (where it's still cut by hand) and thereby perhaps save the economy. Meanwhile, the only people more violently anti-Communist than Cuban refugees are seemingly the people of Jamaica on all class levels; you wonder at times who they must hate more—the mindlessly patronizing American and Canadian tourists, or the Communists. In any case, there's something in the air that you can breathe and taste like emotional cinders, and it isn't love. When you get off the plane in Montego Bay and walk in to get your health card stamped, Disney World calypso natives in straw hats serenade you with backdrop of Holiday Inn sign, poster advertising the beaches of Negril (where all the white hippies go), arid latrine-green plaque warning in two languages that smoking, possession, or sale of ganja ("marijuana," they add in parentheses for naïve hiplets) is a crime punishable by imprisonment. From the plane window, I look down and see a red lake, which I will later discover has been turned that hue and into a quicksand bog by bauxite mining on the part of the Alcoa corporation.

The first sound I heard on arriving in the Kingston airport was the Muzak blasting a Jamaican imitation Otis Redding version of "Hey Jude," which I thought was funny enough until I discovered that Jamaican AM radio almost never plays reggae. After a week of very little beyond Helen Reddy and Neil Diamond, I would be anxious to get the hell out of this place and back home just so I could hear some Toots and the Maytals.

Kingston is very little more than a vast slum surrounding the ominous towers of babel in an enormous plastic palm Sheraton hotel, from which tourists seldom venture and around the swimming pool of which a great deal of Island Records' business is conducted. This place has a Marcus Garvey Room (I peeked in the door; it looked like one of the rooms where I used to give speeches to Rotarian banquets in high school), but that is no reason why, upon arriving or anytime else, you should buy dope, "gold" bracelets or anything from the guys hanging around the parking lot. My colleague from *Rolling Stone*, arriving a virtual rube with no one to warn him, purchased a rather small quantity of not very good herb from one of these characters for the outrageous sum of $25. I have decided that it is a truth, if not a right, that in Kingston you are going to get burned, regardless of race, creed, or color, even if you never go out in the sun at all.

Tuesday. Another writer, the man from *Swank*, comes to my room and turns me on to the legendary herb. It's good, all right, but nowhere near the rep. It didn't move my attention to unexpected places, inflate trivial ideas into fascinating discursions, or even get me deeper into the music like American dope. It did, however, get me stoned.

Later we went with Wooly on a ride through Kingston. It reminded me of a drab melding of California and Detroit, with slums so bad they made the latter's look like the Sheraton. Wooly takes us to the studio of Lee "Scratch" Perry, one of the most prolific Jamaican producers. True to form, Perry is not home. The man from *Time*, who had stayed up all night when he got here finishing his last story and is on a tight schedule, is visibly hassled, and in the car Mr. *Swank* begins to complain about the fact that everybody is waiting around for Marley to be ready to be interviewed. This writer had apparently been promised an audience with Bob yesterday, and is annoyed to learn that he will not be getting one today either.

Wooly patiently explains that no one can get a really good story on Jamaica without getting into the tempo of Jamaican life, and that everybody will take back from Jamaica whatever they bring there. Wooly is, obviously, very much taken with the tempo and lifestyle himself, even if he is staying in the Sheraton.

We go shopping at Aquarius Records, where I first experience the peculiar Jamaican syndrome of walking into one record store after another and asking for top hit singles or albums like *Best of the Maytals*, and being told again and again that they don't have them. I had a long list of records I wanted to buy, and was only able to obtain a few during my stay on the island. I discovered eventually that this was because the music business here (cf. *The Harder They Come*) was almost totally controlled by the producers, most of whom had their own record stores, where you pretty much had to go to obtain the records they had produced. And the records are not cheap, either—most albums are $6.00, one dub album was quoted at ten bucks to Wooly by a guy in Aquarius, and singles are a dollar. I wondered how a country as poor as Jamaica could support the highest per capita singles issue (thirty released a week) in the world, and was told that Jamaicans almost never bought albums—apparently pressed mainly for export and reggae-loving American tourists—but would at times actually go hungry to have money for a single they wanted.

I was also impressed to learn that Jamaica is the only place I've been where people actually like to play music louder than I do. When you go in the record shops it blares at a volume perilously close to the pain threshold, as the clerk plays deejay, switching off between two turntables and two speakers, one in the shop and one on the street. So your head gets rattled back and forth like a pinball between two raucous tracks and one speaker in the distance and another right on top of you. It's jarring, and emphasizes the violence underlying the laid-back "gentle" character of reggae. Many of these records may be little more than a rhythm with a guitar chopping out two or three chords, no solos except a guy hollering things you can barely understand over the whole thing; but that rhythm is rock steady, the guitars chop to kill, and the singer is, often as not, describing class oppression or street war. There is also a sense of listener-as-artist that is one of the most beautifully developed I have ever encountered. In the first place, all the singles have an instrumental version of the hit on the B side, so the deejays can flip them over and improvise their own spaced-out harangues over the rhythm tracks. Since Jamaican radio plays so little reggae, most of these deejays come off the streets, where until recently you could find, periodically, roots discos set up. Out of these emerged deejay-stars like Big Youth and I Roy, and along with producers like Lee Perry and Augustus "King Tubby" Pablo they have pioneered a fascinating form of technologized folk art called dub. An album by I Roy can thank six different producers on the back "for the use of their rhythms." Don't ask me where the publishing rights go. Don't ask anybody, in fact. And don't ask how musicians might feel who play on one session for a flat rate, only to find it turn up on one or more other hit records. The key with dub is spontaneity, the enormously creative sculpting and grafting of whole new counterpoints on records already in existence. And this sense of the guy who plays the record as performer extends down into the record shops, where the clerks shift speakers, tracks and volume levels with deft magicianly fingers as part of a highly intricate dance, creating sonic riot in the store and new productions of their own in their minds: *I control the dials.*

Wednesday. Waiting around the Sheraton pool for Marley. There is a mood of exasperation with the celebrated Jamaican tempo, which many business-minded visitors seem to view with disgust so extreme it turns to amusement. An English musician, here to do sessions, laughed when I asked him if the state of the Jamaican music industry had undergone any significant alteration since *The Harder They Come*. "Things haven't really changed that much. Before Chris Blackwell set up Island, musicians got six dollars a session. Blackwell revolutionized things by giving them *twelve* dollars a session, and I think by now it's up to fifteen. But I'll say this—Blackwell may be the only person I've ever met in the music business, especially in Jamaica, with *any* integrity at all. I mean, all these guys like I Roy, making these hits—do you think any of them have any money?" He laughs again. "Maybe got nice car, mon. Of course we're all still involved in fucking colonialism and exploitation of the people here, with all these record companies. It's inevitable, there's no way around it. But I suppose there's a certain price we pay too, you see. I hate this fucking place, and can't wait to get out, because I can barely get a session started, much less done, because everybody's so fucking laid back you can't depend on anyone to be at a certain place at a certain time or get any work done. Drives me fuckin' crazy. It's all 'Soon come, mon. Soon come.'"

I also have a revealing conversation with a New York music biz veteran who used to manage Mountain. Now he manages one of the top reggae acts in the world, one with records out in the USA, and he is down here trying to sign Peter Tosh, one of Bob Marley's ex-Wailers and writer-singer of the currently big, banned Jamaican hit "Legalize It (And I'll Advertise It)." My New York vet laughs and says: "This is the only fuckin' place I know where the rooster crows while I'm eating lunch. It's the only place I've been where you can buy a 14-karat gold bracelet for ten bucks off a guy in the hotel parking lot, and when you look inside 'karat' is misspelled. I've been here a fuckin' week, waitin' for one tape from Peter Tosh."

"Why didn't you just go get it from him?"

"He never got around to making a copy yet."

"You mean he has it? Then why don't you borrow it from him and make a copy yourself?"

"Well, you see, when you go to the studios, the engineers may or may not be there, and if they are there they may or may not get around to doing this or that. . . . Also Tosh wouldn't talk to the guy from *Time* magazine who wanted to interview him. Too establishment." He laughs again. (I later found out that Tosh did, eventually, speak to the *Time* writer.) As the subject turns to the reggae artist my friend already manages, he says that his charge "can't write very well. When he has to sign his name, he does it so slowly that it's embarrassing."

"Why don't you just tell him to get a rubber stamp?"

"I thought of that. He just tries to avoid having to sign autographs. As far as all the business stuff, of course, it's totally left to me."

"That must be quite a responsibility."

"You're not kidding. He can't sign a contract, but I imagine he gets around to signing the royalty checks when they come."

I believe I just saw, in the tropics yet, the tip of an iceberg.

Dusk. Swank and Stephen Davis, a journalist who is doing a book on Jamaica, are finally getting their interview with Marley, and have asked me to come along. I would just as soon get it out of the way. There is very much the feel that it is an audience, and everyone is anticipating a difficult time with some cat who might well figure himself the Lion of Judah. Wooly drives us there, and we wait by the car as he goes in Bob's house to check out the vibes. The house itself is a rambling ramshackle affair, a sturdy and capacious abode particularly by Jamaican standards yet looking curiously as if someone began a remodeling job three years ago and never got around to finishing it: pieces of the roof are literally falling out, and there are stacks of wood in back that serve no discernible purpose.

When Bob finally does appear, there is a sense of immediate relief: a slim, barefoot, medium-short, intense-countenanced man, he nev-

ertheless projects an amiability that contradicts his reputation. As well
he should: this guy is being billed, implicitly, as some sort of Noble
Savage, a Jamaican cosmic revolutionary, and yet the truth is that
while he was born in Jamaica he spent two years of his life in Wilmington, Delaware, where his mother still lives, and his father was a
white lieutenant in the British armed services. Even though it is getting dark now, there is some feeling in the air that it would be uncool
to do the interview(s) inside Bob's house, so first he leads us out to a
corner of his front yard by the fence. I explain to him that this is no
good, because the fence is by the street, and the noise of the passing
cars will obscure our voices on the tapes. Which will be complicated
already by the fact that like most Jamaicans and all Rastas, Bob talks
in the indigenous patois that is so thick that *The Harder They Come*
may well have been the first English-language movie in history to re-
quire subtitles in the United States. Of course, he could moderate the
sometimes nigh-impenetrable patois enough to facilitate greater understanding, as many other Jamaicans that I met during my stay, from
record producers to cab drivers, did—but then he would not be so
apparently the most prominent media front-man for the Rasta Revolution. So what he does instead is speak more slowly than your average Rasta, and pause occasionally to ask us if we understand. I don't
remember any of us ever saying no, even though we all agreed later
that there were parts of Bob's spiel that went right by us.

We took a short trek across the lawn into Bob's backyard, where he
perched on the hood of his blue BMW, leaned back against the wind-
screen spliff in hand, and answered all our questions between laying
down the gospel of Rastafari. Often there would be spaces between
his statements, grand cumulous cannabinol ellipses, but all was cool.
We three journalists massed our tape recorders together on the hood
in front of Bob, and stood in a semicircle by the bumper, there being
no place for us to sit, all of which helped to emphasize the sensation

of gently ironic ethnocollision. Bob laughed often, dodged sticky questions like an old media hand, and in general maintained himself admirably for somebody who was probably stoned out of his fucking mind, as various other Rastas wandered out to lean on the car and listen in the gathering dark.

Stephen Davis began on mildly shaky ground, asking Bob if he felt any pressure since a lot of Jamaican musicians were waiting for his success to pave the way for reggae to make it big in the outside world. Bob laughed. "I never feel the pressure that much. But theah dat, is dat the reason for? . . . I never know . . ." He laughed again, and began to expound upon what he did know most intimately: "I have a message and I wan' to get it across . . . tha' message is . . . to live . . . y'know . . . like evrabody believe in life an' death . . . anyone can live . . . as a *Rasta*-man . . . so . . . dat is all . . . I come as a *Rasta*-man now . . . so my message call da worl' Rastafari . . ."

"Would you like to see white kids in the U.S. with dreadlocks?" I asked.

"Yeahmon!" He laughed. "Sure! . . . y'see . . . righteousness shall cover d'earth like da water cover d'sea . . . y'unnarstan . . . so . . . as far as we can go . . . we gonna live right . . . we're all jus' children on d'earth . . . but all mind—wiggy-woggy . . . "

"What do the Rastas think is going to happen in Jamaica?"

"Yehmon . . . yehmon, whoever over here has come, Rasta man mus' go over to Africa . . . "

"Will Rasta man settle for making Jamaica more like Africa and staying here?"

"No, no one settle for Jamaica . . . we like Jamaica, y'know, but—Jamaica spoiled . . . in a sense a Rasta man is concerned a history of Jamaica it has prophesy you know is something no one can change. Jus' like if you have an egg an' break, no one can put it together again—Jamaica is like dat. Something a must happen in creation, dat we from

da wes', go back to da eas' . . . Jamaica canna fix for I & I, Rasta man.
The only way Jamaica can be fix is we bow to the colonial type a thing
what dem 'bout . . . "

"Are you as disappointed," wondered Stephen Davis, not quite getting the point yet, "with the current government as a lot of other Rastas seem to be in discussions I've had with them?"

"*Well!* The present government—past, present—only one government me love: the government of Rastafari. Ca' I know it, we don'
live in dem guys' a-things, y'know, we live outside it. Come like a
bird—we gon' check out certain things, because we know what is
going on, we know dat the rule don' come down from uptown, some
a those guys a kick up hell mon, a nothing a goin' on . . . "

"Are you concerned with changing government here in Jamaica, if
Rastas don't vote?" asked Mr. *Swank*.

"This thing'll never change, mon. Y'see da beauty 'bout it, 'bout Jamaica, is dat we come from Africa, and none of the leaders they want
to accept dat. All 'em wan' call it Jamaicans, and we not Jamaicans.
They all live a thing, you mus' say an die here." Will the last person
leaving Jamaica please turn out the lights.

"How many people do you think would go back to Africa if they
gave them what they wanted?" nervously pressed Mr. *Swank*.

"Well, watch me. Today is not the day, mon, but 144,000, plus a
multitude followed."

"What will be the Rasta reaction if there's a lot of violence?"

"Dem guys not dealing with twelve tribes of Israel. We not talking
about govanment now, govanment wrong, we talkin' 'bout de twelve
tribes of Israel. We wan' the unity and the only unity we can get is
troo Rasta. And the only way we can get the message troo right now
is troo reggae."

Mr. *Swank* tried to bring it down to business: "Since Chris Blackwell has come down with Island Records, he seems to be someone

who can communicate very well with you . . . and uh the rest of the people making the music. But CBS records, the big companies in America are catching wind of reggae and starting to come down, what do you see happening in that situation, big people from Babylon coming to exploit the music?"

"It happen faster. Jus' make the people, help to realize what is happnin', quickah. Canna stop it. Because it's not for the money, yoknow, and da big company, and a money, it's soon ovah. Because if weah brothahs da money is nothing between us." Right, and all Bob Dylan started out wanting was some couches and motorcycles. Marley did, however, have some advice for fledgling reggae musicians: "You have to be careful, ca you can get tricked, out deah. People have rob me, y'know, but once you can see dat dis is what happen, I know or I see dat dis happnin', den dat trick don' go on, y'know." He laughed. "You make record an' sell it, don' get no royalties in Jamaica for long time . . . Lak Trojan Records rob me, mon! All Trojans robbers, mon, all dem English companies jus' take Wes' Indian music."

Stephen Davis observed that it seemed that you never heard reggae on the radio in Jamaica. "Because," testified Bob, "da music is da type o' thing would show up the situation in Jamaica dat some people don' like to hear the real trut', y'know. So dem not sayin' what really happnin' down heah. But when dem don' play it on da radio, man, de people 'ave it in dem house. Goin' dance an' hear it. Radio is important, but once de music come out and dem don' wan' play on d'radio, den big promotion is dat once it's banned evrabody wants ta hear it!" He laughed again.

"But," insisted *Swank*, "didn't Manley promise that he wasn't gonna ban songs?"

Bob just smiled. "I dunno abouat, mon . . . Manley can't stop prophesy . . . prophesy well 'ave its coorse . . ." Someone questioned him about the Rastas' reputation for nonviolence, and Bob surprised us all with, "No, Rastas physical. Y'know whai mean, we don' come lak no sheep to da slaughta . . . "

"Like wan time," added a Rasta who had been leaning over the hood of the car, listening. It had gotten so dark that I could barely see Marley's face, and this other guy's dreadlocks looked like a tarantula crawling down his forehead.

"Like wan time," said Bob. "We don' ovalook war."

"With the situation in Kingston now, do you ever fear for your personal safety?" asked Davis.

"Nossah," said Bob. "No mon, me no fraid for them. I mean, if can avoid dem, will avoid dem, goin' down street, see a roadblock, and dere is a street for me to turn off before I reach da roadblock, you bet I'm gon' to turn off! It's no good I ever get searched."

"Ever been in jail?" I wondered. It was a stock question, actually.

"Yeh, wan time."

"For what?"

He took a long toke. "Drivin' witout license." And laughed. So did we all, but then *Swank* took the offensive once more. "Do you feel that this car represents Babylon?"

Bob seemed genuinely surprised. "The car? *System* represent Babylon, system represent death, we livin' in da system—"

"I was just wondering how you could feel you could have this, while—"

"Is no have dis, mon," replied Bob simply, and knocked on the hood of the car. We had been told the day before by Wooly that Bob had said the BMW stood for Bob Marley & the Wailers, so *Swank* offered this out somewhat sarcastically, and Bob came back, good natured as ever, with an even worse joke: "British Made . . . Warcar . . . "

I tried to smooth things over, in my own bumbling liberal way. "So then this car belongs to all your brothers and sisters as well as you?"

"Belongs road, mon!"

Davis asked Bob what he thought about people coming down to ask all these questions. "Well," said Bob, "as long as dem get da right understanding of da answers and write it . . . because plenty time, plenty guys just write for kicks, y'know, like jus' turn in a joke ting is goin' on, an is serious ting . . . "

Marley was not amused by a certain recent interview in which a writer from New York asked him such questions as "Where did you get your jeans?" and "When you were in New York, did you go shopping at Bloomingdale's?"

Still, he did not seem such a solemn fellow when all was said and done, so I asked him, referring to an old Jamaican motor sport, whether he had ever rammed a goat in this car. There was much laughter all around, after which he explained, "No no no, don' think dat, man, people need live good purpose man . . . when you see a goat, you are supposed to stop, communicate to de goat, and make de goat knows de outcome . . . a goat's smart, y'know . . . when you hit a goat, man, you sad!"

"Yes, Rasta," interjected the Rasta on the other side of the hood with the tarantula on his brow. Bob then explained that ramming a goat was considered unlucky. By now most of us were packing up our tape recorders, readying ourselves for the trek back to the Sheraton, but Mr. *Swank* struck for one more shot at social relevance: "This is an election year, isn't it, coming up?"

Bob took a long hit on his spliff. "Yeah? Dat so?"

The Rasta with the tarantula clarified: "You can't serve two masters wan time, y'know." Another, feistier member of the brethren behind him decided to take Mr. *Swank* on: "Do you know about da twelve tribes of Israel?"

This, for *Swank*, was the last straw. "Of course I do—I'm Jewish!"

"Oh yah? What tribe you belong?"

"Well, uh, I'm not exactly sure—"

"Yah? Then how you know you member twelve tribes?"

"Because my *father* told me!"

"Your father???!!!" The Rasta thought, apparently, that *Swank* was referring to his Father in Heaven.

"Yeah, my father and my mother!"

"Oh, you *parents!*"

"Yeah!"

"You read tha Oly Bible?"

"Of *course!*"

"All da way troo?" This guy was obviously not going to be easily convinced; from the beginning, several of those in attendance had been observably suspicious of the motives of these white foreigners with tape recorders. Marley just sat back smoking and laughing. Mr. *Swank*, who in his life had been known to take amphetamines for his weight and est for his personality, was getting frazzled, finally allowing himself to get truly combative after having to wait on Marley and suffer evasive answers. "Yeah, I read it all the way through!"

"How long it take you?" demanded the Rasta.

"Whattaya mean, how long—it was a long time ago!"

Triumph: "You read wan chapter a day, you can read da whole Bible in tree an' a half years!"

Swank backed off enough to see the discretion of not countering with a "So what?" In fact, he didn't have much of anything to say at all, just now, and the Rasta leaped into the breach, accusing him of not really being a member of the twelve tribes of Israel, since he didn't even know which one he belonged to. They argued a bit, and *Swank* eventually allowed as how it was quite probable that he belonged to the tribe of Levi. I think at that moment he would have practically sworn an affidavit to that effect. So now he could slip out of further wranglings, Bob could go in his house for supper, and the

Second and Third Worlds could, for this one evening at least, part gracefully and with a nice buzz on.

Thursday. I am in a cab with John Martyn, bombing through the streets of Kingston on the way to Strawberry Hill. John is an English songwriter who is planning to record part of his next album in Jamaica, but right now we are on our way to a Burning Spear recording session where he is going to do some guitar overdubs. First, however, we have to drive up to Strawberry Hill to pick up the guitar at Chris Blackwell's hilltop estate. The road is long, narrow and whip-winding, with perilous curves and steep drops off the shoulder, but the country around it is beautiful, lavish with brilliant green and yellow. It's a welcome respite, and the only time I will see anything close to still-existing primal Jamaica during my stay. On the way up Martyn points out to me the palatial estate of Blackwell's parents, who made millions of dollars in decades of colonial enterprise in Jamaica. On the way back down we meet, pedaling uphill on a rusty bicycle as if floating, a friend of Martyn's named Country Man. Country Man is a Rasta with university education, gifted, articulate and imbued with enough of the unimpeachably mystical that even a cynic like Martyn (who beats your reporter) believes the accounts of him levitating on occasion. Country Man lives by swimming or rowing far off the coast into the Caribbean, holding onto a rock among the Keys with one arm, and grabbing fish as they swim by. The best story about Country Man is that his wife complained once because he would go off on such expeditions for three days at a time leaving her alone; she wanted, she said, a radio for company. So Country Man sold their house, used the money to buy her a radio, and built a new house the same day.

When we arrive at the Spear session we discover, naturally enough, that we are the first people to show up even though we are over an hour late. So we take a walk around the corner, a risky proposition for

whites in downtown Kingston at any time of the day, and have a couple of drinks in a black bar where sullen youth are playing billiards. I
feel only minor drafts. An old man comes up and asks me where I
come from, and expresses a sentiment I would hear from a few other,
mostly older Jamaicans during my stay: "Many people say bad things
about Jamaica, that is violence, bad place to live. This is not true. You
know, there's an old saying: believe only half of what you see—"

"And none of what you hear," I finished.

He nodded and smiled. "Right"

We go back to the session, which is taking place in Randy's Studios,
which naturally enough is right over Randy's Record Shop, which
may be the best store in Jamaica and is the first place you should go if
you have a shopping list—Randy stocks records by everybody, not
just the output of his studio and star producer, Jack Ruby, who is himself a bit of a legend. Ruby, who has also worked as a hotel waiter,
started producing two and a half years ago and his biggest success to
date has been with Burning Spear, a vocal trio straight out of the hills
whose U.S.-released album, *Marcus Garvey*, epitomizes the more
purely African wing of reggae. There is something almost aboriginal
about Burning Spear—Winston Rodney walks up to the mike and begins to sing a new song about living in the hills, Rupert Willington
and Delroy Hines harmonizing behind him, and there is a haunting
plaintiveness in his voice as he sings of his brother going to the river
to get the water for his family. As he tells this seemingly simple story,
the dozen or so black youths milling about in the control room,
friends of the producer and band, laugh and comment to each other
approvingly. The reason they are doing this is that many of them have
probably experienced what Rodney is singing about—spending a
whole day going back and forth to the nearest river, which may be a
distance of miles, with a bucket on your head, until the drum or bar-
rel which is the family's only water supply is full. In the middle of the

song Rodney sings "These are the sounds of the hills," and begins making bird calls and animal sounds. Martin Denny it isn't. Later Martyn, who has been warming up with some obviously overbusy Eric Clapton runs, will add a few spare, sustained-note and wah wah lines which fill out the track perfectly, especially when he plays an intentionally "wrong" note which in its strange offness somehow is exactly right for Burning Spear, whose sound always remains primal no matter how arranged.

Perhaps most fascinating is that all this goes on with seemingly little direction from producer Ruby. He watches Spear sing awhile, then, *in the middle of a take*, leaves the control board to chat with the visitors and other musicians hanging around the studio, lounging later across the board to read a copy of *Newsweek* I'd brought; then, intermittently, he would unexpectedly snap up from reading or conversation, shout "Spear!" stop the take and bolt into the studio to tell them to bring this up, take that down, change the thing around till the sound is right and tight. All this is in such contrast to conditions in American studios, where not a pin can drop in the control room during a take and there is a red light outside the door barring visitors (who come and go freely in Randy's) when the tape is rolling, that it is mind-blowing. In the midst of such seeming casualness, people talking, joking and rolling endless spliffs everywhere, there is enormous interior discipline; Ruby, while reading *Newsweek* with seeming indifference, is listening intently and in iron control all the way. I mentioned this to him, and he replied, "Of course. I always know the sound I want, and I always get it." He also got two completed takes in one afternoon, which racks up pretty well against the output of any New York producer or studio, for all their comparative uptightness.

Toward the end of the session, the writer and photographer from *Time* arrive to interview Ruby, and later Martyn and I catch a ride back to the Sheraton with them. By now it is nine o'clock at night, not at all a safe time for whites, even in numbers, to be on the streets of Kingston. It is *never* safe for whites to go into Trenchtown. But now the *Time* photog is pointing at the myriad small, brightly lit black rum bars we pass, saying "C'mon, what the fuck, man, I could use a beer, let's just go in." Martyn and I cower in the back, laughing but praying these guys will not stop. Meanwhile, *Time*'s scribe is saying, "I've *got* to figure out a way to get into Trenchtown . . ." I tell him to forget it, and he replies that he's been thinking maybe around five in the morning would be a safe time.

We arrive back at the hotel in a driving rain, running past the poolside bar where under the roof Canadian tourists are singing "Granada" to organ music almost as loud as the speakers in the record stores.

I could use a little bit of cross-cultural relaxation myself. I retire to my room where I watch *Hawaii Five-O* and an old Universal Grade D musical about singing soldiers from the late Thirties, on the TV I had to order when I first checked in. Jamaican TV is weird—there's only one TV network, JBC, which turns up on several channels with things like "An Evening with the Jay-Teens," an hour of young black girls doing folk dances from various cultures against a blank backdrop. (There was no announcer, they looked like a high school dance recital, and moved as stiffly as one through all the corny choreography except when it came time to do African dances, which they performed, of course, fantastically.) The first thing I saw when I turned on my TV on Tuesday morning was a woman demonstrating the use of a steam iron with stilted delivery: "This we use to wash and iron clothes, to keep ourselves clean and our people healthy . . ." Commercials for condoms and birth control pills also run regularly. Every afternoon the station goes off for several hours, leaving a test pattern and radio station playing the usual American pap. The rest of the programming is equally weird and scattered, featuring things like *Bache-*

lor Father, The Six Million Dollar Man (8:45 on Friday night—some
shows come on at times like 6:02, right after headline news) and
Sesame Street, which seems to be a big favorite. I got to watch, since
there was nothing else, the singing-soldiers movies for two nights in
a row, leading me into dark speculations about propaganda, which
were probably paranoid.

Friday. After breakfast I go for a walk around the block immediately
adjacent to the hotel, and look into faces radiating undisguised hatred.
When I stop a youth and ask him for directions to a local record store,
he answers grudgingly in a patois I can't understand anyway. I have not
stopped being uptight in the almost four days I have been here, and
feel a strong yearning to get the hell out of the fucking place.

Back at the hotel, I run into Chris Blackwell by the pool, and he in-
vites me to visit a couple of recording studios with him. Blackwell
himself exudes an air at once sanguine and blasé—he came from
money, now he's making more money, and everything about him indicates that the good life agrees with him. Sandy hair, brilliant tan
that reminded me of many I'd seen in Hollywood, the kind of person
who looks so healthy it's almost obscene, *too* healthy. Or maybe it is
merely endemic to record industry people, this air of bland hedonism.
In any case, Blackwell always looks as if he is either on his way to or
from a tennis court. Now we are in a limousine, riding out to the
home studios of Lee Perry and King Tubby, who live in relatively af-
fluent sections of Kingston; these guys are two of the biggest producers on the island. Their houses look like American working-class
homes circa 1954. At Tubby's I watch an engineer mastering a dub,
and get to meet Vivian "Yabby" Jackson, leader (& producer) of a
group called the Prophets, whose album, *Conquering Lion*, was
recorded at Harry J's studio across town and mixed here; I have just
bought a copy of the album at Micron Records (not coincidentally,

the store and label bear the same name) for five bucks, and show it to
him. Then I lean over and shout in his ear over the booming dub
beat: "How much money did you get for making this?"

"Nothing yet," he says.

Out in Tubby's back yard, I meet U Roy, who is not I Roy, and
whose album, *Dread in a Babylon*, has just been picked up by Virgin
Records in the U.K. We shake hands, and I tell him how much I like
his record. I do not tell him that I thought on the first cut, "Runaway
Girl," his vocal sounded much like Mick Jagger circa *Aftermath*. It is
interesting to note that on the album cover he looks like some ragged
shaman, squatting on the ground almost hidden behind a giant cloud
of ganja smoke, dreadlocks spearing out in every direction. Now, in
person, he is dressed in a beret, red sweater, and brown slacks. He puts
a record on a turntable and the unmistakable, cannonade-in-a-cavern
sound of dub thunders from two giant speakers set up in the dirt in
Tubby's backyard. A little kid dances in front of one of the speakers, on
which "Tubby" is spelled in Chinese-style lettering, pressing his ass
against the speaker cloth, getting off on the vibrations, looking at me
and laughing. The record playing consists of a deep rumble of
Echoplexed drums, out of which, every so often an Echoplexed and
perhaps reverbed male voice (which I will later discover belongs to Big
Youth, one of the most venerable dub artists) hollers, "What the world
needs now, is love, sweet love . . ." I blink. Blackwell laughs: "I wonder
what Burt Bacharach would think of this." I suggest that Blackwell
bring him down here and show it to him. One thing seems certain—
old Burt is not going to get any royalties on this one. Not that he needs
them. I think for a moment that perhaps there is a certain democracy
in the rip-offs permeating Jamaican music, dismiss that as a dangerous
notion, and start babbling to Blackwell about "folk technology." We
agree that dub is fascinating, but neither of us has any idea what to do
with it. Which is perhaps as it should be. The young blacks sitting

around smoking spliffs and listening to this record at the customary earsplitting volume ignore us, except for one who, later in the studio, introduces himself as Clinton Williams and beckons me outside, where he hands me a piece of paper, which looks like a blank invoice, upon which is printed "The Golden-Age Furnishing Co.," along with a phone number. Williams has written his name on one of the lines, and this serves as his card. He tells me he is doing some independent producing in Kingston, has in fact produced five records, and has been a contender for the amateur lightweight boxing championship of Jamaica. I ask him how he finds time both to box and produce records, not bothering to mention that the number he has asked me to call him at seems to be that of a furniture store. He tells me that he wants to become a big-time producer, that the competition is fierce, and that established figures like Tubby and Scratch Perry pretty much have a monopoly on the scene, making it extremely difficult for a young cat to break in. Which sounds a lot like the States, actually. I press him on boxing vs. production; I mean, which is the sideline? He finally laughs. "Boxing." I ask him if he can give me a percentage breakdown on record profits as split between artists, producers and record store owners. Sure, he says. "Usually, about sixty percent goes to the store, thirty percent to the producer, and ten percent to the singer. But sometimes the producers and stores get forty-five percent each."

Back in the limousine and over to Lee Perry's. Perry is a big man in the island's music scene; he produced Bob Marley's early (and superior) sides, and his current star artist is Max Romeo, with "War in a Babylon" by Max Romeo and the Upsetters a hot item in both Jamaica and England. "The Upsetter" is one of Perry's aliases, and it is a measure of what stars producers are in Jamaica that the clerk in Aquarius had showed me an album called *King Tubby Vs. The Upsetter*, a kind of dueling-control-boards, mock-championship-match soundtrack consisting entirely of instrumental dub violence fit to

shatter your eardrums. In Perry's studio, behind his house, he is a little potentate, mixing and playing back his tapes for a steady stream
of admirers who stand in herb awe as he dances around his control
board, changing levels and flicking switches or whirling dials with a
flourish and a knowing smile of infinite humor. I can't say exactly
how or why, but merely to meet and watch him work for a few minutes is to be irrevocably impressed, to know you are in the presence
of genius. The decor of his studio is also instructive: blacklight
posters and big color pictures of Bruce Lee (who is a big hero on the
island, because guns are banned and he fights with his fists) over
walls and ceiling fitted out with an interplay of bright red and green
carpeting, which I found out later are, with gold, the colors in the
flag of Ethiopia.

But this guy was no Rasta, no matter what he or anybody else says.
This was an uptown cat. A hipster. With his hair slicked straight back,
his graying beard, strutting around cocky and amused, a diminutive
lion in his kingdom, he at length danced over to the corner where I
was trying to be inconspicuous, squeezed past me, grabbed a bottle
and, straightening up, stopped a second to look me in the eyes close
as the air, smiling knowingly, and I smiled back. A few minutes later
he walked up to me and said, "You wine man," and handed me a plastic cup and a bottle of something called Winecarnes, which is a local
wine fortified with meat extracts that he seemingly drinks all day
without ever losing his stride.

Now, dear reader, I know that this—one drunk recognizing another—is not the most profound or miraculous occurrence in the
world, but here, in the middle of Herb Heaven, with every righteous
Rasta and American hiplet in sight belittling the rum culture like it
was 1967 all over again, it qualified as outright mind-reading.

As we were leaving Perry's, walking down the driveway to the limousine, I heard a familiar sound and peeked for a moment inside the

open door to the living room of his house. There, on the couch, his kids were watching a Road Runner cartoon on TV.

Back at the hotel, I made arrangements to meet Blackwell for dinner. By the pool I met my colleague from *Rolling Stone,* and over drinks Blackwell asked him what angle he was going to approach his story from. "Oh, I dunno, man," he replied, with no idea who he was talking to, "I'm just gonna use the gonzo approach for this one pretty much. I intend to do my whole story from the poolside bar and go out of the hotel as little as possible. I mean, who gives a fuck, y'know? I'm just in this for the free drinks and to see if I can get laid."

Blackwell looked a little green around the eyeballs, but went on to ask Gonzo what he thought of reggae.

"I can't remember ever hearing any. The last album I really got into was *The Allman Brothers Live at Fillmore East.* Hell, man, I don't even have a record player!"

Blackwell's jaw dropped.

Later at dinner, Blackwell is still staring sourly at Gonzo, who is raving at Michael Butler, a receding face behind a gray Van Dyke who was the producer of *Hair* and is down here getting ready to put together a reggae *Hair* with the projected title of *Babylon.* Don Taylor, Marley's manager, a thin, light-skinned black man in a Toots and the Maytals cap, is telling me and the man from *Melody Maker* that many American blacks resent Jamaican immigrants because, he says, the latter tend to hustle harder and achieve more. He cites his mother, who he says worked at menial jobs but wound up owning her own apartment house, then: "It's just like Bob. He is very dedicated to his music, but when it comes to his money, he is not going to let anyone cheat him out of any portion of his equal share."

Right. No good businessman would. A phrase often used by Rastas and heard in many reggae songs is "I and I." It can mean me, you, we, etc., all balled up in one great big cosmic loving mulch; the old "I am he as you are me as you are we as we are all together" routine. But when push comes to shove . . . well, as John Martyn laughingly put it, "I and I means me so fuck you!" Which may not be exactly what Burning Spear meant when they sang "Give me what is mine," but what the hell—I mean, we're all 20th Century folk here, right?

Saturday. Gonzo and I spend the day getting drunk and smoking dope in his room, reading *Rolling Stone* and *The Village Voice* and listening to the reggae which, for some unaccountable reason, is coming out of the radio. Wooly calls up to see how we're doing, and we tell him we've become Rastas and ask to borrow his cassette recorder so we can listen to Iggy tapes.

That night we are down at the bar when the photog from *Time* shows up and asks us if we want to go to some discos with him. I say sure; Gonzo stays at the bar. This shutterbug and I then drive up to Beverly Hills, the rich folks' ghetto of Kingston, to pick up Clive, son of Randy, who is going to show us where the kids dance in this town. We pass blocks of beautiful houses with sculpted lawns, and the one where the owner of Randy's Records lives is no different from the rest. Clive tells us, in fact, that their next-door neighbor is the French ambassador to Jamaica. A comparison of this picture with Perry's and Tubby's homes seems to confirm Clinton Williams' figures, and I begin to wonder what Burning Spear's house looks like. As for the discos, they look just like American discos: the floor lights up, couples dance to American soul records. The photographer keeps saying he wants more *roots*, and Clive just shrugs, so I translate: "What we're looking for is one of these places with a deejay sitting up there playing dub records and hollering into the microphone while all the guys in the crowd stand around smoking herb and vibrating."

"Oh, those," says Clive. "Not so easy to find now. They never held those like, you know, regular thing. And every time they did, seem like a gunman would show up and start firing. So now they are not allowed."

So much for discos. I suddenly notice that Clive has been taking swigs out of a half-pint bottle of his own. "What's that?" I ask him.

"Roots." He hands it to me, emphasizing that it does not contain what the label says: no rum culture here. I take a swig—liquid cannabis root extract, mixed with something else unmistakable. "There's *wine* in here!"

He smiles slightly. "Yes. A little." And takes the bottle back and pours himself another drink.

After the *Time* man and I take him home, we are driving down a street in a residential district when suddenly we hear a sound like firecrackers; it's pistol shots, and we see people running out of a bar ahead of us on the left, scattering in every direction. The *Time* guy slows down, and I begin to freak. "C'mon, man, let's get the fuck *out* of here! C'mon, turn that corner!" He had almost stopped. I guess he hoped to get an exclusive shot of authentic Jamaican street violence, which I guess is good journalistic instincts. Me, I was more interested in my own skin.

Then again, it may be that the streets of Kingston are, actually, comparatively safe for a honky next to those of Harlem or inner-city Detroit. When we stopped a few minutes later at a MacDonald's (no relation to the American chain) for some curried goat, the steering wheel on my friend's car locked and he couldn't get it started for about 20 minutes. Nobody hassled us; all we got were some black people in a minibus next to us who asked what was wrong and tried to help us get going again. Then again, the bus did say "UNICEF" on the driver's door.

Sunday. This is supposed to be a big day, because we have been told that there is going to be a Grounation, which I can only interpret from the rather vague explanations as some kind of Rasta raveup, which we have been invited to observe. It seems dubious to me that the Rastas would want a bunch of white folk from the United States and Britain sitting in the bleachers gawking at their annual convention, but I am anxious to check this out nevertheless. We are told that it will run from early in the evening until about 1 A.M., and I am already wondering how we can gracefully excuse ourselves around, say, 9:30 if it gets boring. I mean, I'm all for Lowell Thomas, but seven or eight straight hours of the gospel of Rastafari, which the guys in Marley's backyard had already proved every Rasta is ready to testify upon vehemently and at length with little or no provocation, did seem a bit much. Gonzo and I spend the afternoon drinking Bloody Marys by the pool; we have decided to start the booze wing of Rasta and spread the truths of that to the unenlightened, hoping for an eventual migration of all the enlightened back to Seagram's distillery in Waterloo, Ontario. Wooly and photographer Peter Simon, brother of Carly ("I'm Peter Simon, Carly's brother," was how he shook hands with Gonzo) just keep staring at us and shaking their heads as we tell them that the wisdom-inducing properties of Hops are at least equivalent to those of Herb. One thing is for sure: there will not be a bar at the Grounation.

Of course, in Jamaica not even Grounations can come off on time—it's my guess they might be sacrilegious if they did, so we wait well into the evening by the pool with Tom Hayes, an Island employee who, I have been told, is responsible for much of the label's business dealings with artists. So I ask him: "How much does a group like Burning Spear get from Island as an advance?"

"You should ask them that," he replied. "I don't think it would be ethical for me to tell you." He pointed at Gonzo. "That would be like me asking him how much you make; don't you see the unfairness of that?" Then, turning to Gonzo: "Ready for another Heineken's?" And gets up and splits for the bar to buy us a round of drinks.

Later, we're finally ready to go to the Grounation, and when the Rastas are ready for us it seems we've momentarily lost Gonzo, who is flying in the face of experience (namely his burn upon arrival) by trying again to cop dope, I mean herb, from the guy in the hotel parking lot. When he gets in the car, I ask him, "What the fuck is the matter with you? We're going to a *Grounation,* a *festival* of Rastafarians, don't you realize there's going to be more dope there than you could smoke in three lifetimes?"

"I know," he says, "but I gotta have some for later when we get back to the hotel and to get me through my flight back to New York tomorrow. I'm addicted to the shit!"

A few minutes later, Wooly and I somehow get onto the subject of Rasta sexuality. "The Rastas are not a particularly sexual people," he says, adding that "I've never seen one come on to a chick."

"Oh, really? What do you think would be the factors in that?" I had noticed that Jamaican men did seem to believe in keeping the woman home tending to the babies—you seldom saw them in record shops, for instance—although it is well known that the Rasta men do a lot of cooking and will not let the women prepare the food when they are menstruating. In fact, Jamaican men seem to have a whole fixation on the subject of the menstruation cycle—the most popular swear words are "bloodclot" and "bummaclot pussyclot," which are the worst things you can call somebody.

"I think it goes back," answers Wooly, "to the thing you see in lots of primitive societies: the belief that women are polluted, somehow identified with the forces of darkness, like witches . . . "

"I bet I know why they don't care if they fuck or not," interjects Gonzo. "Because they're too *stoned* all the time! Hell, man, I've smoked so much dope before I didn't give a fuck about pussy."

Wooly begins to get defensive—Jesus, man, don't call the Rastas *eunuchs*—and brings up Marley's four wives and numerous children before dropping the subject like a set of barbells even though I want to pursue it further.

The seven of us—Wooly, Gonzo, Peter Simon, his collaborator Stephen Davis, Tom Hayes, me and a Rasta named Killy who is taking us—ride to the Grounation in two cars. I jump in the Volkswagen Killy is driving and begin asking him if he doesn't think this white media influx might dilute the purity of Rasta ritual. He has long thin dread locks running streamers past his shoulders, and is wearing a T-shirt I had seen on Wooly and others this week that says "ROOTS" with picture of same on the front and commemorates Burning Spear's recent gig at the Chela Bay hotel just outside Ocho Rios on the back. I have already been told by Wooly that Killy is not being paid by Island for services like this, so I wonder what his motivation must be. He gives me the standard Rasta sermon, adds that the Rastas want to spread their truths and rights to all the world and this is one way to do it, then gets into something about how "money is energy." Meanwhile, we have stopped off on a side street in a rundown neighborhood that is still middle-class by Kingston standards, where Killy cops some dope for Gonzo, who makes the mistake of not asking for it immediately.

Then we drive off the main boulevards into an area of rusty pothole streets winding around a lot of shacks in the classic mold—corrugated tin, clay, scrap wood and metal, cardboard, windows that cannot be closed and doors with ragged curtains for privacy, into the heart of Poverty Row. And this isn't even Trenchtown, is in fact far better—this is a section called Olympic Gardens, but it doesn't look like any garden. It looks like a slum, because that is what it is, and I doubt if sharecropper shacks in the American South a hundred years ago had much on the housing here. We finally stopped along one lane, got out of the cars and walked up to a small building out of which the least commercialized form of reggae was blasting. Black people were standing all around the outside, and the inside seemed to be jammed, but I peered over neighbors leaning against the wall into a window and saw a stage small enough to fit inside one end of a building about as big as the average middle-class American child's bedroom. On the stage there was a table, and on the table a white cloth, burning candle, pot of red flowers, Bible, and smaller, tattered book which I presumed was a hymnal. Forming a half circle around and behind the table were a group called Ras Michael and the Sons of Negus, who have two albums out in Jamaica: a Chinese-looking organist and drummer, a bassist in the corner by the back door, lead guitarist, primitive amps, and in the middle Ras Michael, a tall thin man in wool cap and striped sweater, singing with ecclesiastical intensity into a microphone. In front of him was another half-circle of musicians sitting in chairs and on the edge of the stage, eight pairs of hands beating on congas and drums more primitive. In front of them about a half dozen rows of benches, which seemed mainly to be filled with little children, though there were women and older people there too. Directly across from the window where I stood I saw, in another window with his back to the street, the mild stringy-bearded face of Peter Simon, bouncing slightly and smiling as if bedazzled. It looked like a good way to get a knife in the ribs.

In a few minutes a space was found for us inside and we were led around to the front of this seeming chapel, through a door and down to the very front, where Gonzo and I were seated amongst a bevy of little black kids who stared at us with a mixture of shyness, fear and laughter. I made a face at one staring at me and she dissolved in giggles. I was not so sure that the same thing would be a wise course of action for me to take, so whenever Gonzo said something funny to me I would stifle my laughter, which naturally had the effect of stifling laughter at the dinner table when you are a child—all those repressed chuckles just kept bubbling ferociously inside, burning to get out in howls while I kept translating them into stoned, beatific smiles as I swayed to the music. It was not that there was anything funny about the situation; I was merely nervous. Or rather, *these* people and this music was not funny—we were funny, our presence here was funny, or was something else more easily accepted as funny, and by the time Gonzo got around to screaming in my ear that "This is better than Thelonious Monk at the Five Spot! I see the light, Lester, I've got religion! And don't ever forget that we could lose our lives at any minute!" I just had to laugh out loud.

Luckily, it was swallowed by the music, which was amazing, or seemed so under the circumstances. Ras Michael sang songs like "None a Jah Jah Children No Cry," "In Zion," and "Glory Dawn," alternating cooking reggae with gospel chants as the drummers smoked spliff after spliff, some of them sitting there in total trance never removing the things from their mouths, sucking the smoke like air, cooking up an enormously complex rhythm conversation which was pure Africa. Killy had sat down at one of the congas, lit up two spliffs, and handed them to me and Gonzo. I smoked and tried to lose myself in the rhythm, as Ras Michael sang of flying away home to Zion and Gonzo screamed in my ear "Right! Right! Fly away home tomorrow!" One particularly driving chant-like number (number?) which sounded like a basal link between African reggae roots and Elvin Jones caught the whole room up and in that moment alone, perhaps, we all were united, flying through the rhythm. The end of each song was signaled by Ras Michael, who would intone loudly into the mike "Jah Rastafari!" to which the little children, women and men present would shout back "Rastafari!" I remember particularly one tot behind me, screaming "Migh-ty God!" It was like a cross between a Wednesday Night Prayer Meet-

ing and a very local garage gig by a band which was itself the link
between the tribal fires of prehistory, American black Revivalist
Christianity, and rock 'n' roll electricity. The guitarist would get
into riffs that occasionally suggested that he had been listening to
Keith Richards, Duane Allman, maybe even Jerry Garcia, but this
was a religious service and nobody clapped. Except Peter Simon,
who kept leaning over and cooing in my ear, "Isn't this *great?* I just
love it, don't you?" He had begun dancing in a manner that I can
only compare to Joan Baez doing the Funky Chicken at the Big Sur
Folk Festival, and little kids in front of him, shifting out of awe-
somely intricate boogaloos of their own, began laughingly to imitate
him. He thought they were all getting together in One World
brotherhood, laughed back and did what he was doing with more
fervor; what he didn't see was that they were having a laugh over his
performance with other children behind him. At the end of the set
(set?) I saw him in the center aisle, palms together and head bowed
in prayerful attitude. Meanwhile, the grass was wearing off, the
bench was hard, and, as at many concerts, I was ready to go home
before the music was over.

I don't mean to sound jaded. It had been intense, both musically
and situationally; it was a capital-E experience, and, as Gonzo said,
"Take a good look, Lester—this is as close as we're ever gonna get to
Africa." But there was a pervasive irony to the Experience, which
could not be escaped. It was in seeing Peter Simon, after Ras Michael
and the band had left the room as the hand-drummers and congregation kept shouting and chanting, mount the stage and stand there behind the table with the Bible and candle, smiling and clapping his
hands as if leading the faithful.

And there was irony a few minutes later, as we were led out of the
chapel into a space behind the house next door, where we were given
herb soup ("As an offering," I was informed) and tokes off the chalice,

a ceremonial, elaborately carved pipe. Ras Michael stood outside; I shook hands with him and told him, "I really dig your music, and I'm going to buy your album tomorrow." We both laughed, there may have been a moment of mutual recognition, and then he launched into the gospel of Rastafari, quoting extensively from the Bible and prophesying Armageddon. It was boring, and after a few minutes I edged politely away, after which it seemed each of our party took his turn at the same course, until Ras Michael got to Peter Simon, whose name he delighted in transposing into Simon Peter, laughing and shaking Simon's hand vigorously. (Upon this rock I will build my church in . . . *Martha's Vineyard?*) We all laughed at this, and a few minutes later I saw Peter Simon inside the house where the Rastas stood smoking herb and testifying to Jah. I could see him, through the smoke, first in the main room, then later coming out of another room in the back. I assumed at the time that that was the john and he had to use it, later realized that was ridiculous since it was almost certain that the only toilet anywhere around here was the ground. The rest of us stood around just inside the door of the house; it was a while before I realized that behind me, in the darkness, all the Rasta women were sitting in chairs or hammocks along the fence, silently watching as their children hopped around them and the men declaimed inside. The only woman I saw inside the house was one young brown-skinned girl about 20, sitting in a chair in a corner with a spliff in her hand upon which she occasionally took another hit; she was beautiful, as yet unbrutalized at least to the eye, but as she stared vacantly into space all the herb in the world could not have been cosmetic for the utter desolation that, in her silence, in her stillness, was radiated by her very youth and beauty.

Older Rastas from the neighborhood came wandering up to the house, some of them ragged, and I looked at them and then at Tom Hayes, who was wearing a pair of pants that probably cost $50, a

Billy Preston T-shirt (I was in my Grand Funk) and a razor cut, and the irony turned to an absurdity so extreme it became a kind of obscenity. It was, at the very least, embarrassing, for me and for these people, and I seriously doubt if for all the talk of brotherhood of Rastafari there is anything beyond that embarrassment which they and I will ever be able to share. What I mean to say is I've been on lots of press junkets before, but this was the first one into Darkest Africa. What I meant to say is that a whole bunch of people were flown, all expenses paid, to Jamaica, so that we could look at these people, and go back and write stories which would help sell albums to white middle-class American kids who think it's romantic to be black and dirt-poor and hungry and illiterate and sick with things you can't name because you've never been to a doctor and sit around all day smoking ganja and beating on bongo drums because you have no other options in life. I know, because I am one of those kids, caught in the contradiction—hell, man, my current favorite group is Burning Spear. But I wouldn't want to organize a press party in that village they come from in those hills they sing about. And not because I don't want to pollute the "purity" of their culture with Babylon, either—because there is something intrinsically insulting about it.

At length we were able to leave. Gonzo had been edgily hunching around the doorway of the house, prodding Wooly and Tom Hayes, who as an upright drinking Englishman was much more amenable, to "get the fuck back to the hotel before the bar closes, man!" We trooped out into the street, and some of the Rastas followed us. A curious thing happened then: they had smoked only herb inside, but as soon as we hit the lane where the cars were parked they started asking for cigarettes, which we of course gave them. As Gonzo put it later: "I felt like we should have had Hershey Bars to distribute." They told us that in the middle of the band's performance (which was not in fact a Grounation at all but rather a religious concert for children—they would never let us come to the adults' affair) the police and soldiers had driven up to the place, looked in the door, and then split. I told them that the same thing happened when a rock 'n' roll band tried to practice in my neighborhood, but somehow it didn't ring quite the same. (Kingston police, I have been told, are not averse to such practices as walking into a house unannounced and for no reason in the middle of the night, interrupting a couple while they are fucking, pulling the man out of bed and hauling him in for interrogation and other sports that can be easily imagined.) I looked up and saw, at the top of a pole on the corner, two strips of black, battered metal, upon which had been crudely written in white paint instructions to go to certain addresses in the neighborhood for the mending of clothes, or to buy fish. "Look," I said to Gonzo and Tom Hayes, "advertisements." The three of us stared up, just stared, and said nothing.

The Rastas stood around or sat on the back bumper of Killy's Volks, polite and friendly conversation was made; they invited us to come back and see them sometime. Right. Eventually, without any true goodbyes, there was kind of a mutual semi-embarrassed separation, as they went back inside and we prepared to get in our cars. It was at this point that we discovered one of our party was missing. Peter Simon was still in the house. Nobody seemed particularly inclined to go in after him, so we just sort of stood around until some of them brought him out, stoned and beaming and holding hands with them like a brother to the world. Killy then told us that he had to take some members of the band home in his car, and we would all have to ride back in Stephen Davis' Toyota, plus we could drive home Chinna, the lead guitarist. Killy also said that he needed gas, produced a hose, and siphoned an indeterminate quantity out of the Toyota and into the Volks. He left us with instructions on how to get out of this neighborhood, said that in any case we had Chinna to guide us, and drove off. Now we had to squeeze seven people into the Toyota—Gonzo, Hayes, Wooly, and myself, three of whom are around six feet tall and in other respects large, into the backseat; in the front seat Stephen Davis driving, Peter Simon straddling the two front seats with his arm around the back of the seat where Chinna rode shotgun. No one spoke to Chinna; in fact, once out on a main road several of us began laughing like maniacs, and I still wonder what he must have been thinking. But some sort of pressure was off, and also the only way four of us could fit in the backseat was for one of Wooly's legs to hang out the window. Stephen Davis almost ran off the road the first time he saw a human foot bobbing up by his window. We drove for miles, followed Chinna's instructions until we arrived at what looked like a suburban 1950s American tract home, except that there were fields around it. It wasn't bad for Jamaica. As Chinna took his guitar through the front door, Gonzo cracked: "I'll bet he's saying, 'Hi, honey, I'm home!'" We wondered if Ras Michael and the rest had left in Killy's Volks for equally middle-class abodes, and Gonzo also revealed that Killy had burned him for the four dollars worth of dope he'd copped for him on the way to the Grounation. He had rolled part of it up into about four joints which he'd passed to us while the band was playing, but when Gonzo asked him for the rest of it at the end he said that we (I and I, Ethiopians and ofays) had smoked it all up. Proving, declared Gonzo, that the Rastas were not Righteous, after all.

Back at the hotel, Tom Hayes, Gonzo and I closed the bar. I had Courvoisier with Heineken chasers. Gonzo said, "Yes, tonight we have been where few white men have dared venture!" Hayes remarked that Peter Simon did not know how lucky he was to be alive.

Stephen Davis, Peter Simon, Wooly and I are driving to Harry J.'s studio. Harry (Johnson) is another prolific island (and Island) producer; Marley has recorded at his studio a lot, and in fact when we get there Wooly sees a car that looks like Marley's BMW and for some reason gets nervous. It seems implicit that if Bob is there visiting Harry J. for any reason, we will have to turn around and go back to the hotel, and it occurs to me that it's a wonder Marley keeps any perspective at all with everybody treating him like this. But it's not his car, after all; we go inside.

In the car all morning Wooly has been saying "Jah Rastafari" and singing Ras Michael's "None a Jah Jah Children No Cry"; the night before, as we stood beside the door, I had asked him if Island was thinking of signing Ras Michael, and he had said no, but that after what we had just seen it might be a good idea. Now he has offered to make me a copy (a dub!) of his tape of Ras Michael's performance, and I tell him I've gotta have a cassette, and that if he can't make one easily not to go through the hassle, because I feel that Ras Michael's show is one of those things where you just would have had to have been there, and I probably won't play it much, especially if it's on reel-to-reel which I don't have equipment for. He insists, though: "Don't you want a tape to play for your friends and turn 'em on?"

It seems to me that the next logical step is home movies. Why didn't somebody give Peter Simon a Portapak?

Inside Harry J.'s studio, Wooly gives him the English edition, on the Island label, of his Jamaican hit with the Heptones, "Mama Say." Harry explodes. "What kinda crap is this? I produced this fucking record, and on this label it credit Danny Holloway [an English producer]. All he did was mix it! This's a fucking bummaclot." I ask him if this kind of thing happens often. "Never before with Chris Blackwell. Always I've trusted him." Something else occurs to me, very belatedly in fact, something so basic I had missed it all through my stay on the island: I ask him if very many Jamaican artists have managers. He looks at me as if I were the most pathetic ignoramus alive. "Not many," he says.

When we get back to the hotel, who do we run into in the lobby but Chris Blackwell himself. He has been in England over the weekend, and is just returning. Wooly is very agitated about Harry's complaint, and tells Blackwell the story. Chris is not perturbed at all. "It's a very simple problem, really. Harry J. has a big ego and so does Danny Holloway." He smiles. "And between the two of them, the Heptones haven't got a chance."

Two hours later. I've checked out of the Sheraton, and am in a cab on my way to the airport. I ask the driver to go by way of the Gun Court, an island attraction I'd heard about and wanted to see before I ever got here, a legend that preceded my tourism. The Gun Court was set up by the Manley regime as a way of dealing with all the berserk pistoleros and violent political agitators. What it means is that anybody caught by the police with even a bullet, even a shell casing, or any type of explosives in his possession, is whisked before a tribunal which asks him why he has these illegal and dangerous items. If he doesn't have the right answer, he is thrown in the stockade behind the Gun Court for life. Sic. 99.9% of Jamaicans who appear before the Gun Court have the wrong answer. And now here it is: high fences with enormous rolls of barbed wire at the top, guard towers, a yard where you can see young blacks milling around. The front of the place painted a garish red. It looks like a concentration camp, and that's what it is. I ask the cab driver what he thinks of it.

"I don' mind Gun Court so much," he says. "Other things bother me much more. On this island there is little real freedom, and now Manley is dealing with the Cubans, and we fear Jamaica will become like Cuba, where there is no freedom. No freedom under Communism, and already I don't feel free here anymore." He pointed to a pile of giant rocks left at some roadside excavation site. "You see those rocks, that's how we feel in Jamaica, like being crushed down by all those, underneath them. Manley is a dictator, of course. Under him today, the people are unhappy, and sometimes driving in the cab I don't say what I think if the rider asks me a question about politics, because I don't know who he is. He might go and tell the police, and I might not be here later. The Rastas are something else—they don' matter at all. I want to always live in Jamaica, but now I am not so sure. All I want now is my freedom."

3

Top Rankin':
The First Great "Third World" Star,
1976–1981

For a brief time, Marley became the major star of the developing world, especially after the original Wailers broke up. The loss of Peter Tosh and Bunny Wailer could have been devastating, but Marley proved to be very resilient.

He reorganized the band into Bob Marley and the Wailers. In place of the sweet and sour harmonies that characterized the Wailers as a trio (their voices were far too idiosyncratic to ever really "blend" in the traditional vocal group manner, and it was one of their greatest strengths) he brought on his wife Rita and two of the most talented vocalists in Jamaica, Judy Mowatt and Marcia Griffiths. (On an ironic note, Griffiths and Bunny Wailer would later have a hit with a song that gets played at every wedding and bar mitzvah in the western world, the "Electric Boogie," aka the "Electric Slide.")

As Bob Marley and the Wailers, Bob continued to write and record songs of protest and earned the respect of conscious thinkers throughout the world. Then they recorded *Kaya*, an album predominantly composed of love songs. This only expanded his audience.

The Rasta Prophet of
Reggae Music Speaks

by Tom Terrell

(Source: MCY.com, January 2001)

This interview was conducted on Monday, October 29, 1979, after Bob Marley and the Wailers' triumphant four-night SRO stand at the legendary Apollo Theater. Young journalist Tom Terrell sat with Bob Marley for a Washington DC Newspaper that has since folded. MCY.com made this exclusive interview available for the first time in over 20 years.

TOM TERRELL: During the early Sixties, what were you into?

MARLEY: School and trade. Welding . . . I went to private school down the road (laughs). You know I was kinda musical. We stand 'pon a street corner at night and sing and beat pan. We had on Spanish Town Road and Ebeneezar Lane . . . a club named Operation Friendship where a man bring a guitar. That's how I get my first guitar—see? This is where it start from. I'm not a good guitarist in one sense; but musically that's how the music start. I got more interested in the singing part, y'know.

TERRELL: American R&B was, and is, popular in Jamaica. Did it have any influences on your vocal style?

MARLEY: Yes. Chuck Jackson, Ben E. King, Wilson Pickett . . . I go back some days and mention "Jim Dandy To The Rescue"—you know them guy there? You know Little Richard? Little Anthony

... the next one named the Drifters, the Platters. A brother sing a tune say "Don't break your promise." Johnny Ace, too.

TERRELL: Joe Higgs was said to have taken you under his wing. Who was he to you?

MARLEY: Joe Higgs was a teacher, y'know. Joe Higgs the man who teach—Bunny, Peter and I; Junior, Cherry and Beverly. Six in all.

TERRELL: On the cover of an early album, you and the other Wailers are dressed in suits, sunglasses . . .

MARLEY: During that time now we were working with a record company, see? And when you work for people you have to make up yourself. But we are rebels, we rebellious—them the singing we do. You see we never really know anything that much about Rasta. The words them a come out but still no know really what goin' on. We just know that something a come out. That the people a say something and it mean something 'bout where we is we never know that reason yet, seen? 'Till them we start to get ourselves independent so start doing what we want do.

TERRELL: Two people that figure prominently in the development of Wailers' music are Lee Perry and Chris Blackwell. What were their roles in shaping your career?

MARLEY: Yeah, Lee Perry. Lee Perry used to work same place. When we leave, him leave too. Him do one business, we do a next one 'til we link up again and do same work. Chris Blackwell come in the music when the music really need someone to get some exposure. Through him now was the one that knew about it more as one in Jamaica can a get. You know Millie Small?

TERRELL: She sang "My Boy Lollipop"?

MARLEY: Good, good. From them time there. It Jimmy Cliff even to the end of *The Harder They Come*, that's when Jimmy Cliff left Island. So him was the man—'cause nobody never know. People used to curse the music because the studio never that up to date like them studio a clear, y'know. Ha' plenty this and that 'pon that, tracks them.

TERRELL: Originally, the Wailers were a vocal group. When did the band take shape?

MARLEY: 'Round 1970, now. Family Man (AKA Aston Barrett; bass) and them was upset at an Island thing and link up with Lee Perry them and thing. In 1968 we start come together y'know. Tyrone (Downie; keyboards) used to go to school . . . used to come record shop when him leave school. We tell him (laughs), "Go home." Now him big, a long time up there.

TERRELL: Bunny and Peter branched out in their own directions. Any comments on the musical paths they've taken?

MARLEY: Well, whatever a man do that pleases him, that is for him right, y'know? This is what our blessing . . . This is how it deal with them.

TERRELL: Are all your songs your sole inspiration or do you co-write with the band?

MARLEY: Well, to me anybody can help me write a song. If not the melody a go and you can almost hear the words them too. Say you hear the words and a man help you put them together. So it happen that way with me plenty times. 'Cause you might hear me. I try say something but you hear what me supposed to say, you know what I mean? Most of my tunes I was writing with my brethren, man. Them all got tell me what to say.

TERRELL: What are you saying to American audiences in your music, and do you think it will translate well to them?

MARLEY: My message is Rastafari, God Almighty, man. The same message to the people. I don't find a man can't understand y'know. What I find out [is] that America is more control. The people is under every control here. Everything is organized. If you come here to do a concert, you have to go through the organization; so it's really organized. You ask why go to Harlem and play reggae music, and the people have a certain amount of pressure 'pon them. So you know them can't even get to listen. The more them hear it, this is a truth here—must come true, dread.

TERRELL: So they can't stop reggae—

MARLEY: They can't stop it; 'cause if they stop it I wouldn't start because there would be no need for me start; be in vain. Me do it because of a cause and until it happen before I feel pleased because that the only thing make feel pleased . . . people them come together in a unity and defend the right. Cause all of them defend capitalism; so what if them conscious them a deal with it. So if the government was Rasta, all of them woulda been Rasta, seen?

TERRELL: Speaking of government, what do you have to say about the political situation in Jamaica?

MARLEY: I don't really feel pleased. Because I and I Rasta. If I tell you say, "I feel pleased," it would be a lie. I and I Rasta. When we are deal with Rasta, we are deal with Rasta, y'know? We not deal with Rasta half enough. Like say we want a different ideology, a different philosophy. When we say we are Rasta we mean we seriously deal with Marcus Garvey, Haile Selassie, seen? So if you live in a country and the country are run by foreigners—we have a country run by foreign ideas—then the country is a foreign country! What happened to Marcus Garvey and Haile Selassie? We are people, we are Black people who want our own. Which is the beginning; our people seeing them run rights again 'pon earth.

TERRELL: Then you're not too happy with [then-current JA Prime Minister] Manley?

MARLEY: That's Ras politics as concerned where I have to say. I don't care what the many want to say. I Rasta, seen? I don't see where a man can do for Rastaman when him is not Rasta. 'Cause only Rasta can help Rasta. Special in a situation where it about government of countries. Government of country and a Rastaman not g'wan help Rasta 'cause Rasta not agree a what he deal with. So it contrary to what him a deal with.

TERRELL: In this country, many musicians become successful then isolate themselves from their beginnings. But you haven't. Why?

MARLEY: Can't isolate, man. Where we come from, man there no deal with isolation. We right there with the people, seen? For there is nothing to me more than to see it. I do not see it yet. When I was small I think it used to happen, but when I grow up and I get to understand—say when I pass through them people with suffering and I just a pass past think everybody in there have dinner and everything. I really grew up big now and started suffering then find plenty of these homes don't have no dinner when evening come. When man have up steak in yard and feed him dog . . . Y'hear me? Until our people live again man, never satisfy.

TERRELL: So your music is definitely oriented towards the Third World?

MARLEY: When them say, "Third World" countries them appeal to say, "Until the philosophies which hold one race superior and another inferior is totally destroyed and abandoned . . . War." I don't think there's 10% Third World, but who is the "First World", who is the "Second World", why is there a "Third World"? I can't dig the "world" business with them.

TERRELL: Returning to your music; has its development been a conscious effort?

MARLEY: Yeah—conscious and deliberate.

TERRELL: One last question—rock critics here have given your album *Survival* and tour lukewarm reviews. At the same time, more people are being turned on to your music. What do you say about that?

MARLEY: That is good, man, that make me understand the people is listening. At the same time there is a lot of people who love it because when I play "Is It Love" and the people say, "Aaaayyy!"— when it start I know one writer can't stop that. First thing I learned from the man I learned how to take the media. That's the first thing God tell me. He look 'pon me and say, "Son, remember . . . them who say a lot of bad things, don't check it bad, when them say a lot of good things don't check it bad." You just remember, say one man write it, he might have a few more people who look over it, but the natural people is out there. Some of them they go an' read it, some of them never ever see that before. The people will make sure of what they know. Every man I see in Harlem them face are not strange. I see them already. Same people, our people.

The Reggae Way to "Salvation"

by J. Bradshaw

(*Source:* New York Times Magazine, *August 14, 1977*)

Out of Jamaica comes a star singing hellfire, revolution and biblical begin-
nings. To the "downpressed" of the third world, Bob Marley is a hero. Now
he takes on America.

So he comes jiggling out onto the stage, this wiry, spindle-shanked
singer, this self-styled black prince of reggae, his clenched fist high
above his head, his dreadlocks flopping round his ears. The crowd rises
to its feet and begins to scream and the singer shouts, "Yes!" and the
crowd shouts, "Yes! Yes! Yes!" And then, with slight menace in his
voice, the singer says, "Jesu, light the fire to my salvation. Whom shall
I fear? Jah. Ras Tafari." And the crowd screams, "Jah, Jah, Ras Tafari"
and begins to whistle and clap and the band begins to play and the
singer slides into one of his early songs called "Lively Up Yourself."

It is the final concert of Bob Marley and the Wailers' European
tour at the Rainbow Theater in London. His American tour begins
next Thursday at New York City's Paladium. After six albums in the
last five years, Bob Marley has emerged as Jamaica's chief cultural
hero, its Cassandra, singing wonderfully well of doom and desolation.
Despite the growing popularity of reggae (pronounced REGgay)
music, it is most odd that this Caribbean wild man, with his dreadlocks, his ganja-inspired revelations, has attracted such a hysterical
following. A gospel of death to the "downpressors" does not seem in
keeping with these tame times.

But here he is in front of an overcrowded house, half of them black, half of them white, singing of burning and looting, of revolution, of lightning, thunder, brimstone and fire, On the stage behind Marley is a lurid backdrop, complete with huts, fires and telegraph poles— meant to resemble Trenchtown, the squalid Kingston ghetto where he was raised. To the right of the stage is the flag of Ethiopia and a banner depicting the Conquering Lion of Judah. At Marley's previous London concert, there were numerous stabbings and tonight the police and vigilant groups of black security men prowl through the theater. It is a young audience and the kids have taken to turning up at Marley's concerts in natty urban-guerrilla gear. Boots, berets and clenched-fist salutes are popular. The theater is thick with the sharp aroma of burning marijuana.

Marley breaks into "War," a speech of Haile Selassie's he set to music. It is like an invocation. "Until the philosophy which holds one race superior and another inferior is finally and permanently discredited and abandoned, everywhere is war. Me say war," he chants. Behind Marley the five Wailers strike up and, to the side, the I-Threes, the female back-up singers (including Rita, Marley's common-law wife) in tribal dress, turbans and beaded necklaces pick up the harmonies. Marley tends to act out his songs with exaggerated rage and anguish, throwing his head into his hands, crying or strutting up and down the stage as he sings. "Until the color of a man's skin is of no more significance than the color of his eyes, there will be war, everywhere war," he sings and all these clean and fresh-faced kids who wouldn't know the difference between an Ingram M10 and a machete scream and throw their fists in the air.

In a contemporary rock world devoid of the revolutionary caterwauls of the '60s, Marley and his rebel music have inspired a genuine cult. Although his albums sell well in America (the recently released "Exodus" is currently a candidate for No. 1), Marley's significance goes far beyond his commercial success. His popularity in the Caribbean, in West Africa (where such pop stars as the Nigerian dissident Fela have long emulated him) and in the large black communities in England and on the Continent is attributable to his fervent jeremiads against the system, "the hypocrites of Babylon" as he calls them, and his music is flavored with tribute to the God of his Rastafarian beliefs. It has taken Bob Marley nearly 15 years of failure and false starts, but he has become the third world's first real superstar.

Strictly speaking, Bob Marley does not live anywhere, at least for long. Occasionally, he may be found in London or at his mother's home in Wilmington, Del., or while on tour in one or another of the European capitals. He is always difficult to find and he is fond of saying, "Me jus' possin' tat." When he is in Jamaica, which he rarely is anymore, he can usually be found at his rambling house on Hope Road in Kingston.

The large yellow wooden house, with rust-red shutters and a green tin roof (the colors of the Ethiopian flag) is set back from the road behind white pillars and a white fence in two acres of lightly forested land. It is an old house in which I, coincidentally, lived briefly some 10 years ago. Except for recent renovations and the ragtag group of Rastas smoking herb in the back yard, comparatively little has changed.

I had had two appointments to see Marley but he had been asleep or around the corner on both occasions, which is not surprising in a country where the cocks are said to crow at noon, where punctuality is considered rude and the national saying seems to be "Soon come, soon come."

We are talking in the back yard under the large poinciana tree. Doctor birds squawk overhead and a large buzzard bisects the sky. Outside the gate, speeding cars and a scruffy herd of goats pass down Hope Road. Marley's silver BMW is parked in the yard and Marley pretends to believe he purchased it because he thought BMW stood for Bob Marley and the Wailers.

Off-stage, Marley is quiet and curiously withdrawn. He has a nice smile and laughs a lot. A short fellow with a wispy goatee, he wears a red and white striped tam, which covers most of his 14-inch-long dreadlocks. He chain-smokes the herb, or spliffs as they are called, smoking about a pound a week. He has the glazed eyes of a man who likes to dream.

For 15 years Marley has been singing of a benighted people caught up in the octopal tentacles of an inept and often corrupt government. Songs such as "Concrete Jungle," "Rebel Music," "Burnin' and Lootin'," "Them Belly Full" and "I Shot the Sheriff" articulate the plight of the Jamaican ghettos—urging change and preaching revolution should change not come.

The songs are filled with such lines as "A hungry mob is an angry mob," "Cold ground was my bed last night, rockstone was my pillow too," "It takes a revolution to make a solution," "If you are the big tree, we are the small ax sharpened to cut you down" and "Rise up all you fallen fighters, rise up and make your stand again." Marley, of course, refers specifically to Jamaica but the analogies to much of the rest of the world are exact and obvious.

After 15 years of independence, the Jamaican Government is broke. Prime Minister Michael Manley was swept into power in 1972 and again in 1976 and promised the usual new dawns. In 1972, a reggae song called "Better Must Come" became his campaign slogan, and it was a hit in the island. But better has not yet come.

Because of widespread urban terrorism, a state of emergency was invoked in June of last year; it was lifted just two months ago. During 1976 there were some 200 politically motivated killings. Unemployment in Jamaica is currently running at 24 percent. The Government has recently passed import restrictions on a wide variety of manufactured goods. Manley wishes to turn Jamaica into a republic of demo-cratic socialism within the British Commonwealth. Tourism is down by 35 percent from last year and many hotels have closed. Since 1972, some 245 million Jamaican dollars have been spirited out of the coun-try. Some 40,000 Jamaicans have left, mostly the middle classes, who fear new outbreaks of violence, socialism, or both. There are, for ex-ample, only 95 dentists left in the island, or one for every 22,000 peo-ple. Given Michael Manley's recent alliances with Fidel Castro, many of his countrymen have taken to calling him "Miguelito."

The Rastafarians like to say that bauxite and tourism are down and ganja and reggae are up and they are not far wrong. Since Manley has been in power, Marley has been singing that the system was down-pressing the people, that capitalism was a plague and that Babylon would burn. Last year, Island Records (Marley's label) attempted to persuade the Jamaican Government to sanction reggae as the coun-try's national music in much the way that bossa nova has become the national music of Brazil. They were turned down. How can you have a national music that does little more than snipe at the nation? "Look round you," said Marley in his low, lilting Jamaican patois, "dere's a war goin' on. Da system we live in is wrong. Right now, the devil him have plenty influence. De devil him struttin' everywhere."

"De Government is tramplin' over de people's sweat and tears. Comin' down hard, hard. We're oppressed, so we sing oppressed songs and sometime people find themselves guilty. And dey can't stand do terrible weight of it. But Babylon don' want peace, Babylon want power, Babylon want to keep the people down. We mus' fight against the darkness. It is better to die fightin' for your freedom den to be a prisoner all do days of your life. It is better dat righteousness cover do earth like water cover de sea."

Marley laughs and picks his teeth with a chew stick. "We're not talkin' bout burnin' and lootin' for material goods. We want to burn capitalistic illusions. Anyway, Jamaica jus' run outta politics today. Me no deal with politics. Me sing and deal with de trot' de best I can. Me sing de song and hope de people catch de tune and mark do words. People have plenty misunderstanding, mon. No ting is important dat much. Love life and live it, dat's all."

Bob Marley was born on Feb. 6, 1945, in the village of Rhoden Hall in the parish of St. Ann on the northern side of Jamaica. Marley prefers to say he was born in Babylon. His father, a white British Army captain, came to Jamaica during the war and married Marley's mother—a black woman from the interior. Marley has two brothers and a sister. He does not remember his father at all. "Don' remember me father, only hear of his death," he says. "Don' know what he died of, no, no, not really. He jus' die, mon."

In St. Ann's, the family farmed—coffee, bananas and yams—and Marley became proficient at milking goats and raising food. When he was 9, his mother moved the family to Kingston—Waltham Park and thence to Trenchtown—ghettos not unlike those of Bombay or the South Bronx. Despite new Government building, Trenchtown remains a hideous place—row upon row of stucco buildings and shanties built of tarpaper, corrugated tin and chicken wire.

Marley remained at school until he was 16 and then found work as an electrical welder. The times were difficult. The family had little money. They lived in a two-room shack on Second Street and Marley's mother ran a cookshop and did housework on the side.

Marley had picked up a little music while still in school. "During school break, de teacher she say, 'Who can talk, talk, who can make anything, make, who can sing, sing.' And me sing." The music was everywhere, blaring into the streets from radios and jukeboxes and from the countless little record shacks—American soul music, Otis Redding, the Drifters, James Brown, calypso, steel band, meringue, Curtis Mayfield, Nat (King) Cole, Fats Domino, Ricky Nelson, Elvis

Presley and the Jamaican big-band sounds such as Byron Lee and the
Skatallites. "Dere was plenty music, plenty music," Marley recalls,
"all comin' like a spirit strong, strong into me."

Alvin (Seeco) Patterson, the Wailers' percussion man, met Marley in Trenchtown in 1963. Marley was 17. They used to sit outside
time neighborhood kitchens in the evenings and sing. None of them
played an instrument. "That year," said Seeco, "Bob win some talent contest and me know right away he would be a de-angerous
showman. He learn plenty quick. Anything you do, rude or no rude,
Bob him write a song 'bout it. All de talent in Jamaica was in
Trenchtown den and it was a nice place to live. No riot. No violence. People, dey get along. Politricks change dat later." Seeco always calls it politricks.

Marley soon gave up welding and with Rita opened up a record
shop, called Wailin' Soul, in a little shack about the size of two bath-
rooms. There was a speaker outside on the step blasting the current
ska, which was a kind blend of syncopated Caribbean music, bebop
and American soul, into the crowded streets. The shop never made
any money, but it gave Marley a chance to play in public singles of his
own that he had begun to record.

The Wailers began as a vocal group, picking up instruments when
they learned to play and when they could afford to buy them. He
called his group the Wailers, as in those who are oppressed, and in
1963 Robert Marley and the Wailers recorded their first song. It was-
called "Judge Not" and Marley was paid $50. It was not a success.

Throughout the '60s, Jamaican music was undergoing enormous
change. The influences were extremely varied, ranging from calypso
to the theme song of the movie "The Good, the Bad and the Ugly,"
which went to No. 1 in Jamaica in 1967. In the early and mid-'60s,
ska was followed by rock steady, a laid-back form of ska with less im-
provisation and more calypso.

The derivations of reggae are rather more obscure. Toots Hibbert, the lead singer of Toots and the Maytals, is generally credited with coining the word in 1966 with his song "Do the Reggay." But the word had been in the streets for years. During the mid-'60s I remember certain Jamaican girls were occasionally called "streggai"—meaning they were slatterns. "Me used to hear people say you can't use dat word or you go to jail," said Marley. "Used to say dat 'bout a low lady. If she hear you say it she don't feel too good 'bout it. Not a bad word, but if the lady hear, the Lord don' like it." Whatever its derivations, reggae—with its syncopated rhythms, Caribbean lilt, American black soul, biblical chantings and ganja-high detachment—had evolved into the Jamaican sound by the early 70's and was being heard outside the island for the first time.

Prior to 1972, Marley and the Wailers released four albums in Jamaica. They were the island's biggest reggae stars and yet Marley made little more than $200 for his efforts. In those days, Jamaican artists were constantly ripped off by their producers and tales of the plunder are commonplace. "In de beginnin' every people rob and cheat you," said Marley. "Dem was some bad pirates, too, comin' down like Dracula on reggae. On payment was mean and me know plenty artists driven mad by Babylon."

In 1972, Marley signed with Chris Blackwell of Island Records and, at last, had international distribution. Blackwell, a wealthy white Jamaican who started Island in 1962, knew what he was doing. "Blackwell is as good with money as some men are good with dogs. Blackwell would make money in a lazaretto." The first albums Island released in America—"Catch a Fire," "Burnin'," "Natty Dread" and "Rastaman Vibrations"—did not do as well as expected, but reggae was becoming fashionable. By 1975, Taj Mahal, Barbara Streisand, and Johnny Nash had all recorded Marley songs. Nash had two American hits with "Guava Jelly" and "Stir It Up," and in 1976 Eric Clapton recorded "I

Shot the Sheriff," which promptly went to No.1 on the charts. Reggae was on its way. And with it came the popularizing of the Rastafarian faith, of which Bob Marley was to become the most famous disciple.

For nearly 50 years, the Rastafarians have been feared and persecuted in Jamaica. They have been accused of being rabble-rousers, layabouts or dealers in the lucrative ganja trade. But what began as a small, rural religious cult has now become a popular movement. By some estimates, there may be some 20,000 Rastas in Jamaica and nearly as many among the 400,000 Jamaicans in New York City.

The Rastafarian movement was started by Marcus Garvey, who founded the Universal Negro Improvement Association in Harlem during the '20s. He preached "Africa for the Africans" and urged his countrymen "to look to the mother country, where a black King shall be crowned, for the Day of Deliverance is near."

Garvey's activities in Harlem led to his arrest and he was deported to Jamaica in 1927. Three years later, Lij Ras Tafari Makonnen ascended to the throne of Ethiopia as His Imperial Majesty, Haile Selassie I, Power of the Holy Trinity, 225th Emperor of the 3,000-year-old Ethiopian Empire, Elect of God, Lord of Lords, King of Kings, Heir to the Throne of Solomon, Conquering Lion of the Tribe of Judah. His coronation received front-page coverage in *The Jamaica Daily Gleaner* and Rastafarians hailed Selassie as Jah, the living God on earth.

Today, Rastafarians differ among themselves on specific dogma, but generally they believe they are black Hebrews exiled in Babylon, the true Israelites, that Haile Selassie is the direct descendant of Solomon and Sheba and that God is black. Most white men, they believe, have been worshiping a dead god and have attempted to teach the blacks to do likewise. They believe the Bible was distorted by King James I, that the black race sinned and was punished by God with slavery and conquest. They see Ethiopia as Zion, the Western world as Babylon. They believe that one day they will be repatriated to Zion and that Armageddon is now. They preach peace, love and reconciliation among the races, but also warn of imminent dread judgment on the downpressors.

They don't vote, tend to be vegetarians, abhor alcohol and wear their hair in long, tin-combed plaits called dreadlocks or natty dreads; the hair is never cut, since it Is part of the spirit and should neither be combed out or cut off. The Rastas say "I-and-I" for "we" and tend to shift "I" to the front of all important words, such as "I-tal" for "natural" and "I-nointed" for "anointed." They never use the word "last," since it expresses retrogression and a Rastaman can only go forward. Grass or ganja is the holy herb; it is regarded as a sacramental gift and the Bible is quoted as proof of this ("And thou shalt eat the barb of the field," Genesis 3:18). In Jamaica, where it remains illegal, an estimated 65 percent of the population smokes ganja, the highest grade of which the Rastas call lamb's bread.

Haile Selassie always denied his divinity, although he did give the Rastas encouragement. Land grants were given to Rastas who went to Ethiopia, and the brethren were always favorably received at his palace. In 1966, Selassie traveled to Jamaica. Seeco remembers thousands of Rastas, dressed in rags and carrying wooden sticks, lined along the airport road, praying, screaming and bowing down. It is said that many of them were amazed to see that God was 5 feet 4. Haile Selassie died in 1975 at the age of 83, but this did little to alter Rastafarian conviction that he was the living God. Some Rastas claim that he was reincarnated, while others claim he is not dead at all.

"Check me now," Marley says, "many people, dey scoffers, many people say to me, 'Backside, your God he dead.' How can he be dead? How can God die, mon? Dese people dey don't tink too clear, y'know, dey have de devil in 'em and dat devil he some trick devil. He smart de eyes and vex de brain. Dat's why me wrote 'Jah Lives.'"

In the Kingston ghettos of Marley's youth, Rastafarianism must have been a powerful siren song. It was, as it remains, a way out, a deliverance, the high road to Avalon. But Marley sees it in another light: "You don' suddenly become a Rasta, you mus' be a Rastaman from creation. Me was always Rasta . . . On whole earth start in Africa, de whole creation. Goin' back to Africa is not de ting. We don' go back to Africa, we go forward. Me want to go to Africa but me don' want to leave my brethren behind. Me no leader, jus' an ordinary sheep in da pasture. All I know is dat Rastaman is of the Twelve Tribes of Israel and dat dere comin' back together. And people no like dat. Dam vexed."

Whether he chooses to think so or not, Marley is a powerful political voice in Jamaica and it is, perhaps, this along with his Rastafarian beliefs and his criticisms of his country that instigated "the incident" last December.

On the night of Dec. 3, Marley and the Wailers were rehearsing in his Hope Road home in Kingston for a free concert they were to give in the city's National Arena two days later. At the time, Jamaica was in the throes of a violent election campaign between Michael Manley's People's National Party and Edward Seaga's Jamaica Labor Party. Throughout 1970, Kingston seemed more and more like a black Belfast. Manley claimed repeatedly that the C.I.A. was engineering the violence. Bob Marley had supported Michael Manley during the 1972 election but had since become disenchanted. "When me decide to play da concert," he said, "no politics were involved. Me jus' want to play for de love of da people." He had, however, received anonymous warnings not to play.

At about 9 o'clock, Don Taylor, Marley's manager, drove through the gates of Hope Road and parked his car. He could hear the band playing "Jah Lives" inside. It was very dark. Taylor had come to see Chris Blackwell and, though he didn't know it at the time, the fortunate Blackwell would arrive, as is his custom, several hours late. A few minutes later the band took a break. There were eight musicians in the front room, along with the three girl singers and the usual hangers-on. Marley told the group to work on some of the bridges, while he went to get something to eat.

When Don Taylor walked into the brightly lit kitchen at the rear of the house, the back door was open and Marley was standing in the corner eating grapefruit. He asked Marley for a piece. Marley smiled and held it out. Taylor walked toward him and heard what he took to be the sound of a fire cracker. Marley suddenly spun round, dropping the grapefruit to the floor. Taylor continued to walk toward Marley, passing in front of the open kitchen door, when he heard the sound of fire-crackers again, many of them this time, and felt a terrible pain in his side. He stumbled in front of Marley, felt another stab of pain in his side and, dragging Marley with him, fell to the floor and blacked out.

Don Taylor had been hit three times—once in each thigh and in the side. He was in hospital for six weeks. Marley was shot in the left elbow and another bullet grazed his chest below the heart. The bullets were homemade. There seemed little doubt that the shooting was the work of political hirelings, but many other extravagant rumors circulated and nothing was proved one way or the other. No one was ever apprehended.

Two days later, Marley showed up at the concert and was mobbed by 80,000 fans—including Michael Manley. Marley had intended to play one number and leave, but he played about an hour and shall and exhibited his wound to the crowd. He had a hit single, "Smile Jamaica," at the time and he pledged its proceeds to the poor of Trenchtown.

Several months later, Marley sat on the floor in a small drawing room of his mother's house in Delaware and smoked a spliff the size of a carrot. "Dem say de gunmen get clean away. So dem say. But me know dey couldn't shoot de Prime Minister or de Chief of Police and jus' disappear. Dat could never happen." He shrugged. "But dat's cool, mon. It's in de past now." He shook his head. "Don't know, maybe it wasn't politics."

"It politricks," said Seeco.

"Maybe jealousy," said Marley. "Jealousy's a disease inside plenty people's brain. It stirs 'em up and twist 'em round toward wickedness. Dat's do trot'. And when you know do trot' you can't get annoyed."

He lit up another spliff. "Herb is a natural t'ing," he said, apropos of nothing. "It grow like de tree. It is de healin' of de nation. I cannot use it jus' to get high. Me no do dat. An herb inspires. It clears ya out." Marley has been busted only once, in England last year, and he told the judge that he had smoked grass "since a you" and saw nothing wrong with it. The judge fined him $75 and asked him to try to restrain himself while he remained in England.

Since the shooting, Marley has not returned to Jamaica; and in the near future, at least, he is not likely to. "You can' sing your song in strange land," he says. But his music is everywhere—particularly "Exodus," the title song of his new album.

During the Jamaican election last December. Michael Manley's campaign slogan was "We know where we're going." Shortly afterward, Marley wrote "Exodus" and the Rastafarian brethren believe the song was the appropriate reply to Manley's assertion. "Open your eyes and look within," Marley wrote, "are you satisfied with the life you're living? We know where we're going, we know where we're from, we're leaving Babylon into our father's land." The song has become the No. 1 hit in Jamaica. It is also No. 1 in England and Germany.

It is, of course, difficult to predict whether Marley will exert the same influence in this country. To date, his American audiences have been predominantly white. "Exodus" is the first of his albums to have captured the black audience. Marley has been told that many of his black American brethren have not been able to afford tickets to his concerts.

"That only part true," says Tyrone Downie, the Wailers' keyboard player. "The blacks in America are into glitter; they're into platform shoes, fur coats and Cadillacs. They're tame, man, and they ain't about to let their pretty Afros down. All that talk of revolution—it vex 'em, man, it vex 'em bad."

But in Europe and throughout the third world, Marley has become a figure of almost messianic proportions. His fans come to his concerts for the music but it's the message they take away. To watch their stem, clenched-fist salutes, to hear their fervent chants of "Everywhere be war" and "Death to the downpressors" is to believe, however momentarily, that the revolution is near.

"Me don' understand politics," said Marley, "me don' understand big words like 'democratic socialism.' What me say is what de Bible say, but because people don' read de Bible no more, dey tink me talk politics. Hah! It's de Bible what have it written and it strong, it powerful."

"Yeah," he said, lighting up his spliff again, "now is wicked time. De trot' is always dere, you got to seek it out, dat's all. Dere is plenty of wisdom on dis earth dat people don't know. God is my boss and he tell me what to do, so I don't make no plans." Marley lay lack on the flour and looked up at the ceiling. "Sometime I talk and I don' understand what I hear, but I know what I mean, y'know?" When questioned about the spreading of his message in America, Marley smiled and looked away. The question bored him. The spliff had gone out. Lying on the flour, he closed his eyes. He appeared to have gone to sleep.

And then: "Me not know if they be ready here," he said. "In Africa, dey prepare for Zion. It is for dem me sing de song. Me only want to sing and spread do word. It slow to start, y'know, and now it creep up and do time is right. On time is come to rise up against Babylon. It have to be," he said, spreading his arms, "in America, all over de world. It in prophecy. And dat, no man can change."

Bob Marley:
Movement of Jah People

by Vivien Goldman

(Source: **Sounds,** *May 28, 1977)*

"Isn't it a nice feeling . . . isn't it a nice day . . . isn't it a nice feeling . . ." Bob Marley croons, strumming on an acoustic guitar. He's glowing, planted on the neutral modern sofa, in this sunlit hotel room. Outside the sliding plate-glass windows there's a balcony. Stand on the balcony and the river Isar rushes in a yellow froth far below, bubbling through spans of green leafy trees. We're in—where are we again? Oh yeah. Munich. The Hilton.

It's because, for example, Family Man never knows where the hell we are, that the Wailers travel in such a tight, closed unit. A real family on the road. It could be, and usually is, anywhere outside, but the Wailers' world is secure. A mobile Jamdown in a Babylon. European Dread.

Looking around this light, spacious living-room of the corner suite, some of the family are taking their ease. This Saturday a.m. is brilliant. There's a natural mystic flowing through the air, and everything happens crystal clear, because it's Saturday morning, and it's a day off the bus.

And everybody's either singing, beating time on a coffee table, or just aware of the sweet music dancing like sunlight through the room. You can hear the river bubble, the hissing wind through the trees, you can hear the distant sound of cars on the highway, and above it all you can hear Bob singing this tune, mellow as the river, fresh/free as the wind.

The melody swirls like incense in the air, interlocking everyone into a mood of peaceful unity, breathing in synchompatibility. The tennis on the colour T.V. is turned down low. The positive vibrations are turned up higher than high. Photographer Kate Simon says, "Now I'm gonna shoot some black and white," firmly switching cameras.

"Hey sister," someone interrupts, "Why dontcha shoot some black and black. No offence."

"That's cool," Kate says brightly, beaming like she's just scored the cover of the *National Geographic*, "I'll see what I can do." And shoots off another dozen pics while she speaks. And when that film's developed, there it'll be, black on black.

Roland Kirk called it Blacknuss, playing just the black notes on the piano to make sweet rebel music, telling his brothers and sisters not to worry 'bout a thing, 'cos every little thing's gonna be alright.

Bob Marley and the Wailers call it Rastafari.

"We know where we're going, we know where we're from, we live in Babylon" ('Exodus')

I've been on the road with all kinds of bands, and so's Kate, but never on a tour quite as hermetically sealed as the Wailers'. Mick Cater, the man-on-the-road from Alec Leslie who set up the tour (very efficiently, I might add) had this to say:

"It's easy to arrange a Wailers tour. All they want is a room where they can be left alone to eat their ital (natural) food, and not be hassled. The only reason why they're staying in Hiltons and expensive hotels like that is because they're the only places with private kitchens."

The Wailers follow the Rastafarian way, they like everything to be natural.

And what's a more natural part of life than FOOD? Right! Where other bands hit the night-spots, the Wailers chow down.

The Wailers are the exact reverse of junk food junkies. You can't imagine Family queuing up at the Blue Boar for a plate of egg and chips, it just doesn't work that way. No, the Wailers have Gilly and Inez in official green/yellow tour jacket ON THE BUS to take care of their stomachs.

Gilly looks like a cross between a swashbuckling seafaring man and a giant doorman from the Arabian Nights, with scimitar and turban. He rolls as he walks, and he has a way of looming over you as he talks that can be almost alarming. At gigs, he positions himself by Tyrone's keyboards at the side of the stage, stepping solemnly in his imposing solar topee. Then he rushes to the kitchen and concocts those fabulous, indecipherable Jamaican brews. Standing sternly over the blender, he adds a splat of red, a smidgeon of brown, and whirrrrrrrrs. Yumyumyum. What's this, Gilly?

"This life protoplasm, mon."

Seen. Not much answer to that, is there?

Like everybody connected with the Wailers, he's fiercely loyal and protective. Inez was almost reduced to tears when she arrived at the Heidelberg hotel and found NO KITCHEN. (Turns out they had space reserved in the main hotel cookery, so everything, of course, turned out to be ALRIGHT. Don't worry 'bout a thing.)

Neville Garrick, the Wailers' willowy art director bred'rens hovers on the blender, eyes glued to the Life Protoplasm. As soon as the first lot's done, he knocks a glass back, then says, "Where's the skip?" and sprints solicitously off with the machine to ensure that Bob gets a generous dose of the life-giving juices.

Bob's a man who spent a good few formative years being ripped off, and the result is, as Mick Cater said, "Where business is concerned, Marley doesn't trust anybody. That's the only way to be."

Members of Marley's entourage took the accounts of the last tour away from Alec Leslie's offices for inspection before this tour. (AL Enterprises weren't obliged to show the books, but they did quite happily.) Marley representatives cover every aspect of the money-gathering procedure—double-checking. And on this tour, everybody's on the case.

Kate and I were sitting in the back-up singers, the I-Threes', room one night—they share a room together on the road, kind of like the Girls Dorm—Rita Marley, Judy Mowatt and Marcia Griffiths were lounging around on the gilded beds, offering us delicious cold spicy chicken they'd saved over from supper.

Rita's small, dark and lithe, with a cheeky snub nose and a warm, urchin's smile. She was tidying away her clothes in a big cardboard drum she travels with, folding tops and skirts away. A red-green-gold Ethiopian lion flag drapes over the mock Louis Quinze lampshade, softening the light. They've made this baroque one-night stop-over room look homely, inviting.

I tell them how much I enjoy watching them onstage—they always look like they're having a party going on in the corner of the stage, looking at each other, whispering between numbers and laughing, generally vibing each other up while they sing those frighteningly perfect-to-the-point-of-sublime harmonies. Then towards the end of the set, perhaps during 'Lively Up Yourself', Bob dances over to them and flings an arm over Judy's shoulders, swinging his hips against hers, eyes closed in concentration, singing along with them—"yes, lively up yourself," . . . and sure enough, Judy, who all through the set has been performing with exquisite purity (tongue delicately poking out in concentration as she swings through the gun-shooting mime that accompanies 'I Shot The Sheriff') SPARKLES! even more. Marcia, pale moon-face serenely lovely, looks up and laughs. "Yes, we all brighten up when the big boss is around . . . "

And what she means by that is not that everyone suddenly starts working extra-hard when Marley's at hand, just that his energy is inspirational. Serious t'ing, me a tell ya.

Kate said to Bob, "You know, Bob, when you smile it's like seeing the sun come out."

She's right. It was like the sun emerging on the horizon when his head bobbed up behind Seeco's seat on the bus when they brought out the champagne to celebrate Seeco's birthday. The gnarled conga-player (he's had a meteoric rise in the Wailers' ranks—starting out as a roadie who kept on crashing out in the dressing-room, he was promoted to cook, but couldn't, and finally metamorphosed into the nifty congas person he is) was grinning with shy pleasure, his girlfriend squirming with modest glee beside him, as the entire bus sang an affectionate, spirited HAPPY BIRTHDAY to him.

Neville says, "It's funny, everyone has birthdays on this trip . . ." Family's sitting next to me, his usual blissed-out self, eyelashes curling tight over the swell of his cheek—and I comment on the—well, the nicer atmosphere on this bus.

"Yeah, mon," Fams sighs happily, "there always is."

The bus moves on through the night, bearing an extraordinary cargo of talent. Movement of Jah people.

Backtrack to the interview, London, 30th April 1977

As a man sow shall he reap and we know that talk is cheap ('Heathen').

Another bright Saturday, this time in Chelsea.

I'm climbing the white wrought-iron spiral staircase to Bob Marley's eyrie. When my head reaches floor-level, I see him asleep after a hectic soccer game in the park, on the beige couch, legs dangling over the end in their faded khaki trousers, militant-style, one foot bandaged from a soccer mishap.

On the colour TV the Saturday afternoon sitcom is playing away to itself. The floor's covered in cassettes, a bag of cashew nuts. The room basks in late Saturday stillness, light rippling through the trees outside in waves that wash over Bob asleep.

Hmmm. Asleep. What to do . . .

Just then, Bob looks round. Sees me. Closes his eyes again, as if to sort out whether he's awake or asleep. Decides to be awake. Sorry to disturb you, Bob, but you said I could call by . . . "Na. cool. One minute . . . "

. . . and vanishes downstairs to collect his thoughts.

Moments later he re-appears, and establishes himself cozily back on the couch, ready to talk . . .

"You see me here? The first thing you must know about me is that I always stand for what I stand for. Good? The second thing you must know about yourself listening to me, is that words are very tricky. So when you know what me a stand for, when me explain a thing to you, you must never try to look 'pon it in a different way from what me a stand for."

He's an unusually participant interviewee, always asking me questions—

"What you think about now? How you feel in life? You feel like you gonna live, or you feel like you must die? . . . "

I feel . . . movement.

"You feel like you're gonna live . . . that's a good thing. You have people feel seh, yes bwaoy, they gonna die so nothing makes any difference . . . "

Basically, this interviewee's as interested in checking out the interviewer as vice versa (and that's unusual). Reason being: "Speaking truly, when people write about me, me no specially like it, y'know. Me no really deal with—make and break, that type of word. Whatever I have to say, I wouldn't like it to be a personal thing, like what me think about meself.

"If you want to do some good, you should say some good things about Rasta, so that people can get some enlightenment.

"Like today, we talk kind of personal, I don't come down on you really with blood and fire, earthquake and lightning, but you must know seh that within me all of that exists too . . . "

Marley's keen to remind me that he's not just a man, he's a spokesman.

Patiently, he explains ("every writer same procedure") that he no longer regards it as excusable when writers refer to His Majesty Haile Selassie as 'deceased'; Jah Live, and Marley reckons that it's about time, with the quantity that's been written about Rasta, that everybody realized it.

A brief crosscut

Just 'cos you're a righteous man doesn't mean you're not human too. Two contrasting encounters illuminate Marley's chemistry.

Munich

Marley's manager, Don Taylor, presents me with my first ever ceremonial bowl of steaming hot Irish Moss (a JA beverage). The city electric spreads out far down below, nothing but shadowy concrete hulks strung about with necklaces of sulphuric fluorescent light. Bob scans the Telegraph, then the Express (Jah only knows how they got here) and tosses them aside. Sighs, puts his feet in their broken-down Roman sandals (plus bandaged toe—some injury) on the chrome 'n' glass table.

What's new in the papers, Bob?

"Nothing, mon. Same thing every day."

He moves closer up the table.

"You like that?"

Sure I do, it's great. I can't begin to imagine what it is, but there's cinnamon and nutmeg, it's faintly acrid and faintly sweet . . . Bob's eyes are twinkling.

"That's good for ya . . . you know that?" His eyes twinkle. "Make your pom-pom wet."

London

I think it was the night they were mixing 'Heathen', Bob was sitting on a tall stool by the studio kitchen bar, holding forth about politics with Mikey Campbell, Trevor and some other breddas, locks piled into a towering natural wool hat. Suddenly he swings towards me, pinning me with his eyes.

"Why you no write about Africa?"

Well, Bob, as you know I write for *Sounds* and they're a rock 'n' roll paper which tends to stick pretty darn close to music.

"Seen." Nodding, meditative, eyes downcast. Looks up. "And if you did write about it, the editors would probably take it out."

Back to the interview

"Me love talk about Bethlehem, Jerusalem, Nazareth, y'know," he continues, extra-animated, "me feel stronger. Me feel like a celestial thing happen to me, yes mon. Me just feel—different. So, see it, there come a stage where I check that these writers purely defend Babylon, just a different pure bloodclaat BABYLON. Although dem smile at me and laugh at me every day . . .

"Ten, twelve years me a sing—am I always gonna sing about aggression and frustration and captivity and all dem t'ing? Well now, you think it's my pride to really keep on doing that? The thing is, that must end when it must end. Me no gwan sing 'bout dat. Me is ahead. Not A HEAD of a people," he cautiously interrupts himself, mindful as ever of possible misinterpretations of arrogance, "but ahead of certain things.

"How long must I sing the same song? I must break it sometime, and sing 'Turn The Light Down Low', and deal with a woman, talk to some LADY, y'know?" He laughs again, jubilant as—well, as I am, listening to *Exodus*, the new Wailers album.

When I interviewed Bob, he wasn't sure of the final running order of the album. He was unaware of the 'hard/sweet' contrast between the sides, but very aware of the shift towards overt romance in his music.

"After the shooting . . . me never want to . . . to just t'ink 'bout shooting. So me just ease up me mind and go in a different bag. What me stand for me always stand for. Jah is my strength."

Things are very different now from the days over a decade ago when he, Peter Tosh, Bunny Wailer and Beverley Kelso started out as the Wailing Wailers, cutting tracks that seem incongruous in relation to his present-day persona—"What's New Pussycat", for example.

"Yes, Coxsone [Dodd] our first producer, he tell me a do that. We do all the Beatles, too—'And I Love Her'." He glances up in amusement from where he's lying on the couch.

"At the time, it no seem strange. 'Cos we not really trained singers, y'know, we just like singing—learn harmony, like the sound . . . "

The memories linger on. The decade old "One Love" re-appears on *Exodus*, and a new version of the equally old "Kaya" is among the dozen odd tracks in the can for possible inclusion in the next album.

"Sometimes me just like record old songs," Marley comments simply. "Yes, mon, we used to have some nice times singing . . . "

But in 1977, we're dealing with forward movement. An onward, upward motion flowing like the breezy rhythms of "Jamming"— "Yeah, 'jamming in the name of the lord'." Marley quotes softly, "You can be sure of that . . . 'right straight from yard!' (i.e., JA).

"Every song we sing come true, y'know," he adds abruptly. "It all happen in real life. Some songs are too early, some happen immediately, but all of them happen. Burning and looting happen—so much time, it's a shame. The curfew. Yeeeeees mon, everything happen. Same thing with 'Guiltiness'. 'These are the big fish that always try to eat up the small fish, they would do anything to materialize their every wish . . . ' You always have big fish, 'cos they manufacture them. That's all. I don't have to sing no more song, just that one line—just, 'guiltiness rest on their conscience . . . '"

Sitting in the placid Chelsea comfort, as Marley intones the biting lyrics, I flash back to an equally placid night in Jamaica. The evening cool settled on Marley's Hope Road home, many brothers and sisters crammed into the tiny bedroom beneath Family Man's floor. Bob's sitting on the single bed, legs crossed at the ankle, in frayed denim shorts, playing an acoustic guitar. He's staring into the eyes of a pretty young fan who stares transfixed as he sings a song so resonant and moving I'm practically slithering through the floorboards—potent Biblical lyrics about big fish eating small fish, who eat the bread of sorrow every day . . .

I couldn't forget the song, and when I hear it again eight months later, propped up against a brown-carpeted studio wall in West London, the slither-effect comes back with double force. All the magic and mystery of Jamaica returns—a naturally mystic land, where duppies (ghosts) are tangible as gunmen. So I don't blink when Bob says, "JA one of the heaviest places in the West spiritually, regardless of what a go on," and tells me about the 'Three Little Birds' of the song—

"That really happened, that's where I get my inspiration." Birds sang to Marley, "don't worry 'bout a thing, 'cos every little thing's gonna be alright . . . "

Marley's sung similar positive messages before now, but this sounds strangely slick on first hearing, in its chirpy, nursery-rhyme setting.

"The people that me deal with in my music," Marley replies confidently, "them know seh what I mean. People are gonna like that song, people that don't even know about Rasta, and it will make them want to find out more.

"Like with that song, 'Waiting In Vain'. That nice tune, mon, that from long time back. It's for people who never dig the Wailers from long time, 'cos dem just couldn't relate. So, what I do now is a tune like 'Waiting In Vain' so dem might like it and wonder what a go on. A different light. It's movement time."

Family Man is the band leader. He's called Family Man (going strictly on vibes this time) because he's the perfect image of a family man, warm, sympathetic, easygoing, humorous . . . in fact, he's got eight kids, so the name fits in more ways than one.

I remember wanting to meet him in Jamaica and Dirty Harry the horn player telling me, "Just follow the music. You'll always find Family there."

He was absolutely right. At home in Kingston, Family breaks into a sturdy, stepping dance, arms swinging rhythmically, head bent gazing down at the expanse of floorboards in this big, square, light room; the wall backing onto the verandah is lined with records, tapes, record, cassette, and reel-to-reel equipment; Family's dancing by huge box speakers. A piano, mikes, guitars and basses, no other furniture (except a little three-legged stool by the Revox, for threading ease, and a fridge full of fruit).

In Chelsea, Family dances on plush neutral carpet in a smaller room full of Habitat-catalogue furniture, round white tables and a fitted white slatted cupboard with built-in sink, crinoline lampshade . . .

Family counteracts the antiseptic Holiday Inn decor with—what else?—music. A mini-mixer between the speakers, singles all over the white lace bedspread, "Black Skin Boy" lying top of the pile . . . marked contrast to Bob's portable mini-cassette machine.

And on the bus, Family's toasting along to his massive portable cassette; a huge ends upturned grin slicing his silky apple cheeks, just like the man in the moon. He toasts and sings along to Dillinger's 'Bionic Dread', the Meditations, Culture, 'The Aggrovators Meet The Revolutionaries', Rico's 'Man From Wareika', and lots of rocker 45's.

In the studio. Family takes control. You think he's asleep, leaning back in the padded swivel chair, with hands folded on his turn. Then oh-so-slowly, he leans forward, eyes half-closed, rests a well-shaped finger on an echo button and pushes briefly. The music shifts, deepens, as Family closes his eyes with a satisfied half-sigh, and folds his hand on his turn again, settling back into meditating on the music like a shiny black Buddha.

And outside, Bob's playing table football.

The table football machine's a welcome variant in the on-the-road staples of life: food and colour T.V. The patterns repeat, like Wagnerian leitmotifs—after a while it seems like one long round of watching a Clint Eastwood movie on TV (when a hapless soldier falls from the top of a building in flames, Neville cries exuberantly, "See it deh: Catch A Fire!", and everybody yells "EXODUS!" when the prisoners escape from the dungeons . . .) while tucking into ackee and saltfish and dumplings 'n' drinking that Life Protoplasm . . . so the table football machine becomes a cathartic mirror for the emotions of the day. When everything's going well, when a track's near completion, Bob plays a keen attacking game.

"Come, Aswad," he shouts, "I-man gonna' mash up all o' dem!" Angus Gaye jumps to the table, and balls fly towards the coffee dispenser as they rock the machine. At 5.30 in the morning, when 'Jamming' is into what seems its 18th mix, Bob muffs shot after shot. He's tense; he can't understand why every track takes so long to mix . . . "Energy low", he mutters, as he turns away.

Other nights the energy's so high it seems as if the whole studio's about to fly on wings to the sky. Chris Blackwell says, "Call the skip, now," and someone fetches Bob. Standing on the platform behind the mixing desk, arms folded against the wall behind him, Bob shuts his eyes and listens intently to the final mix of "Exodus."

Suddenly his eyes snap into superlife; he beams, he shines with joy. It's almost Jekyll and Hyde, Bob dances, transfigured, flinging himself in the free, athletic, MOTION that thrills onstage. Even here in the dark basement studio, it's as if a Northern Lights aura throbs round every move. Everyone in the studio's exultant, it's a moment of triumph. Could anyone but a geriatric basket case with severe arthritis refuse this invitation to dance, dance, dance?

The "Exodus" party carries over quite naturally to the stage. The band are called back (invariably; they're magnificent) and perform a ravishing "Get Up, Stand Up," that has the entire audience swaying in mass ecstasy, then the beat shifts to the intense pulse of 'Exodus', shaking the air like the tread of an army crossing the desert to Africa, to freedom, irresistible as the flow of the Nile to the sea.

Marley trembles like a pillar of fire on the stage, thundering a challenge that's a command.

"OPEN YOUR EYES AND LOOK WITHIN, ARE YOU SATISFIED WITH THE LIFE YOU'RE LIVING, WE KNOW WHERE WE'RE GOING, WE KNOW WHERE WE'RE FROM, WE LIVE IN BABYLON, WE'RE GOING TO OUR FATHER'S LAND—SEND US ANOTHER BROTHER MOSES FROM ACROSS THE RED SEA . . .

"MOVEMENT OF JAH PEOPLE!"

Tuff Gong:
Bob Marley's Unsung Story

by Carol Cooper

(Source: **The Village Voice,** *September 10, 1980)*

BOB Marley and the Wailers are coming to Madison Square Garden next Friday and Saturday, September 19 and 20, to kick off a three-month American tour. They will end by making a neat, solicitous loop, landing back in New York for more performances early in December. Herewith a preview, a folio of impressions of my quest to penetrate the hype, mystique and misunderstanding surrounding Rasta reggae. *"Ain't no rules, ain't no vow, we can do it anyhow/I and I will see you through,/ 'Cause every day we pay the price, we're the living sacrifice . . . "* When faced with lyrics like those in Marley's "Jamming," one wonders first if the Rastafarians are serious, and then, just what they are serious *about.* Is reggae more than music or less than mysticism? That was the question I started with.

Ever since 1976 when *Natty Dread* was favorably reviewed in *Playboy,* the American media coverage of Bob Marley in particular and reggae music in general has been strangely elliptical. When critics waxed enthusiastic, they managed to rave about the imagery and spectacle of Rastafarian music without ever really touching on the heart of the message.

Despite such colorful corollaries as kayamysticism and Coptic (Christian) Ethiopianism, the kind of reggae Marley exemplifies has arisen to accomplish a particular international goal: to resurrect the political ethic of Garveyism.

Garveyism. How many Americans, black or white, remember that from 1914 to 1927 the black nationalist movement started by Marcus Mosiah Garvey managed to organize over 800 chapters in 40 countries on four continents, with nearly a million working members and two or three times as many sympathizers and lay participants? Black Puerto Rican Arthur A. Schomburg compiled his extensive collection of black and African research material as a result of his involvement in the Organization. The present-day Schomburg Research and Study Center in Harlem is a pan-African library developed as a direct outgrowth of Garvey's ideology.

The national amnesia among black Americans concerning Garveyism and its expression in reggae music seems to have well-calculated origins. An ideological war was fought between the NAACP and Garvey's UNIA (United Negro Improvement Association) during the early twenties; the outcome determined the current ineffectual direction of black political organizing. The "victory" of the NAACP has left much of black America (and indeed, the black diaspora) with two bitter truths that it systematically refuses to face: First, that the power brokers of America *never* intend to release its black masses from their economically convenient position at the bottom of the American social ladder; and second, that a self-deluded black elite (at that time mostly light skinned and college educated) sold out the Garvey movement because they believed the growing white liberal/leftist movements of the twenties would help them bring about immediate and total racial equality. Indeed they were promised such instant social integration before the crash of '29; a promise one can only assume black American leadership is still waiting for, after two and a half international wars and a Great Depression that has remained with the black community for half a century.

Recently the TV show *Like It Is* broadcast a lengthy interview with the widow of W.E.B. Dubois, discussing the evolution of the pan-

African liberation concept—which they credited to NAACP founder Dubois. Nowhere in the segment did they mention the Garvey movement, or the bitter feud between Garvey and Dubois that culminated in the deportation of the man whose philosophy prompted the successful anti-colonialist revolutions in Kenya and the Congo, and about whom Ghana's Kwame Nkrumah said in 1968: "Long before many of us were even conscious of our own degradation, Marcus Garvey fought for African national and racial equality."

There is evidence that Dubois later regretted the decision to oppose Garvey, and that his intention in doing so was more to supplant than destroy him. One year after forcing Garvey's deportation, Dubois wrote in the NAACP's organ, the *Crisis*: "Shorn of its bombast . . . the main lines of the Garvey plan are perfectly feasible . . . American Negroes can, by accumulating and administering their own capital, organize industry, join the black centers of the Atlantic by commercial enterprise, and in this way, ultimately redeem Africa as a free and fit home for black men."

Five years later, Dubois again adopted the stance of a Garveyite: "*—as* consumers (Negroes in America and the West Indies), *must at the very lowest estimate spend ten billion dollars a year. . . . We furnish such capital today to the white industrial world. There is no reason on earth why it should not be spent to establish a black industrial world.*"

The significance of the Rasta revival provoked and promoted by Marley and other reggae masters is that they not only understand this chapter of black history, they realize that the final global conflicts will be fought over Africa and her natural resources; not the Middle East, not Indochina, not the Americas. They know the current disunity and lack of self-determination among victims of the African diaspora leave Africa vulnerable to recolonization, and maintain the economic serfdom of black communities around the world. When Marley sings "Africa Unite" he speaks not to the continent alone, but to millions of blacks everywhere. In the newest LP when he renders hymns like "Comin' in from the Cold," "Zion Train," and "Work," he is expressing an explicit platform for black liberation and social reform which finds its active manifestation in the Wailers' tours and their Tuff Gong business organization.

When the word went out last year that Bob Marley and the Wailers would play the Apollo Theatre in Harlem, and not just once, but four nights in succession, there was more than a hint of snide incredulity expressed by the press. The smug assumption on the part of many in England and the U.S. who considered themselves the "first called" fans of the Wailer mystique was that black Americans could not possibly be the real objects of Marley's evangelism. That even aside from traditional rivalries between Caribbean and mainland Afro-Americans, American blacks were somehow not sufficiently clever or *moral* enough to be attracted by Marley's call to revolt and reform. This view was reflected by British writer Neil Spencer, who covered the Apollo concerts for his tabloid, *New Musical Express:* ". . . it's a long way from the sharp strutting, jive talkin' coke sniffin' get-down paaarrty world of popular black American idealization to the resolute Rastafarian idealism" (11/10/79).

Marley's residency at the Apollo was a sold-out affair. The racial and cultural mix was impressive, with an appreciable number of Asians and Hispanics among the salt and pepper crowd. Japanese and Italian television sent crews down to document the concerts and the event attracted ethnic programming from several cities as well as mention on network TV.

All this attention centered on an artist who critics had been saying "has lost his moment." In truth, Marley may just have expanded beyond the narrow theatre of operations the white media had prescribed for him, thereby becoming—for them—intangible.

It can be discomfiting to the skeptic to know that many Rastas believe in telepathy, and then to watch what they do with it. People appear with glasses before you have said you are thirsty; the subject of an interview will state or answer your question before you ask it. Yeah, yeah, anticipation, you say. Glass face, you say. But over a period of days the coincidences mount up, and one becomes convinced that either one is merely the butt of a conspiratorial joke, or these people *do* use some form of effective communal intuition.

It can be disconcerting to spend time around a group of people who have repeatedly read the Bible cover to cover and quote devastating segments at you as offhand conversation. During a two-hour interview taped for local black radio station WDAS in a Philadelphia hotel room, Marley discusses rising Klan activism, the then ongoing MOVE trials, biblical history, black history, world politics, the Pope, and possible dealings with the Philly-based Black Music Association. Afterwards a heated debate erupts between a "self-exiled" Jamaican and Marley. The two move rapidly from general politics to the situation in Jamaica, and the patois becomes both elevated and profane. The transplanted one urges Marley to seize the time, to use his popularity to organize a physical revolt against the Manley government. Marley argues him down by questioning his altruism, then his bravado ("Why don't *you* do it then? Do you know how many Rasta die every day?"). But what deals the telling blow is recourse to the hotel's Gideon Bible. Brandishing the book like a brick, Marley heaves it towards the challenger making him read aloud chapter and verse to refute and shame his own arguments. The man still tries to defend himself, only to be deftly cut down by yet another chapter and verse. And so it goes.

I've traveled twice to Kingston recently to see Marley's record company in operation. Tuff Gong Records International, formerly Tuff Gong Records Ltd., began as a tiny record store managed pri-

marily by Bob and his wife Rita long before the Wailers achieved anything approaching international fame. It has since grown into an ex-
panding Garveyite experiment in reassessing human potential and
employing black youth. A "ghetto" in Jamaica is often no more than
an area where black people without social connections live; thus Tuff
Gong makes a point of welcoming the "ghetto element," people
whose inborn talents have been neglected and rejected for reasons of
color or poverty. At the same time, Marley's fame and Tuff Gong's uptown location at 56 Hope Road have attracted many "society" people:
but whether they just pass through or remain attached in some con-
structive capacity depends on how well they understand the kinds of
personal sacrifice required in ambitious social reform.

In the media-hyped eased and fury that passed for a black nationalist movement during the late '60s in the U.S., middle-class ac-
tivists were often accused of being too moderate or bullied into
being recklessly radical, while the ostensibly lower classes were favorite objects of media ridicule and martyrdom, and used as pawns
by the poverty-pimp. Within the Tuff Gong environment such
party factionalism is not eliminated—after all, we are not dealing
with any miraculous utopia, only an intelligent alternative in a
healthy state of becoming—but it's eased.

From a Rasta point of view, most people, oppressed and oppressor,
have been miseducated as to what life and work should be about, so
the only solution is for everyone to be re-educated from scratch. The
process of entering the Tuff Gong operation is one of undertaking
systematic Rasta training—including diet and physical exercise—
geared to provoke spontaneous retrieval of innate knowledge. There
are no formal lectures, I saw no indoctrination. Only conversation or
"reasoning" which are sparked anytime the curious have a question,
and the knowledgeable have the urge to respond. Even though business activity in the Hope Road compound is almost constant, any

moment in the day might suddenly be used to expound upon a meta-physical idea that often results in practical, material application. Gifts of inspiration, these ideas are valued in Rasta communities much the way American governmental and business institutions value their think tanks.

With the completion of its 16-track studio last year, Tuff Gong has become a totally self-contained operation. It owns and runs its own pressing plant and is in the process of completing en extra, 16-track studio in a separate building to serve as training ground—for the newer, younger talent. Because Tuff Gong is in part the industrial arm of the socioreligious Twelve Tribes organization—one of the largest Rasta groups in Jamaica—there is considerable raw man-power at its disposal. The goal, I am told by more than one of the Wailers, is employment for all. But first training is necessary, and there are not yet enough skilled specialists to teach and supervise. Yet there is general confidence among the Tuff Gong people in gradual, unstoppable growth.

Women occupy key positions in runnings, some traditional, some not. In general the word "secretary" in Jamaica has broad connota-tions. Mostly in their twenties (but younger girls are constantly sit-ting in) they field the local complexities of international calls, keep track of personnel that may be in any city on three continents, plus the comparatively mundane chores of screening visitors for parasites, handling studio bookings, promotional items, correspondence, and inventory from the adjacent record shop. I mention to Miss Collins, with some envy, that in just the last year or two she must have seen plenty—and could write a helluva book. She agrees, but with gentle disinterest; there are important things to do, and she, like other young men and women on the premises, is into the music, with sev-eral works already in production. Aston "Family Man" Barrett, the Wailers' music director, had told me earlier what the game plan was:

Tuff Gong as the new Motown—Motown "from a more 'roots' per-spective." At present the Tuff Gong stable includes an impressive col-lection of male, female and child talent: Bob and Rita's four children form the Melody Makers and already have two singles. Burning Spear, suffering from an inequitable contract with EMI, has gotten Tuff Gong to distribute the new, brilliant, *Hail H.I.M.* LP. Singles from each of the I-Threes as well as an I-Threes album are available, while the new wave market, easily wowed by Chrissie Hynde and Cristina might snap up a beautiful, eerie tune called "Don't Feel No Way" by Dahima. Best of all is a 12-year-old discovery, Nadine Sutherland, whose single "Starvation on the Land" should make her competition in the States worry.

I speak to Freddie McGregor, another writer-producer-arranger in the Tuff Gong family, about the mechanics of distribution. Just 24, he and his group One Vibe were instrumental in the recording of Judy Mowatt's *Black Woman* LP as well as solo projects. London has been a base for quite a few years, but a Tuff Gong *store* has just arrived on Hyde Park Blvd. in Los Angeles. Although it may seem as if they want to bypass the international conglomerates, Tuff Gong artists are not averse to additional distribution deals. Rita Marley recently signed one with Hansa in France, while Freddy has an album Island is distributing in Europe. The key to survival is what it has always been: diversification, and maximization of total resources.

I visited Tuff Gong most recently in July while the Wailers were on European tour. Diane Jobson, Rasta lawyer and all-around business-woman, was running the show in the meantime. I watched her navi-gate a 12-hour day with seemingly endless energy, attention, and lit-tle wasted motion, but she chafed at the pressure from time to time. In addition to holding marketing and sales meetings for the new Wailers album, she is there to handle various foreign business in-quiries. Plagued by Jamaican import bans and taxes, she has to insure certain technical equipment is in stock or on order, she must regulate and prevent undue studio traffic, and attend to any one of dozens of daily snafus connected with the constricting Jamaican economy. Ultimately responsible should anything major go wrong, and woefully understaffed at the time, Miss Jobson had to keep the hammer down. I spoke with her briefly about it.

"In the music business the reality is you always have the groupies, the leeches, the idlers," she begins, "and worse, the ones who want to absorb you, who are only there because you are famous. They are the worst—but these are just the conditions of the business and you have to work around them." I mention being impressed by the professionalism and discipline I see in her young staff, automatically comparing it with the total dearth of such commitment back home. "If that's what you see you're already wrong," she responds. "It needs plenty more." Her standards are high: being functional is not sufficient.

Her attitude toward the media is brusque and pragmatic, perhaps because of a recent *Gleaner* item lambasting the establishment for being dirty, noisy, and generally casting a "ghetto environment" in the otherwise nicey-nice New Kingston suburb. This, even though the Tourist Board had prominently featured Tuff Gong studios and Rita Marley's Ganette Mander Restaurant as major attractions in its Sunsplash tourist package. Even in a black country, black people are arbitrarily accused of ruining the neighborhood. We talk a bit about the possibility of the print media ever doing justice to the concept of Rasta, and it becomes clear that she feels it unlikely. "How can you spend two weeks in Jamaica and write about Rasta?" she asks. And later, "Do you know black Americans are the last people to catch on to Bob's music?" This is the third time she has asked this; and although I know the answer to her implicit question, I am not really ready to say, and she is not really ready to hear. We drift to another topic; my terribly non-specific religious orientation. Non-specificity has always been my personal survival tactic.

"Rasta is the way to God," Diane says, and here, for all of me, we are in perfect accord. For up to this minute, everything I have ever conceived being divinity to be in relationship to human life is epitomized in the Rasta approach. And if we come no closer than that to an instant consensus, it is momentarily enough. Before leaving she asks if I've read Proverbs 31. I have to think a little . . . but yes, in doing some research I had made note of it, together with Proverbs 8 and 9. She reads it for me and says it should mean a lot to me. It does—but more as a testament to Diane, or Rita, or my mother— than myself. *She looketh well to the ways of her household, and eateth not the bread of idleness . . .*

And Bob Marley, where is he in all this? Playing for 180,000 Italians in two days? Flown by special jet to play for the Zimbabwean independence celebration? Taken by private plane on a public relations visit to Brazil? Take your pick. He has done all of the above and more within the past six months.

Marley's attitude toward Africa does Garvey one better at present; he often says that money made in Africa must stay there. The Wailers insisted on underwriting the entire cost of the Zimbabwe trip. And in recent concerts in Gabon and Zimbabwe, Marley took the opportunity to assess local needs and insure that whatever money he left there went into projects that served the needy and not the bureaucratic elite.

If the past six months are any indication, Marley's international impact is just beginning to be felt. In Jamaica he is known and respected as priest, prophet, shrewd entrepreneur, and, yes, something of a folk hero. But what about the man?

A king forever in his kingdom, Marley is seldom alone. In his communal environment there is always someone to teach, to console, to learn from, to talk, play, plan with. Marley has not so much assumed power over his "members" as it has been thrust upon him. To minimize the growing awe in which he is held by some, he now tries to defer as much as possible to the decisions and opinions of those he respects. Nevertheless anyone will tell you Marley is the leader of an ever increasing following. At a word or a motion people tend to move.

"Marcus Garvey said, 'When the black people in America get ready, the Jamaican must get ready.' It's working in a different way, in a sense, but still, it's gonna work like Marcus Garvey said." In an interview held just after the four-night Apollo gig Marley told me this, and in a loose, speculative way we talked about the tribalization of black American communities, and the fact that the increasing internal conflicts might finally force them to hear the solution in his music.

"I feel communication will be good," he said. "Because people are starting to pay attention. And that is the thing, we want black people to *look*. 'Cause we don't have anything against the white man in the sense of color prejudice, but black is right!"

Herb and dreadlocks were the next items on the long list of things that have inhibited most of black America from investigating reggae and Rasta for 10 years. It might amuse Marley to note how dreaded up New York has become since his last visit. What with corn-rows, natty-Muslims, "fashion-dread" and the sudden migration of genuine locksmen to the city on business or escaping the political heat back in J.A., there has been a wider dissemination of the hairstyle than the philosophy—and the biblical injunction—behind it.

"I used to trim y'know," he confided, "and brush and comb . . . especially when the black power business start. But one day I just said: 'It's myself still, but it not fit-up myself to look that way'. . . and me just break from it and say no, *dread*. So plenty people kinda 'fraid of it 'cause it get"—he laughed—"*bad propaganda*. Them say everything about it. But it's because the white man knows . . . suppose every black man look so? See everyone doing the same thing? But the beauty of it is you don't have to look so still, you can have the unity, but you must be *free*, to do whatever you want to do."

About herb, Bob is less diplomatic. He knows many people fear it and admits they might have good reason: "Them say it might get you mad. But all this is true! 'Cause them never make themselves, they don't know what power, what strength them have . . . and the more they look 'pon the thing, they get afraid of *themselves*. 'Cause if you can eat tomato you can smoke herb. But it's better if you start to smoke herb when you're young, 'cause it gives you a conscience, you know right from wrong. But you got plenty people who only come upon herb when they're 30, 40 so when they check it for the first time, it mash-up their head! Because it looks back too far in your life. It makes you check out from your beginning to today before you can go any further. And if you're wrong down the line, then you have to go down and straighten it out."

What an immense, and painful, introspection that must be—a kind of self-confrontation that Marley sees as crucial and inevitable. It is here that I glimpse the heart of Rasta, the reason why in spite of the awesome odds against it, the reggae message has captured international attention. Through herb, presently the most maligned of all Rasta accoutrements, they manage to reconnect modern man to a sense of spiritual sacrament—a ritual designed to bumble man in the face of those things in the world that he did not make, and therefore is not *superior to*. To humble an individual before nature so that he feels his interdependence within the environment is to make it almost impossible for him to support any system that destroys that environment. It is this type of deconditioning or "awakening" that Rasta advocates—by any means necessary.

"So it's a hard job?" I ask.

"Yeah, that's why plenty people don't like it. It's like some parts of the Bible the preacher don't like to read, because like herb, it brings out yourself too much."

Once we both realized that I realized Rasta is fundamentally suggesting truths that everyone is afraid of and therefore don't want to hear, the choice was to get very grim, or to laugh. Because as underscored by the test of Marley's *Uprising*, people are clearly being offered either continued serfdom under political technocracies and feigned "integration" or freedom through internationally applied Garveyism. And it seems that only the most desperate man or woman, who experience the gravest social misery, will choose freedom.

Because they have nothing to lose.

And we laugh.

4

Blackman Redemption: The Death of Bob Marley and His "Second Coming," 1981-2002

After Bob Marley died of cancer in 1981, his impact only grew. Among Rastafarians, he was practically deified. Some went so far as to say that, like Selassie, Bob didn't die. His music became a sort of Rastafarian gospel, offering a far more grounded truth than most religions: "If you know what life is worth, you would look for yours on earth."

The deification didn't stop in Jamaica or among Rastas. Throughout most of the "developing nations" of the world, especially in Africa, Bob Marley's image is ubiquitous, his legend profound. He's a national hero in Zimbabwe; for years he was more respected in Africa than by official channels in Jamaica, which always regarded Rastafarians with suspicion and their musical mouthpiece with the most mistrust of all.

A whole sect of conspiracy theorists speculated that this mistrust led the Jamaican government to enlist the CIA's help in ridding them of a potentially dangerous leader. Others believe that the CIA did it on their own to either destabilize or stabilize Jamaica. Take your pick.

Marley never copped to being a prophet and certainly disdained "politricks." He saw his music as a way for Jah to speak through him; the message he delivered was so beautifully universal that anyone could appreciate it, and the way he delivered it could make the dead wanna dance.

For these reasons, the posthumous best-of album *Legend* continues to rank high on the *Billboard* charts. Bob Marley has also become the topic of learned papers, several museums, and albums that recycle his recordings from as early as 1962. And, oh yeah, books. Many of them.

The Chapel of Love:
Bob Marley's Last Resting Place

by Chris Salewicz

(Source: **The Face,** *June 1983)*

On a hillside in a peaceful corner of Jamaica's lush rural hinterland— Natural Mystic Country—perches the simple white-washed chapel erected on the spot where Bob Marley is buried. Standing in a small garden alongside a single, carefully tended ganja plant and two doves of peace, the chapel overlooks the tranquil hills and valleys where Marley returned to end his days with friends and family before his death in a Miami hospital on May 11, 1981. It was here, in the village of Nine Mile in the parish of St. Anne's, that he was born 38 years ago, spent a poor childhood and the first years of his marriage to Rita. Their home for the first six years was a small hut. Here was where he was laid to rest in a gold coffin—dressed in a denim suit with his guitar in one hand and his bible in the other—after an ostentatious state funeral in Kingston and a cross-island motorcade carrying the body to this remote spot. On the second anniversary of his death Tuff Gong and Island Records are releasing a "new" Marley album. Chris Salewicz traveled to Jamaica to discover that the wound left by Bob's tragic death has almost healed but that the musical and political legacy of his life and work has not faded with time.

With the red, gold and green Ethiopian flags flying high in a heat haze either side of a fortress-like gateway, the headquarters of Tuff Gong International these days resembles not so much a source of Love and Unity as a mediaeval Moorish castle.

This semi-barricaded state, which is really closer in style to a Kingston adventure playground, is in the tradition of most Jamaican businesses. Channel One, the Jamaican Broadcasting Corporation, and the Red Stripe factory are all similarly protected from unwelcome visitors by high walls, barbed wire fences and officious gatekeepers. And these days Tuff Gong is definitely a business. Rita Marley and her posse of able female aides even brought in a firm of management consultants to advise how the company may best turn its millions of dollars of assets into a profitable investment.

Perhaps these business experts are behind such neat signs as the one in front of the main house that reads "No Ball-playing". To see this next to the yard where Bob Marley loved to play football all day long does ring a little oddly. But it is only intended to discourage the multitude of hangers-on who became permanent fixtures at 56 Hope Road. None of Bob's true friends have been excluded—Vincent Ford, the dread who lost both legs in a car crash and to whom Bob gave his songwriting credit for "No Woman No Cry" and several other tunes, is still there in his wheelchair.

If you seek significant slogans, the Tuff Gong motto is a truer touchstone—"We Free the People with Music". Or pay heed to the words painted large on the building's stairwell—"Do Good and Good Will Follow You". These speak of the real spirit of Tuff Gong.

For years reggae had confidently developed in the slipstream of its figurehead; Bob Marley's death in May 1981 stunned the music and stunted its growth. Developments that did occur were tangential, as though no-one had the confidence to make a major move: the rise of the New Wave DJ and DJ double-acts has been the most significant advance of the past two years. Figures like Eek-A-Mouse, Brigadier Jerry, and women toasters like Sister Nancy helped move the music on, or at least prevented it from falling back. A toasting superstar like Yellowman was an adequate jokey distraction but hardly fulfilled reggae's need for a leader.

But the wound seems to have almost healed. A number of acts on major labels have achieved real international success—Black Uhuru, Gregory Isaacs, Third World, Peter Tosh. Moreover, reggae is now a thoroughly integrated influence in contemporary music: Radio One pop is packed with reggae rhythms.

Now, on May 11, the second anniversary of Bob's death, Tuff Gong, through Island Records, will release a new Bob Marley album, *Confrontation*. Some of the songs are out-takes from the *Survival* and *Uprising* sessions, others have been worked up from demo tapes, with The Wailers and The I-Threes adding overdubs. Bob Marley was in my view the only popular musical figure who never released a bad song. So it is good to be able to report that all the *Confrontation* numbers match his own inspiring standard.

Briefly, they are: "Mix-up, Mix-up," built up from a two-track that had Bob's voice on one track and his own scratchy ska-like guitar and a drum machine on the other—edited down from an original eight minutes, it has a rhythm uncannily close to that of Marvin Gaye's "Sexual Healing"; "Give Thanks," similar in rhythm and melody to "If the Cap Fits" on *Rastaman Vibration*, and written at the same time; "Jump Nyabingi," again from a 2-track demo, a master having been lost; "Chant-down Babylon"; "Blackman Redemption," released as a single on Tuff Gong in 1979; "Trenchtown," currently a Tuff Gong single; "Stiff-necked Fool"; "I Know," a *Rastaman Vibration* out-take; "Buffalo Soldier," which will be released as a single and has as its subject the American Indians.

As a fierce tropical rainstorm suddenly enshrouds in thick cloud his house in the Blue Mountains overlooking Kingston, Island Records owner Chris Blackwell, who has produced *Confrontation*, points out that "Buffalo Soldier" is a particularly meaningful song. For in the fact that reggae proclaims self-determination, so American Indians found a soul brother in Bob Marley. Many young Apaches consider him to have been a kind of re-born Indian chief—Marley's cry at the beginning of "Crazy Baldhead" is identical to that of an Apache war-whoop.

Blackwell points out that in Jamaica itself it was Bob Marley who destroyed the tradition that your success was almost always in direct proportion to the lightness of your skin. "Before Bob," he stresses, "the only thing that anyone with Rasta hair could succeed at was being a carpenter or a fisherman. But Bob just had it naturally. He was a really exceptional person. When I first met him, I immediately trusted him. People at first would say to me, 'Those guys, The Wailers, are real trouble.' Which usually means that the people in question want to be treated like human beings."

It was Bob Marley's simple, clear perception of life, believes Blackwell, that allowed the musician to realize the greatness he was destined to attain. In the hamlet of Nine Mile, deep amidst the steep valleys of the rural interior of Jamaica, he spent an intensely poor childhood. Yet that upbringing indelibly stamped basic country truths on Bob Marley, like the time it takes for things to grow; in his career he would always let time run its course, which is hardly typical of many hustling, would-be reggae stars.

Nine Mile is now overlooked by the humble chapel in which Bob
Marley was laid to rest. Perched at the top of a sharply sloping
hillock, it is a small, serene building with white-painted walls and red,
gold and green wood-work. From an Ethiopian stained glass window
a lion gazes down at a house in the small valley behind, where Bob's
grandmother once lived.

There is a small garden, with a pair of doves of peace near to a soli-
tary ganja plant growing in a pot. One of several relatives who dedicat-
edly tend this area tells how it was predicted by a local seer who read in
Bob's hand as a child that he would grow to become a very great man.
He does not say whether she also foresaw what a companion helper
claims: that Bob Marley was a victim of a CIA conspiracy. On one of his
trips "in foreign", Babylon somehow ensured his body turned cancer-
ous, to destroy the man who was uniting the world's oppressed.

The story has a romantic appeal. But it is unlikely; Chris Blackwell
insists the standard explanation is the truth. The cancer was a direct
result of a football injury to a toe that happened in France in 1977. An
English doctor examined the lesion, and diagnosed that the toe
should be amputated; a doctor in Miami said he need not resort to
such a severe remedy; a Rastafarian doctor also said he believed amputation was unnecessary—"which is what he wanted to hear."

His one-time manager Don Taylor also dismisses the conspiracy
theory. He claims that Bob's melanoma cancer was hereditary—he
understands his father also died from it. Taylor also is sure that if Bob
Marley had survived his illness he would have found himself considered by Rastafarians on a par with Haile Selassie. Marcia Griffiths of
the I-Threes offers an echo of this idea when she gently mentions
that, as Christ's disciples carried on His work after He was crucified,
so Bob's music carries on his work.

Hardly the picture of a black music manager—he is probably the
only man who can wear a £140 black silk shirt from Bond Street and

make it look as though he picked it up for a handful of dollars in downtown Kingston—Don Taylor puts this view another way: "Because there won't be many more new records from Bob Marley, people will now have time to actually listen to his lyrics, to the gospel of his revolutionary ideas."

It seems accepted as a matter of course that Bob Marley's legend and influence are as yet in their infancy. For example, Jah Lloyd— "elected by the elders of Haile Selassie's theocratic government to represent the divine structure to the secular powers of Jamaica"— places him alongside such Jamaican national heroes as the nineteenth century rebels Sam Sharpe and Paul Bogle.

As well as the *Confrontation* record, Tuff Gong has another major release scheduled for this spring, *The Trip* by The Melody Makers. The Melody Makers are four of Bob's children: 14-year-old David 'Ziggy' Marley sings and plays rhythm guitar; nine-year-old Steve plays drums and even writes some of the songs; 17-year-old Sharon and 15-year-old Cedella also sing. The Wailers provide most of the musical backing. When The Melody Makers' excellent "What A Plot" single came out at the end of last year on Tuff Gong, the uncanny similarity between Ziggy's vocals and those of his father was immediately apparent—but this may not be so noticeable on the LP, as his voice has been breaking during its recording. *The Trip* is being produced by Ricky Walters, Grub Cooper, and Steve Golding, the team that also produced Rita Marley's fine *Harambe* LP, a big Jamaican seller at the end of 1982.

Also in production at Tuff Gong is an I-Threes album, with The Wailers again providing the backing. It is being produced by the stately figure of Cedella Booker, Bob's mother. This seems a rather strange idea, a bit like your mum producing The Clash.

Out at Bull Bay, ten miles to the east of Kingston, the sun sets, its last rays of the day finally cracking wide open a previously overcast sky.

On the delicious Caribbean waters the fishing-boats bob peacefully up and down, as they must have done in the days of the Arawak Indians. Twenty yards back from this beach—Bob Marley's favorite when he wanted to swim—Bongo, a 76-year-old dread who joined the Rastafarian faith in 1929, stands framed in the doorway of his shack.

He listens as a young-back dread from Grenada pours out a variant on the Bob Marley death conspiracy theory. "Everyone of us came here to do a portion of Jah's work. "I'm rise up as a songster . . . He died because Babylon killed him. He went innocently into their hands. He is mixing with the wrong sort of people. They began to call him the King of Reggae, when there is only one King. His Majesty Haile Selassie I . . . His blood is spattered all over Europe. Europe is responsible for his death . . . They gave him cocaine," he asserts, as though privy to secret information. "They can cut into that cancer germ . . . and his death is on the shoulders of that harlot in Britain!"

At the end of this harangue Bongo smiles, waits a moment, then offers his own thoughtful interpretation. "They try to seduce Bob Marley. But he is well alive. Death is not in our language. I and I deal with rest."

Late one evening by the front porch of the Tuff Gong house, a white dread, a former American DJ who—inspired by the *Natty Dread* LP—moved to Jamaica to become a Rastafarian, is standing and reasoning with the gathered brethren. He has heard from Rita Marley, he says, that there are sufficient Bob Marley songs remaining for at least one, possibly two more LPs. With the solemnity of a Biblical prophet, he reels off the titles of Bob Marley's albums, his tone drawing out the significance in which they string together: *Catch A Fire! Burning! Natty Dread! . . . Kaya! . . . Survival! . . . Uprising! . . .* And now: *Con-fron-tay-shun!*

"Yes-I!" He exclaims. "So the next LP, it must be given the title— JUDGEMENT!!!"

So Much Things to Say:
The Journey of Bob Marley

by Isaac Fergusson

(Source: **The Village Voice,** *May 18, 1982)*

HE sat with his friends smoking and rapping. Bob Marley. During his lifetime this man had become a mythical figure, yet nothing in his easygoing manner identified a superstar. He did not overshadow or separate himself from the dozen or so Rastamen milling about his Essex House suite. His laughter was uproarious, unpretentious, and free. He blended so snugly with his peers that I could not have picked him out had his face not decorated record jackets, T-shirts, and posters everywhere. A year after his death his words still sustain and warn and fulfill.

I had read about the millions of records Marley sold worldwide and that he was a multimillionaire. Still, I found it hard to reconcile the slightly built, denim-clad man with the explosive entertainer who danced across the stages of huge arenas or penetrated me with his stare from the cover of *Rolling Stone.* Marley got up, and politely took leave of the jolly group. He led me to the bedroom. Lying casually across the bed he carefully thumbed through a Bible. Tonight he will talk with me about Rastafari; tomorrow he will go up to Harlem's Apollo Theater and make more history, more legend.

Marley recorded his first song, "Judge Not," in 1961; he was 16 years old then. A helter-skelter music industry was just developing in Kingston where the unemployment rate was 35 per cent and Marley scuffed out a living as a welder. "Me grow stubborn, you know," he recalled when we talked. "Me grow without mother and father. Me no have no parent te have no big influence pon me. Me just grow in a de ghetto with de youth. Stubborn, no obey no one; but we had qualities and we were good to one another." In 1964 Marley, Peter Tosh, and Bunny Wailer formed the Wailing Wailers. From the beginning Marley strove to convey meaningful content in his lyrics: "Nothing I do is in vain. There is nothing I ever do that goes away in the wind. Whatever I do shall prosper. Because I and I no compromise I and I music. I'm one of dem tough ones," Marley said.

Soon the world discovered that Marley was no ordinary singer whose words were designed to be hummed for moments and forgotten; here was a messenger whose lyrics call attention to our condition, to the reasons for suffering. The music brings lightness to the feet and makes them dance, but the best is a marching drum, a call to struggle: "Get up, stand up,/Stand up for your rights/Get up, stand up,/Don't give up the fight."

Marley came to be widely respected as a songwriter with a reach that was broad and deep. Eric Clapton had a big hit with Marley's "I Shot the Sheriff," Johnny Nash scored with Marley's "Stir It Up" and "Guava Jelly." In 1972 Marley and the Wailers signed with Island Records, a small London-based company headed by Chris Blackwell, a white Jamaican. Marley, who writes his songs and arranged his music, made 10 albums with Island. They all went gold; 500,000 copies sold within the first year in England, Europe and Canada. Two albums, *Rastaman Vibrations* and *Uprising*, made gold in the U.S. His only comment when asked about his success was, "The man who does his work well, he shall be rewarded."

During the late '60s the Wailers became the first popular Jamaican group to make Rastafari philosophies and Rasta drumming the main thrusts of their music. Inspired by the back-to-Africa beliefs of Rastafari, Marley took a deep interest in Africa and the slave trade and wrote some of the most devastating statements of black rage ever recorded. His songs were designed both to tell history and to instill pride and hope in a people indoctrinated with the lie of inferiority. "In my music I and I want people to see themselves," he said. "I and I are of the house of David. Our home is Timbuktu, Ethiopia, Africa where we enjoyed a rich civilization long before the coming of the European. Marcus Garvey said that a people without knowledge of their past is like a tree without roots."

Soon, more and more of Jamaica's top musicians became Rastas, and reggae, the dominant music of Jamaica, became the main vehicle of expression for the Rastafari movement. Its radical ideas were carried by radio into every home and soon Rastafari permeated the society. Reggae singers like Marley became more than mere entertainers, they became "revolutionary workers" and representatives of Kingston's poor. "Them belly full but we hungry/A hungry mob is an angry mob/A rains fall but the dirt it tough/A pots cook but the food no 'nough." Sung with simplicity and the clarity of Marley's skeletal voice, these ideas were easily understood and quickly absorbed by even the most illiterate among the poor. Through music, Marley and other Rasta musicians attacked Jamaica's skinocratic system that placed whites at the top, mulattos in the middle, and blacks nowhere. Marley sang in "Crazy Baldhead": "I and I build the cabin/I and I plant the corn/Didn't my people before me slave for this country/ Now you look me with a scorn/Then you eat up all my corn."

The singer became the high priest, prophet and pied piper of Rasta and captivated the people of the third world. Unlike most religious cults Rastafari has no written rules or procedures; its members are united by certain common beliefs and uncommon rituals. The rituals and even the beliefs vary from one Rasta group to another. Bongo-U, a college-trained pharmacologist and now a Rasta medicine man in Montego Bay, says: "You will never know the Rastaman through books. You can tell the Rastaman through deeds, but to know the Rastaman you must live the experience—it's the only way." Some Rastas are devoutly religious and of exemplary moral character; others are thieves and criminals. Some Rastas are hardworking and industrious; others believe employment means surrendering to "Babylon." The only two beliefs all Rastas hold in common are: Haile Selassie is God; repatriation to Africa is the only true salvation for black people.

"Rasta is the most dominant, most important thing in my life," Marley once told me. "You have one man defend capitalist and other man defend socialist . . . finally you have I and I who defend Rastafari." Marley believed that in the Rastafari way of life there was an urgent message for the rest of the world. He believed that it was his divine mission to spread the word of the living, almighty "Jah," and also to inform blacks in the West that they are a lost tribe of Israelites sold into slavery in a Western hell called "Babylon." Marley came to help an uprooted and displaced people establish an identity. Bob Marley, who worked to explode the myth of a white God in a black society, was the first person to tell me that Israel was a man and not a place. He said the people who live in the country of that name are imposters. To Marley and all orthodox Rastas, blacks are the true Hebrews.

Rastas refer to themselves as "I and I," speaking always in the plural because they believe that God lives inside them. To express this divine presence they change the numeral in the title of Selassie I of Ethiopia and pronounce it like the personal) pronoun. Most Rastas adhere to a strict vegetarian diet.

In the strictest Rastafari sect, called Niyabingi, Rasta take an oath pledging "death to black and white oppressors." Yet they refuse to carry weapons: "Violence," Bongo-U explains, "is left to Jah. God alone has the right to destroy." Niyabingi Rastas cite Genesis, saying that God made the earth with words—"Let there be light, Jah said, and there was light." They believe that when all Jah's children are united in one cry—"death to black and white oppressors"—destruction will surely come to the exploiters. "Rastas believe in mind power and in the power of the elements, lightning, earthquake, and thunder," Bongo-U says.

From the Book of Numbers Marley and other Rastas took the command never to cut their hair: "All the days of the vow of his separation there shall no razor come upon his head, he shall be holy, and shall let the locks of the hair of his head grow." This is the oath of the Nazarites, which Jesus took. According to biblical injunction, Rastas cannot eat while others starve. They live communally, sharing goods and services among their community.

In the mid-'60s when there was an unprecedented rise in gang warfare and violent robberies in the West Kingston ghettos—police and politicians alike blamed the Rastas. The government ordered an offensive against Rasta communes and police viciously routed them and burned their homes. The worst attack involved the July 1966 destruction of Back-O-Wall, the worst part of the slums where numerous Rastas had settled in makeshift tin-and-board shacks. At dawn heavily armed police ringed the settlement with bulldozers while the occupants slept. Without warning they leveled the settlement, injuring and arresting scores of Rasta men, women, and children. This attack failed to destroy the Rastafari movement; instead it was scattered throughout Kingston and the rest of the island and soon began to challenge the norms, beliefs, and habits of Jamaicans throughout the island.

Once entrenched all over Kingston, the Rastafari, who had a history of self-reliance based on fishing, farming, and handicrafts, now inspired the youths to seek alternative employment outside the "shitstem!" Their call to "come out of Babylon" spurred an explosion of creative art and today Rasta painters and wood-carvers are transforming Kingston into a showplace of talent that generates considerable tourist business for Jamaica. But the most important product of the Rasta artistic renaissance is reggae music. Numerous drumming brotherhoods developed in the Kingston ghetto as unemployed youths and former rude boys turned to music as a profession and creative outlet.

Until 1966 Marley's music consisted mostly of glorifications of the rude boy desperado life style. He had had hits with "Rude Boy," "Rule Them Rudy," "I'm the Toughest," and the rude boy anthem "Stepping Razor." But Marley came under the influence of Mortimo Planno, a high priest and a force among the West Kingston Rastafari, and his transformation began. Marley said Planno guided him to a consciousness which we always saw in him and which he only had to recognize. He emphasized that no one can make a person a Rasta: "You have to look inside yourself to see Rasta," he said. "Every black is a Rasta, dem only have to look inside themselves. No one had to tell me, Jah told me himself. I and I looked inside I-self and I saw Jah Rastafari."

After Planno, Vernon Carrington Gad, the Prophet to Rastas and the founder of the Twelve Tribes of Israel Rastafari sect to which Marley belonged, took the singer even further into Rastafari: "Gad revealed back to I and I the secret of the lost Twelve Tribes," said Marley, who learned that each person is assigned to a tribe according to the month of their birth. "I was born in February so I'm from the tribe of Joseph," he explained. "Somebody born in April 1 could say they are Aries and that's what they will be because the word is power and you live it. But if you say you are Reuben, then you realize you find your roots because you become Jacob's children, which is Israel. Jacob said thou art Reuben, thou art my firstborn, the beginning of my strength, the excellency of my dignity."

In "Redemption Song" Marley identified himself as the present-day incarnation of Joseph, son of Jacob: "But my hand was strengthened by the hand of the almighty." Genesis 49:24 says of Joseph: "But his bow abode in strength and his hand was made strong by the hand of the almighty." Ramdeen, an East Indian dread, pointed to this biblical verse and said, "Same man that Bob Marley. Jah gave him the gift to write that music and put those words together. His mission was to deliver Israel through songs of redemption."

In 1967 Marley quit recording, left Kingston and returned to the St. Ann's mountain village where he was born. There in those hills he made a covenant with a new God, Jah Rastafari. This was to prove a pivotal event in his life, in his musical direction and in the history of the Rastafari movement itself. For a year Marley roamed the hills and practiced the ways of Rasta and soon Rastafari permeated his entire being. When Marley returned to Kingston in late 1968 he brought with him a new music and also a mission to take the word of Jah Rastafari to the people. His religion became the content of his music, and the music therefore became the medium through which he set out to take Rastafari to the world. Jamaica's ex-prime minister Michael Manley said, "Marley took what was a subculture in Jamaica and elevated it to a dominant culture. He took a folk art," he continued, "and he elevated it into a universal language of communication."

Marley's first song of religious testimony, "Selassie I Is the Temple," came in late 1968. This was followed by "Duppy Conqueror," "Small Ax," "Trenchtown Rock"—these songs zeroed in on poverty, injustice, and the evil of power politics. Marley had experienced a rebirth, and ready or not, Jamaica and the Rastafari had a new prophet. By constantly calling attention to the social inequities and by threatening and demanding redress, Marley and the Rastafari, mainly through music, moved not just the poor, but also middle-class intellectuals to question the ethics of Jamaican society and the conduct of government officials. Tremendous pressure was brought to bear on politicians as the music urged the people to view them with distrust. During the months preceding the 1972 elections, the ruling Jamaica Labor Party (led by Prime Minister Hugh Shearer) reacted by banning such songs from the radio. But a brisk black market developed in reggae and the music still played a big role in the defeat that year of the JLP by Michael Manley's People's National Party.

Without ever getting involved in power politics Bob Marley, who said, "me no sing politics, me sing 'bout freedom," became a political force to be reckoned with. He was quoted and courted by both factions of Jamaica's political establishment. Jamaican Albert Reid, a 63-year-old tractor operator, swore that if "Bob alone was in power in Jamaica we would have a lovely, peaceful country."

In Jamaica and abroad, Bob Marley transcended barriers of race, color, and class. Marley said to me, "The different peoples of the earth are the different flowers of the earth. Jah made them all." Indeed, people all over the world perceived that despite his pro-black stand he was not a racist, they knew he stood for love and respect for all peoples. Wailer vocalist Judy Mowatt says that, "even people of different languages and different cultures understood because his message was simple. He sang about the need for love and unity amongst all people." The universality of the Rastafari message is perhaps the most important factor in the worldwide acceptance of Marley's music. Reggae music is also infusing new radical content into British and American popular music—the Wailers, Steel Pulse, Burning Spear, are topping the charts. At the Garden concert, Oja, a black American Rastaman, spoke of its connection to blacks here: "Reggae can make the music much more relevant to the real life experiences of black people in America. We listen to our radios more than we read or watch television and what does most of the music say to us? Party, party, dance, dance, get down, get down. But a reggae song might deal with the lack of food for the people, or about the war in Zimbabwe, or the need for blacks to unite. That's why it's so important for our people to hear reggae."

In strife-torn Africa where various nations are in struggle for political power and self-determination, songs like Marley's "War" inspired the revolutionaries to keep up the struggle: ". . . Until the ignoble and unhappy regime/That now hold our brothers/In Angola,/In Mozambique,/South Africa,/In subhuman bondage,/Have been toppled/Utterly destroyed/Everywhere is war." His "Zimbabwe" became a war cry for SWAPO and ZANU guerillas on the battlefield in what was then Rhodesia. This song internationalized the struggle and helped to win world support for Zimbabwe's liberators. In 1978 the Senegalese Delegation to the United Nations presented Marley with the Third World Peace Medal, in tribute to his influence as a revolutionary artist.

Marley went even further in contributing to Zimbabwe—he headlined a concert at Boston's Harvard Stadium and raised money for the new nation. For the first time in modern history a popular singer had thereby demonstrated that he could use his music and his popularity to influence the outcome of a war. This action won Marley worldwide acclaim, but also earned him enemies. As Marley developed he became increasingly secular and international in scope. Consider his 1979 release, "Babylon System," which deals with workers passing their lives toiling in the capitalist profit machinery: "We've been treading on the/Wine press much too long,/Rebel, rebel/Babylon system is a vampire,/Sucking the children day by day,/Sucking the blood of the sufferers." Marley called on the sufferers to take action to change their own lives. Such lyrics can be interpreted as anticapitalist and progressive, merely liberal, or anarchist—depending on the perspective of the listener: like the Rastafari ideology from which it comes, the reggae message is open-ended. And as Rastafari and reggae become more widespread, people of diverse political ideologies read their own meanings into the religion and the music.

Some Marxists read and interpret the songs as invocations to the international working class to unite and overthrow capitalism. "Marley's reggae is the world's most powerful battle cry," said leftist economist Teresa Turner. "The task at hand is collecting the survivors of centuries of exploitation, racism, and degeneration—people who, as explained by Marx, are necessarily left out of the mainstream of society. Those survivors are potential revolutionaries and Marley's reggae invokes them to keep up the fight as the life's work of this generation. The mission of Rasta is to recreate society on a moral basis of equality."

But theocratic Rastas like Marley are both anticapitalist and anticommunist, saying that both systems are evil and designed to oppress and destroy. They give allegiance to no authority but Jah Rastafari. Says Bongo-U: "We shall set politics against religion, religion against commerce, capitalism against communism, and set them to war! And they shall destroy themselves." Since Rastas are in constant contact with God—reading a chapter of the Bible every day—there is no need for intermediaries. Thus there are no conventional leaders in the movement.

For the five years that preceded the diagnosis of cancer Rasta prophet Bob Marley had been working incessantly, ignoring the advice of doctors and close associates that he stop and obtain a thorough medical examination. No, he wouldn't stop, he would have to quit the stage and it would take years to recoup the momentum. This was his time and he seized upon it. Whenever he went into his studio to record he did enough songs for two albums. Marley would drink his fish tea, eat his rice and peas stew, roll himself about six spliffs and go to work. With incredible energy and determination he kept strumming his guitar, maybe 12 hours, sometimes till daybreak; but he had to get just what he wanted, always the perfectionist.

When Marley and the Wailers arrived in New York in September 1980 for the concert at Madison Square Garden straight away I sought them out. Minion Phillips, a close friend of Marley who traveled with the Wailers, was even then extremely worried about Marley. She had had some terrifying dreams. In one she dreamt that Bob stood before her and she saw a big serpent curled up and moving round and round in his stomach, eating it out. "I'm afraid for Bob," she said. "I have a feeling something terrible will happen. I don't think this tour will be completed."

"Marley! Marley! Marley! Marley!" resounded under the huge Madison Square Garden dome, then amid thunderous applause the audience of 20,000 jumped to its feet. There he stood. About five feet four inches, a slim man in denim jacket, jeans, and construction boots with his guitar held fast before him like a machine gun. He threw his ropelike head of hair about and it became a whirlwind around his small black face. The crack of a drum exploded into bass, into organ. And high above the roar of the audience, the sinewy tenor sliced through the inky space like the shrill call of a sea gull: "There's a natural mystic flowing through the air/If you listen carefully now you will hear/This could be the first trumpet, might as well be the last/Many more will have to suffer/Many more will have to die."

He became rock-still and intent at the microphone, a presence at once shocking and magical, totally in control. His eyes were dark holes in cheeks of slate. A huge crown of matted locks haloed his face and fell onto his back and shoulders. I jumped the barriers between seats and moved to different ends of the Garden, searching hard for signs of any weakness. Marley seemed in excellent form and the audience screamed for more each time he completed a song. "He's okay," I told myself, "he's got to be okay to perform like this."

The band was silent. Marley picked out a low note on his acoustic guitar. "Emancipate yourself from mental slavery/None but ourselves can free our minds/Have no fear of atomic energy/None of them can stop the time . . . These songs of freedom is all l ever had . . ." But why was he singing this one alone? And why the past tense—"all I ever had?" The next day, Sunday, Marley collapsed while jogging in Central Park. Tuesday the same thing happened in Pittsburgh during what became his last concert. The following Saturday I visited Rita Marley and Judy Mowatt. "How's Bob?" I asked. Rita took my hand.

"We don't know for sure," she answered, "the doctors say he has a tumor in his brain." I looked up at Minion Phillips and she was staring straight into my eyes. We both knew. The horror choked me.

The knowledge that Bob Marley might soon die haunted me for those months he spent fighting for his life in Dr. Joseph Issel's cancer clinic in West Germany. Still I was shocked when I heard that he had died in Miami on Monday, May 11, en route to Jamaica. He knew the work was over. While in the hospital he told his mother, Cedella Booker, that he had had enough of the needles which for seven months pricked at his flesh. Less than 70 pounds, he was too weak to lift the guitar he hardly left alone for 20 years. Says Mrs. Booker, "He wasn't afraid or bitter at the end. He said he was going into the hills to rest for a while."

Bob slept and Rita Marley flew back to Jamaica. She journeyed to the mountains of Nine Miles Village, St. Ann's. Marley had lived in a small house built by his father on the side of a steep hill overlooking the village in the valley below. There on that hill, Bob sat on a huge stone and wrote his classic, "Trenchtown Rock." There she had spent some of the happiest days of her life. Bob's tomb would stand beside the house right where the stone sat. She carefully chose the spot.

Rita decided then to build a temple with a roof and space enough for her to sit and talk with Bob. He would not be buried under the earth, but rest in a vault five feet above ground. She would embalm his body in the same way Egyptians and tribal Africans preserved their kings. Generations to come will be able to break the seals, draw Bob out and gaze upon him. She would take him to his resting place with the pomp and glory befitting a king.

When a king dies everyone has a theory; the reggae king is no exception. Some, like Fatso who sat behind me on the flight to Kingston, say that Marley committed suicide. Did Marley work himself to death at age 36, or did he work so furiously because he knew he would die young? Marley was always rubbing his forehead and grimacing while performing. Did he know something no one else knew? "Who feels it knows it Lord," he sang in his "Running Away" in 1978. "Bob spent too much time up in the ozone layer, that messed up his health," said his photographer friend, Fikisha.

There is talk of foul play, despite what police say. One dread told me Bob was killed because he was an important revolutionary. He argued that "laser beams" were hooked up between the spotlights while Bob performed and they "burn out 'im brain." Jamaican police sergeant Vernal Savane was certain marijuana killed Marley. "Ganja has destroyed a lot of youths," he insisted. To Rastas that claim is ridiculous. Rasta George, a Niyabingi dread, said, "The holy herb can kill no one, it can only heal I and I."

But the most controversial belief of the strict Niyabingi Rastafari is their total rejection of death. "Don't expect a man like Bunny Wailer and Peter Tosh at Bob's funeral," said Niyabingi Rasta Ras Joe, "them men are livers—they do not deal with death." Psalms 6:5 says, "For in the grave there is no remembrance of thee," thus Niyabingi Rastas like Peter Tosh and Bunny Wailer say let the dead bury the dead. They do not attend funerals. No hard feelings exist between the three founding members of the Wailers, indeed, if Peter died, Bob would not have shown up to his burial.

Marley, like other Rastas, believed that a person manifests himself again and again in the flesh. Thus Selassie is the same man, David. Marley has given up one body, but he will manifest himself again in a new body in the days to come. To Rastas who believe Marley was the "fleshical manifestation of Joseph, son of Jacob," his passing merely marked the departure of a great prophet and there was no sadness. Dread I-One, a one-legged Rastaman taxi driver, pointed into the starry blue sky and said there was no need to be sad because "we are numerous as the stars. Every prophet that fails, 12 are born."

Wednesday, May 20, was a national day of mourning, and by noon 12,000 persons had beaten me to the Arena, viewed the body and left. Another 10,000 gathered outside the Arena trying to get in before 5 p.m. Thousands rushed the gate and police resorted to tear gas to repel them. Sister Sissy, aged 80, held fast to a young man she did not know and fought her way forward as if she could not feel the tear gas biting at her skin. "Me never get tear gas on me befo," she said, "but me tek it only for Bob Marley. I never knew him, but oh I loved him. God knows he was a true prophet. I had to see 'pon his face before they bury him."

I stood there staring at what looked like a doll with Marley's face. It was a very eerie experience, hearing his voice, watching him lie there. His handsome face looked scrubbed, plastic from embalming, but the trance only increased its mystic magnetism. His majestic locks, scorched by radiation aimed at his brain, were laid in twisted ropes almost down to his waist. He was still wearing his gold, red, and green undervest and knitted wool cap in the colors of the Rastafari, and his usual jeans and denim jacket. The stream of faces of a thousand different colors flowed slowly along in step to his voice wailing from huge loudspeakers: "So old man river don't cry for me/Cause I've got a running stream of love you see/And no matter what stages/ . . . No matter what rages. . . changes/Rages they put us through/ We'll never be blue."

At 6 p.m. on Thursday, May 21, over 200 police officers and thousands of Jamaicans lined the street outside Kingston Max Field Park Ethiopian Church. His Eminence Archbishop Abouna Yesehey, the Western church head, came to Kingston to officiate at a members-and-invited-guests-only ceremony which began at eight inside the gates the bishops gathered, arrayed in splendid gowns of gold, silver, and crimson. Like wise kings from the East they mumbled prayers in Amharic and Geez as the archbishop lit frankincense, which filled the church. Drums pounded amid the tinkling of bells and the humming of songs and prayers. Journalists and television crews hustled in to take all the space between the altar and the congregation, blocking the view of church members and guests.

A motorcade quickly assembled after the service and cruised across West Kingston, passing by Marley's Tuff Gong Studios and then turning into the National Arena, where a state ceremony had to commence at 11 a.m. The huge arena was filled to capacity. State politicians, ambassadors, international media, music stars and thousands of Rastas dressed in white with red, green, and gold caps mingled and talked, and then the politicians took turns making speeches: Sir Florizel Glasspole, Michael Manley, and finally Prime Minister Edward Seaga. He announced that a statue of Marley standing with his guitar is to be the first erected in Jamaica Park, a shrine for distinguished Jamaican heroes. "May his soul find contentment in the achievements of his life and rejoice in the embrace of Jah Rastafari," said Seaga, and the audience jumped to its feet. Thunderous shouts of "Rastafari! Rastafari!" punctuated the applause—in death official society finally recognized Marley and his God.

At the end, Wailer musicians, incensed at the way the establishment co-opted the funeral, pushed aside police pallbearers, and Marley's lifelong companions bore him outside. Horse-mounted police forced a path through the huge crowd and the motorcade moved. People piled into trucks and buses, some rode motorcycles, others set out on foot. Down through Spanish Town, down past a thousand shanties, up into the mountain passes and through villages where people gathered in solid walls along both sides of the road, deeper and deeper into the heart of Jamaica, they traveled back to the hills from which Bob Marley came.

I arrived at a steep hill atop which the mausoleum stood and fought my way up. I pushed a black-suited man aside and came face to face with a smiling Edward Seaga standing on the threshold of Marley's tomb. Black-jacketed men flanked him. Seaga arrived by helicopter, avoiding the slow and grueling 55-mile trip in a 90-degree sunsplash. Yes, he had seen Jamaica come out that day. No, he had never seen a funeral like this, yes, it was an incredible sight. He moved aside, I stepped around him and saw the open vault waiting.

I heard the crowd exclaiming and there came the police pallbearers battling uphill like packhorses straining under their heavy load. They headed straight for the vault and pushed the coffin in. "Bob Marley, king of reggae, has chosen to come here to rest," someone announced over a loudspeaker. And 10,000 voices all rose up. Did they shout, "hail him"? Or was it, "praise him"? Coherence was lost in a roar that reached up to the sky. Again and again, they hailed him.

The photographers scrambled to tree tops and clambered to the roof of Bob's father's house. A trumpet pealed. The sun burst between the silhouettes atop the mountain and illuminated Bob's ledge. His wife and mother sang: "Angels of mercy, angels of light singing to welcome the pilgrim of the night." The sun dropped behind the mountain and immediately it was cooler. Only the bishop's voice broke the silence, reading the final sermon. A stout man placed a red metal plate with a gold star of David—this was the first seal. One by one he inserted the studs and fastened them. A heavy steel-wire grill was bolted on—the second seal. They fastened a plyboard sheet in and poured buckets of wet cement between plyboard and metal—this formed the third seal.

Darkness falls swiftly once the sun leaves those hills. The television crews, the police, and the politicians hurriedly boarded vehicles, engines roared, trucks and cars negotiated tricky turnabouts and rumbled downhill at 7 p.m. African drummer Olatunji walked around Marley's tomb ringing an agogo, a ceremonial bell. The drummer struck out a range of different pitches and rhythms. He stopped at Marley's head and rang out a long penetrating peal that ricocheted off the mountain sides and lingered in the still darkness. The mountains became giant lumps of coal. Down in the riverbed a fire burned before a small house. Shadows danced and moved in and about the yard. Powerful speakers drove Marley's voice out the door. It resounded against the hills and filled the night. "How long shall they kill our prophets/ While we stand aside and look/Some say it's just a part of it/We've got to fulfill the bock./Won't you help to sing/These songs of freedom . . . redemption songs."

One-legged Abraham Moriah came hopping uphill to the tomb on his crutch to welcome Bob home. "Bob made us hold our beads up. He has to call my father uncle, all of us in the village is one family. He gave us a message of honesty. I believe he is a prophet because many things he talk fulfill."

One Love

by Robert Palmer

(Source: **Rolling Stone,** *February 24, 1994)*

MEMORY pictures coming in: two snapshots of Bob Marley. In the first, the Wailers are playing one of their mid-'70s New York City concerts to a theater thick with ganja and dreads. The music unwinds from the first note like an impossibly sinuous Slinky, the groove steady, one song shading into the next without pause or change of key. Marley is a blur of motion, bobbing, weaving, dreadlocks flying, never seeming to quite touch the stage. It's as if the thick clouds of smoke and the rapt concentration of the mostly Jamaican audience are somehow buoying him up; he's hovering. No matter how much I squint and stare, his feet seem to be floating a few inches above the boards. Maybe it's the ganja. Maybe not.

In the second picture, Marley is sitting on the couch in a posh midtown hotel suite, surrounded by protectively huddling brethren and sistren, looking pale, drawn, severe. It's 1980, and the Wailers—now playing Madison Square Garden—have taken over an entire floor of the hotel, muting the lights in the hall to perpetual twilight, filling their stuffy, carpeted precinct with the unaccustomed smells of ital cooking and, of course, ganja.

There's been a disquieting change in Marley's demeanor. In the past, he would deliver even his most biting critiques of Babylon with an unmistakable generosity of spirit, his face friendly and open, his body language expansive. Each toss of his head set his mane of dreadlocks flying.

"It take many a year, mon, and maybe some bloodshed must be, but righteousness someday prevail," Marley would say. And it would come across more like a prayer than a warning.

This time, Marley sits very still, his head almost swallowed by the knitted cap he's wearing. His critique of the "politricks" of exploitation is as trenchant as ever, but now it's straight on, lacking the warmth and humor that were once such outstanding signifiers of his Rasta state of grace. Warmth? Humor? In less than a year, Marley will succumb to the cancer that only his inner circle knows is eating him alive.

The world Bob Marley came from, the Third World of the political philosophers, is a dog-eat-dog world: Trenchtown, a chaotic maze of shacks and dirt and footpaths and concrete jungle slung precariously along the edge of the 20th-century abyss. His life story has many of this century's most characteristic and horrific leitmotifs—the New World Order's rape of the planet's organic and spiritual resources; the obscenity of plenty and poverty living cheek to jowl under the gun; naked force opposed by visionary religion and deep cultural magic.

There really is only one way out, as Marley sang in "Trenchtown Rock": "One good thing about music/ When it hits, you feel no pain." With his induction this year into the Rock & Roll Hall of Fame, he is being honored for his music, which celebrates life even as it embodies struggle. But the music will not let us forget that this is a dog-eat-dog story and that even the big dog gets eaten in the end.

Marley's extraordinary body of work spans the entire history of modern Jamaican music, from ska to rock steady to reggae. But he never lost sight of the emotional center of his art—his people, the sufferers of Trenchtown, of greater Kingston, of all the world's ghettos. They placed their faith and hope in him, and he did not let them down. Later works such as "Survival," "Zimbabwe" and "Coming in from the Cold" are as passionately committed as anything from earlier years.

"It something really serious, is not entertainment," Marley once said of his music. "You entertain people who are satisfied. Hungry people can't be entertained—or people who are afraid. You can't entertain a man who has no food."

No one in rock & roll has left a musical legacy that matters more or one that matters in such fundamental ways. Yet there has been a reluctance in some quarters to accept Marley's music and reggae in general as a part of rock & roll. For their part, reggae musicians have been understandably reluctant to identify themselves with rock & roll's passing parade.

"Me have to laugh sometimes when dem scribes seh me like Mick Jagger or some superstar thing like that," Marley told *Rolling Stone* in 1976. "Dem have to listen close to the music, 'cause the message not the same. Nooo, mon, the reggae not the twist, mon!"

That was Marley's sense of humor at work. He clarified his position in an interview with author Stephen Davis: "Reggae music, soul music, rock music—every song is a sign. But ya have te be careful of this type of song and vibration that ya give te the people, for 'Woe be unto them they who lead my people astray.'"

Marley's election to the Hall of Fame provides the opportunity for a reassessment of this issue—or perhaps a reintegration. He was right to make a distinction between his music's singleness of purpose and various pop ephemeras; that doesn't mean one should separate it from the rest of music in its own proud but insulated ghetto. Because it isn't enough to identify the man as the crown prince of reggae or the Third World's first pop-music superstar. As an artist, he was always playing in the big leagues. No matter what category you put him in, his stature stands undiminished.

For that matter, it's probably high time we stopped looking at Jamaican music as a reflection or derivation of developments on the American mainland. The realities are more complex than that. Memphis, Tenn., and New Orleans created and sustained their own distinctive rock & roll traditions, and so did Jamaica. The processes that shaped all these musics are, in fact, very nearly identical. Arguably, the way these processes work defines rock & roll itself.

It works something like this. Ships come in bringing slaves from Africa, bringing music. In a climate of brutal oppression, the music toughs it out, assuming the importance it had in Africa as the culture's psychic and social foundation. As in Africa, there is an emphasis on rhythms, and the rhythms have a story to tell—often literally as speech-inflected patterns—and work to do. They bring people together, draw them into participation and serve as mediators between the individual, the community and the world beyond the world, the world of the spirits.

As the culture evolves and slavery's death grip at last begins to falter, rhythmic fundamentals begin to spread beyond the ritual setting. As populations leave the countryside for the cities looking for opportunity, dance music built on sacred rhythms spreads into urban dance halls, bars and theaters. There the music encounters the mediums of radio and recording: flashpoint. Suddenly, the venerable rhythms are the latest thing, a pop sensation. From plantation drumming and voodoo ceremonies to country-church "shouts" to Bo Diddley to James Brown: That's the North American version of the tale. The Jamaican version runs from the drumming of the Maroons (runaway-slave societies) to the pocomania and Revival Zion churches to the Rastafarians to mento, ska, rock steady, reggae and Bob Marley.

Robert Nesta Marley was born Feb. 6, 1945, in the heavily forested country of St. Ann's Parish, the child of 19-year-old country girl Cedella Booker and a white colonial then working in the area, Captain Norval Sinclair Marley. The captain did marry Cedella, then abandoned her. Bob grew up in a back-country world whose values and beliefs were still profoundly African, a world more permeable to superhuman forces both natural and supernatural than any city child could know. His grandfather Omeriah Malcolm was a respected man in the parish, a myalman adept in the ways of sorcery and spirit propitiation. Long before he embraced Rastafarianism as a spiritual philosophy and a way of life, Bob Marley was on intimate terms with his culture's deepest mysteries.

When the teen-age Marley arrived in Kingston, Jamaican music was entering a period of unprecedented expansion and growth. Mento, an acoustic popular music comparable to the calypso of Trinidad and Tobago, was being displaced from the forefront by an increasingly Jamaicanized take on Southern R&B and soul music. As the new ska sound developed, it began to exert a subtle but increasingly significant influence on North American soul.

Island rhythms had been an important ingredient in New Orleans' musical gumbo since the early days of jazz. Professor Longhair, the founding father of New Orleans' piano-based R&B, specifically mentioned his wartime experience playing with "West Indian boys" as a factor shaping his influential polyrhythms of the 1940s and '50s. By the mid-'60s—when Jamaican tempos slowed, its grooves deepened, and its bass moved out front in the mix, creating the style dubbed rock steady—Jamaican rhythmic ideas were beginning to surface in Memphis soul music as well.

Al Jackson Jr., the seminal Booker T. and the MG's-Stax Records session drummer, began vacationing in Jamaica, buying records, visiting sessions. Listen to Jackson's rhythm arrangement on Wilson Pickett's "In the Midnight Hour" back to back with the Silvertones' rock-steady cover of the tune, and you will readily hear the connections. All rock & roll styles are derivative of earlier musics in the beginning. Jamaican music quickly grew out of this phase, becoming part of a two-way rhythmic dialogue, transcending geographical and national boundaries.

Marley did not spend much time watching these events from the sidelines. A precocious musician with an already distinctive vocal style, he began making records in 1962. He sounded nervous, high-pitched, painfully adolescent on his debut ska recording, "Judge Not." But already he was drawing on Biblical imagery and themes in original lyrics that had an important social dimension as well as a spiritual and moral imperative: "While you talk about me/Someone else is judging you."

Marley's earliest ska recordings were solo efforts, but the '60s were the heyday of Jamaican vocal groups, and Marley had been woodshedding with a loose group of friends from Trenchtown. When he became dissatisfied with his original recording situation, he auditioned with the group for No. 1 sound-system man Clement "Sir Coxsone" Dodd.

Of the original group members, Junior Braithwaite and Beverly Kelso soon dropped out, leaving a tighter-than-tight trio of running partners to carry on. Neville "Bunny" Livingston, later Bunny Wailer, was one of Bob's earliest and closest childhood friends from St. Ann's Parish. Marley's mother and Wailer's father were living together in Trenchtown when Bob and Bunny met Peter McIntosh, later Peter Tosh, who completed the triumvirate.

This trio's mesh of voices was never conventionally pretty. The three voices didn't so much blend as create a constantly shifting ensemble texture, tightly interwoven but with each singer's timbre remaining distinct. Unlike most singers on the way up, Marley, Tosh and Livingston refused to cosmeticize their back-of-town rawness, realizing from the first that their origins were one of their greatest strengths. They had in fact chosen a group name that called attention to these origins; they were Wailers, they said, because they were ghetto sufferers, born wailing. Dog eat dog; that was the reality of life in the ghetto and in Kingston's music and recording scene. Producers ruled the roost, paying musicians and singers a nominal one-time fee for recording and reaping the subsequent profits. Nevertheless, in 1966, the Wailers took on the system, leaving Sir Coxsone's stable (a move tantamount to professional suicide) to start their own record label, Wail 'M' Soul 'M', and produce the sessions themselves.

"Yes, people rob me and try te trick me, but now I have experience," Marley said, adding later, "I know, and I see, and I don't get tricked. Everybody that deals with West Indian music . . . thieves!"

If you're listening chronologically to Island's exemplary four-CD set *Bob Marley: Songs of Freedom*, the move into self-production comes as a dramatic departure. For the first time, the singers and musicians seem to be breathing the same air, producing a superbly organic group sound. The Wailers' 1967–68 rock-steady sides for Wail 'M' Soul 'M' are the trio's first unalloyed masterpieces: "Mellow Mood," "Bend Down Low," "Thank You Lord" and the rest still move, instruct and delight.

After Marley took time off to write songs for the American pop-soul singer Johnny Nash (who recorded "Stir It Up" and "Guava Jelly"), the Wailers met Lee Perry, a former sound-system DJ for Sir Coxsone who was beginning to bring a new sense of space and mystery to Jamaican music. Among the session players who worked for Perry were the two Barrett brothers, drummer Carlton ("Carly") and bassist Aston ("Family Man"). As rock steady mutated into the even trickier, more fluid grooves of reggae, the Barrett brothers staked their claim as the music's definitive rhythm section. With the hyper-creative Perry, aka Dread at the Control, behind the mixing desk, the wailing Wailers and the Barrett brothers made an imaginative leap into a new and entirely unanticipated sonic landscape. Marley was now a songwriter in a class by himself, and the Wailers-Barretts-Perry team was able to create and sustain a powerfully specific mood and presence for each of his gems. Many hard-core reggae fans consider these recordings, collected on such albums as *Soul Rebels* and *African Herbsman*, the high point of Marley's entire career. That's debatable; the music's blinding brilliance is not.

Dog eat dog

Almost 10 years in the forefront of one of the most hectic, intensely creative music scenes on the planet, and what did the Wailers have to show for it? They were still living in Trenchtown, below the poverty line. They never heard their records played on Jamaican radio. "It's because the music shows the real situation in Jamaica," Marley said. "Some people don't like to hear the real truth." And outside Jamaica and the West Indian communities in the U.K., they were utterly unknown, as was reggae itself.

Through Marley's Johnny Nash connection, the Wailers, Barretts in tow, went to England, hoping to tour and stir up some interest on the part of a major record label. They managed to secure a bit of session work, record some demos and play a handful of dates in clubs and schools. They awoke one morning—cold and hungry—to find that their erstwhile management had left the country, stranding them cold and penniless.

Enter Chris Blackwell, a white Jamaican who had done well leasing hits from Kingston for the U.K. on his Island Records label and who was currently scoring major pop successes with the likes of Traffic and Cat Stevens. He still thought reggae could win an audience in the wider world, and to that end he gave the Wailers the budget to record an album. This in itself was an innovative move. Any other label honcho would surely have seen the group's outspoken stand against oppression and exploitation and its embrace of a Rastafarian belief system as potential impediments to commercial success at best. Blackwell encouraged the Wailers to be themselves.

The Wailers' first two Island albums, *Catch a Fire* and *Burnin'* (both from 1973), represent another new beginning for Marley. Both albums freely raided his enormous back catalog of songs, and while some of the versions issued earlier may be the definitive ones, as albums, *Catch a Fire* and *Burnin'* are themselves definitive Marley records. They are the powerful, unified masterworks of an artist at the height of his powers.

With the release of *Catch a Fire*, the pressure was on. After a U.S. tour that found the Wailers driving thousands of miles to play for audiences that were frequently small and uncomprehending, Wailer and Tosh elected to drop out of the rat race and go solo. This development broke up one of the era's greatest vocal groups, but Marley assembled the I-Threes (Rita Marley, Marcia Griffiths, Judy Mowatt) to fill out the band's vocal sound and kept touring. He was a man with a mission.

"God sent me on earth," Marley once said. "He send me to do something, and nobody can stop me. If God want to stop me, then I stop. Man never can." Marley's next three studio albums—*Natty Dread* (1974), *Rastaman Vibration* (1976) and *Exodus* (1977)—made him an international star. The Wailers were now officially Bob Marley's band, still piloted through the rhythmic rapids by the incomparable Barrett brothers but now expanded to include a clutch of superb musical individualists who were fundamentally team players, including guitarists Al Anderson and Junior Marvin and keyboard men Earl "Wia" Lindo and Bernard "Touter" Harvey.

Brutal as the Wailers' nonstop touring schedule was, the real brutality was waiting for Marley back home. Jamaica in the middle and late '70s seemed to be a society coming apart at the seams. The country's two rival political parties both employed gangs of ghetto gunmen to settle their differences. They also leaned hard on Marley for public support. At the same time, there was a great deal of resentment in the air. Jamaica's ruling class traditionally despised the Rastafarians for offering scathing critiques of the "shitstem" while refusing to take part in it. The emergence of a dreadlocked Rasta as Jamaica's No. 1 citizen to the world was seen as a public-relations disaster and, for many, a personal affront.

No rock & roller has ever had so many formidable and sinister forces arrayed against him. Marley found it expedient to maintain social relationships with gunmen and politicians from both political parties. "The devil ain't got no power over me," he asserted. "The devil come, and me shake hands with the devil. Devil have his part to play. Devil's a good friend, too . . . because when you don't know him, that's the time he can mosh you down."

Marley proved miraculously adept at advocating justice and an end to neocolonial exploitation of the increasingly beleaguered island while maintaining a sovereign's indifference to the machinations of partisan politics. But attempts to manipulate him for political gain continued unabated, and Marley well knew that the slightest miscalculation could have fatal consequences.

In 1976, representatives of the country's ruling, nominally socialist government persuaded Marley to headline a free outdoor concert in Kingston that would be strictly apolitical, a plea for peace among the ghetto's warring factions and a celebration of "one love, one heart." Two nights before the concert, two carloads of gunmen broke into Marley's house with barrels blazing. Astonishingly, no one was killed, though Marley and several associates were wounded. Showing remarkable courage, Marley honored his promise to sing at the concert. Showing good sense, he left the island the next day and didn't return for more than a year.

"They claim that I was supporting a political party, which is not true," Marley insisted afterward. "If it was really true that I was defending politics, then I would have died that night, because me know that the politician is the devil. . . . My job is to come between these politicians and become something else for the people."

Throughout these difficult years, Marley remained committed to his Rastafarian ideals and to self-determination for his people. In the Third World, especially where liberation struggles were in progress, he was seen as both a popular musician and a revolutionary ally. When Zimbabwe won its freedom from the white Rhodesian regime in 1980, the Wailers played at the independence celebration. Through it all, Marley continued to forge a visionary music that opposed the tide of violence and celebrated the rhythms of life.

His diligence never faltered; finally, it was his own rebellious cells that brought him down. The cancer that finally killed him on May 11, 1981, had apparently developed from an untreated soccer injury—although in circumstances such as these, one can never be entirely certain what happened or why. One can only be certain of Marley's enduring musical legacy.

The beauty of Marley's music is that while it holds a special significance for the sufferers of this world, it speaks to any listener with an open heart. You don't have to understand the sociopolitical background or the Rasta subculture—or even Marley's Trenchtown patois—to get it. The rhythms are as close as your heartbeat, the voice speaks a language the spirit understands. And, yes, when it hits, you feel no pain.

Chanting Down Babylon: The CIA & the Death of Bob Marley

by Alex Constantine

(Source: High Times, *February 2002)*

DID a soccer accident really cause Bob Marley's death, as has been widely reported? Or was the dark hand of CIA covert operations behind the death of the greatest countercultural prophet of our time?

Marley knew the drill—in Jamaica, at the height of his success, when music and politics were still one, before the fog of censorship rolled into the island, old wounds were opened by a wave of destabilization politics. Stories appeared in the local, regional and international press downsizing the achievements of the quasi-socialist Jamaican government under Prime Minister Michael Manley. In the late 1970s, the island was flooded with cheap guns, heroin, cocaine, right-wing propaganda, death-squad rule and, as Grenada's Prime Minister Maurice Bishop described it three years later, the CIA's "pernicious attempts [to] wreck the economy."

"Destabilization," Bishop told the emergent New Jewel Party, "is the name given the most recently developed method of controlling and exploiting the lives and resources of a country and its people by a bigger and more powerful country through bullying, intimidation and violence."

In response to the fascistic machinations of the CIA, Marley wove his lyrics into a revolutionary crucifix to ward off the cloak-and-dagger "vampires" descending upon the island. June 1976: Then-Governor-General Florizel Glasspole placed Jamaica under martial law to stanch the bloody pre-election violence. Prime Minister Manley's People's National Party asked the Wailers to play at the Smile Jamaica concert in December. Despite the rising political mayhem, Marley agreed to perform.

In late November, a death squad slipped beneath the gates at Marley's home on Hope Road in Kingston. As biographer Timothy White tells it, at about 9 PM, "the torpor of the quiet tropical night was interrupted by a queer noise that was not quite like a firecracker." Marley was in the kitchen at the rear of the house eating a grapefruit when he heard the bursts of automatic gunfire. Don Taylor, Marley's manager, had been talking to the musician when the bullets ripped through the back of his legs. The men were "peppering the house with a barrage of rifle and pistol fire, shattering windows and splintering plaster and woodwork on the first floor." Rita Marley, trying to escape with her children and a reporter from the *Jamaica Daily News*, was shot by one of the men in the front yard. The bullet caught her in the head, lifting her off her feet as it burrowed between scalp and skull.

Meanwhile, a man with an automatic rifle had burst through the back door off the pantry, pushing past a fleeing Secco Patterson, the Wailers' percussionist, to aim beyond Don Taylor at Bob Marley. The gunman got off eight shots. One bullet struck a counter, another buried itself in the ceiling, and five tore into Taylor. He fell but remained conscious, with four bullets in his legs and one buried at the base of his spine. The last shot creased Marley's breast below his heart and drilled deep into his arm.

The survival of the reggae singer and his entire entourage appeared to be the work of Rasta. "The firepower these guys apparently brought with them was immense," Wailers publicist Jeff Walker recalls. "There were bullet holes everywhere. In the kitchen, the bathroom, the living room, floors, ceilings, doorways and outside." There has since been widespread belief that the CIA arranged the hit on Hope Road. Neville Garrick, a Marley insider and former art director of the *Jamaica Daily News*, had film of "suspicious characters" lurking near the house before the assassination attempt. The day of the shooting, he had snapped some photos of Marley standing beside a Volkswagen in a pool of mango-tree shade. The strangers in the background made Marley nervous; he told Garrick that they appeared to be "scouting" the property. In the prints, however, their features were too blurred by shadow to make out. After the concert, Garrick took the photographs and prints to Nassau. Sadly, while the Wailers and crew prepared to board a flight to London, he discovered that the film had been stolen. Many of the CIA's files on Bob Marley remain classified to the present day. However, on December 5, 1976, a week after the assault on Hope Road, the Wailers appeared at the Smile Jamaica fest, despite their wounds, to perform one long, defiant anthem of rage directed at the CIA—"War"—suggesting the Wailers' own attitude toward the "vampires" from Langley:

> *Until the ignoble and unhappy regimes*
> *That now hold our brothers*
> *In Angola, in Mozambique,*
> *South Africa*
> *In subhuman bondage*
> *Have been toppled,*
> *Utterly destroyed,*
> *Everywhere is war. . .*

Only a handful of Marley's most trusted comrades knew of the band's whereabouts before the festival. Yet a member of the film crew, or so he claimed—reportedly, he didn't have a camera—managed to talk his way past machete-bearing Rastas to enter the Hope Road encampment: one Carl Colby, son of the late CIA director William Colby.

While the band prepared for the concert, a gift was delivered, according to a witness at the enclave—a new pair of boots for Bob Marley. Former Los Angeles cinematographer Lee Lew-Lee (his camera work can be seen in the Oscar-winning documentary *The Panama Deception*) was close friends with members of the Wailers, and he believes that Marley's cancer can be traced to the boots: "He put his foot in and said, 'Ow!' A friend got in there. . . he said, 'let's [get] in the boot,' and he pulled a length of copper wire out—it was embedded in the boot."

Had the wire been treated chemically with a carcinogenic toxin? The appearance of Colby at Marley's compound was certainly provocative. (And so was Colby's subsequent part in the fall of another black cultural icon, O.J. Simpson, nearly 20 years later. At Simpson's preliminary hearing in 1995, Colby—who resided next door to Nicole Simpson on Gretna Green Way in Brentwood, a mile from her residence on Bundy—and his wife both took the stand to testify for the prosecution that Nicole's ex-husband had badgered and threatened her. Colby's testimony was instrumental in the formal charge of murder filed against Simpson and the nationally televised fiasco known as the "Trial of the Century.")

Seventeen years after the Hope Road assault, Don Taylor published a memoir, *Marley and Me*, in which he alleges that a "senior CIA agent" had been planted among the crew as part of the plan to "assassinate" Marley. It's possible that this lapse in security allowed Colby entrance to the compound. It's clear that the CIA wanted Marley out of the picture. After the assassination attempt, a rumor circulated that the CIA was going to finish Marley off. The source of the rumor was the agency itself. The Wailers had set out on a world tour, and CIA agents informed Marley that should he return to Jamaica before the election, he would be murdered.

Taylor and others close to Marley suspect that it was more than a threat. Lew-Lee recalls: "I didn't think so at the time, but I've always had my suspicions because Marley later broke his toe playing soccer, and when the bone wouldn't mend the doctors found that the toe had cancer. The cancer metastasized throughout his body, but [Marley] believed he could fight this thing." British researcher Michael Conally observes: "They certainly had reasons for wanting to. For one, Marley's highly charged message music made him an important figure that the rest of the world was beginning to notice. It was an influence that was hard to ignore, least of all because everywhere you went you saw middle- and upper-class white people sprouting dreadlocks, smoking spliffs and adopting the Rastafarian lifestyle. This sort of thing didn't sit well with traditionalists and authoritarian types."

The soccer game took place in Paris in 1977, five months after the boot incident. Marley took to the field with one of the leading teams in the country to break the monotony of the Wailers' "Exodus" tour. His right toe was injured in a tackle. The toenail came off. At first, it wasn't considered a serious wound.

But it would not heal. Marley was limping by July and consulted a physician, who was shocked by the toe's appearance. It was so eaten away that doctors in London advised it be amputated. Marley's religion forbade it: "Rasta no abide amputation," he insisted. He told the physician, "De living God, His Imperial Majesty Haile Selassie I, Ras Tafari, Conquering Lion of the Tribe of Judah. . . He will heal me wit' de meditations of me ganja chalice." No scalpel, he said, "will crease me flesh. . . . C'yant kill Rasta. Rastaman live out."

He flew to Miami and Dr. William Bacon performed a skin graft on the lesion. The disease lingered undiagnosed and spread throughout his body.

Isaac Fergusson, a friend and devotee, observed the slow death of Bob Marley firsthand. In the three years separating soccer injury from cancer diagnosis, Marley remained immersed in music, "ignoring the advice of doctors and close associates that he stop and obtain a thorough medical examination." He refused to give up recording and touring long enough to consult a doctor. Marley "would have to quit the stage and it would take years to recoup the momentum. This was his time and he seized upon it. Whenever he went into the studio to record, he did enough for two albums. Marley would drink his fish tea, eat his rice-and-peas stew, roll himself about six spliffs and go to work. With incredible energy and determination, he kept strumming his guitar, maybe 12 hours, sometimes till daybreak." Reggae artist Jimmy Cliff observed after Marley's death: "What I know now is that Bob finished all he had to do on this earth." Marley was aware by 1977 that he was dying, and set out to condense a lifetime of music into the few years remaining.

Bob Marley's Star Finally Rises in Jamaica

by Howard Campell

*(Source: **The Michigan Citizen**, February 27–March 4, 2000)*

ONCE shunned by Jamaica's ruling class, Bob Marley is now being lauded by the island's luminaries, from talk show hosts and religious leaders to politicians, as a champion against oppression during week-long celebrations commemorating his 55th birthday.

Unlike previous years, when the reggae legend's Feb. 6 birth date was recognized with token homage from civic leaders and one day of

increased airplay of his music, Marley's image took on added significance in his homeland in 2000.

Full-page color ads appeared in newspapers proclaiming Marley as
the "Millennium Man." The leading television stations supported
events honoring Marley, as well as advertising Marley "specials" in
the weeks leading up to his birth date.

This wave of popularity has been triggered by a recent spate of accolades from prominent Western media, which have cited Marley's
role as a Third World musical icon. None has made more of an impression in Jamaica than *Time* magazine naming in December Marley's *Exodus* as Album of the Century.

The acknowledgement from one of the world's most well-known
publications received front-page treatment in Jamaica, with newspaper
columnists and government leaders alike lauding the achievement.

Earlier in 1999, the British Broadcasting Corporation (BBC)
named his single "One Love" Song of the Century. Both distinctions
have sent Marley's stock soaring in Jamaica, which has traditionally
shunned followers of his Rastafarian faith.

Time's proclamation made the *Exodus* album a hot item, with retail-
ers reporting strong sales for the 1977 album, which is distributed by
Island Records.

"That publication has made a lot of difference. We are selling a lot
of Marley CDs, especially *Exodus*," said Robert Khouri, the manager
of a leading Kingston record store.

Khouri reported that *Exodus* has appealed to an older demographic,
but says that a younger generation is also being exposed to Marley
through *Chant Down Babylon*, an album that fuses Marley's vocals with
those of several big-name hip-hop acts.

Clive Kennedy, manager at the Aquarius record store, says his establishment was also benefiting from the new love affair with Bob
Marley.

"*Exodus* has been in demand since January and we can't get any more from Tuff Gong (Marley's company)," said Kennedy.

Ironically, *Exodus* was inspired by a near-fatal incident involving the dreadlocked vocalist in 1976. Marley's Kingston home came under fire from gunmen during the state of emergency that was called to crack down on crime in the country. Marley was shot in the arm.

Shortly after performing at the Smile Jamaica concert organized to ease political tensions in Jamaica, Marley retreated into a self-imposed exile that ended with his headlining the One Love concert in Kingston in 1978.

At the time of the assassination attempt, Marley was being hailed as the next big thing in music. He had appeared in *Time* and *People* magazines and was the subject of numerous television specials throughout Europe.

Though he had a grassroots following at home, he was never popular among the middle and upper classes, who not only looked down on the Rasta movement, but also blamed it for leading many uppercrust children astray.

But his funeral in May 1981 attracted the country's most influential minds.

And 19 years after his death, even followers of different religious persuasions are hailing Marley's contribution as a musician who had a major impact on society.

Ian Boyne, leader of the Jamaican chapter of the Worldwide Church of God, conceded that the *Time* and BBC acknowledgements went a long way in winning Marley new fans among Jamaica's ruling class.

"His icon status has been solidified by the elite in Jamaica because two of its most credible international voices (*Time* and the BBC) have acknowledged his superstar status," Boyne wrote in a column in the *Gleaner* newspaper.

"There is nothing like a little validation from outside for us good colonials to feel good about ourselves."

For all the acclaim Marley has been receiving since late 1999, his timeless music still receives only token airplay in a country entranced by dancehall and hip-hop, out of North America.

Rastafarian leaders have consistently called for Marley to be made a national hero, and for his ideas to be taught at the university level.

Until such proposals are reality, Marley's call for one love will remain just a pretty song in his homeland.

5

Judge Not: The Marley Estate
and Other Legalities,
1982–2004

J ust as Bob Marley's artistic credibility and status as a prophet of
Rastafarianism grew immensely after his death, so did his fortune.
The legalities surrounding that estate became one of the most tangled
legal issues in the history of music, and many battles are yet to be resolved.

Ever distrustful of legal documents as harbingers of Babylon, Marley died intestate. From there, through a labyrinth of he-said-she-
said, the estate fell into the hands of a trustee who made it available to
the highest bidder. This put the Marley family in the odd position of
having to bid for its own birthright, which they eventually won with
the help of Chris Blackwell.

These legalities begat other legalities and also unearthed other issues as well. It brought the Marley name together with such boy
scouts from the jamboree (see the introduction to Section 1) as Morris Levy.

Beyond this, wealth can make someone a legal target: A variety of
people have sued the Marley estate for a wide range of reasons. It all
keeps the attorneys very busy.

Marley's Ghost in Babylon: A $30 Million Wrangle over a Tangled Estate

by Jerry Adler with Howard Manly

(Source: Newsweek, *April 8, 1991)*

IN life, the reggae singer Bob Marley disdained the impediments of what he called "Babylon"—modern Western civilization—such as lawyers, preachers and barbers. His philosophy was a radical Caribbean romanticism, surcharged with the Biblical cult of Rastafarianism. His habits ran to regular indulgence in cigar-sized joints of powerful marijuana. Neither was conducive to an orthodox personal life. He did business with his band on the basis of a handshake, paying them when and what he chose; he fathered at least seven children by as many women, not counting four by his wife, Rita; and when he was dying of cancer in 1981 at 36, he refused to make out a will. Preferring to believe he would live forever, he ordered a new Mercedes Benz. A decade later, the car is one small piece of a monumental legal tangle over Marley's $30 million estate that just goes to show, as he might have put it, that "Babylon" always wins in the end.

At the center of the dispute are Rita, 46, a former dancer with Marley's band whom he married in 1966, and J. Louis Byles, the court-appointed administrator of the singer's estate. Under Jamaican law, Marley's widow would have been entitled to half his estate, with the remainder divided equally among his children. But Byles charges that for much of the 1980s money that should have gone to the estate was diverted to offshore corporations controlled by Rita and her lawyers. After the 1984 release of Marley's *Legend* album, a compilation of his great hits, Marley's royalties jumped from around $200,000 a year to $1 million, and eventually much more, but the estate never saw most of the money; a subsequent audit found discrepancies totaling around $16 million. Rita admitted in court forging her husband's signature on backdated documents transferring ownership of Marley's companies to her. She did this, she told *Newsweek*, on the advice of her lawyers and in the belief that since she was the prime heir anyway, "how can I steal from myself?" The court dismissed her as one of Marley's original executors, but she was not charged with a crime; the estate has sued her lawyer to get the money back and, after more than four years, a federal court in New York is expected to rule later this year. "I did nothing of my own thought," Rita added. "I was a lowly wife who went on stage and danced when Bob told me to dance."

Byles—a conservative 79-year-old Kingston banker who never cared for Marley when he was alive—has been hunting down the estate's assets with a relentlessness that has disconcerted even some of the heirs whose interests he is protecting. Since Marley never bothered to legally transfer to his mother the $400,000 house in Miami he bought for her in 1978, the estate's lawyers tried to evict her and put the house on the market. Chris Blackwell, the Island Records producer who gave Marley his start, eventually bought the property and gave it to her. "These people [the estate's lawyers] are so bright and so evil," Marley's mother says. "They are the devil's tools." The Mercedes Marley bought on his deathbed didn't arrive until after he died, and was paid for by the estate. When Byles discovered that Rita had been driving it since 1981, he began legal proceedings to reclaim the car, which by now has more than 90,000 miles on it. His efforts to make the strictest principles of English probate law fit the circumstances of a Jamaican folk hero and Rastafarian mystic have not endeared him to the Jamaican public, and he has been wounded by the bad publicity. "I can honestly say I have regretted the day I agreed to take this job," he says. "It has indirectly caused me three major operations and the addition of a pacemaker."

Cash settlements

Then there are the other heirs. Marley once said he wanted as many children as there were "shells in the sea," and appears to have made good on the boast. When the courts advertised for potential heirs, hundreds of would-be Marleys appeared from all over the world. Rita herself helped winnow the claimants down to seven. But the heirs, most of them poor, must have been quite disappointed to discover that their share of the great singer's estate at first came to approximately $210 every three months. The situation has improved somewhat since then. Five of the heirs have reached their majority and gotten cash settlements of around $70,000. They will receive more when the estate finally sells the rights to Marley's music, but the sale has been held up while the courts decide whether the price, $8.2 million, is fair.

Meanwhile, the estate gave about $100,000 to the heirs last year. This compares to roughly $2 million for "professional services" in the same year. The "stiff-necked baldheads," as Marley described Jamaica's ruling class of professionals and politicians, got it all, at the going rate of $300 an hour for the estate's lawyers. The one thing they couldn't take cuts of, though, was Marley's own indomitable spirit, which appears to have been passed down more or less intact to his and Rita's son Ziggy, 22. A reggae singer himself with several Grammys to his credit, Ziggy filed a statement in Florida's Dade County Court expressing his desire to be rid of the whole mess. "Let them have it," he said. "Me can go out and make me own money."

Talkin' Over: Marley Estate Case Ends; Island Logic, Family Can Purchase Assets

by Maureen Sheridan

(Source: **Billboard,** *December 21, 1991)*

As the voice of Bob Marley, singing "Get up, stand up, stand up for your rights," plaintively echoed from a car parked outside a downtown Kingston courtroom, the prolonged and bitter battle over the rights to his estate finally came to an end. Chris Blackwell's Island Logic, widow Rita Marley, and the six adult (of the 11 total) sons and daughters of Bob Marley have been collectively awarded the right to buy the music-related assets of the late reggae singer's estate.

In a decision handed down by Justice Walker Dec. 9 in the Supreme Court of Jamaica, the Island Logic/Marley family offer of $11.5 million was deemed more "certain" than the MCA conditional bid of a "maximum" of $15.2 million, which had, said the judge, "too much uncertainty surrounding it."

Chris Blackwell, who was in London when the hearing on the sale was concluded, declared himself "thrilled with the decision," but admitted to being "a little afraid to believe that it's finally over and that we've won. For two years we've been on semi-hold and we couldn't really go forward with anything. We can really get behind it now, and I'm looking forward to getting on with the job of running the future." Said Rita Marley's attorney, Michael Hylton, "the future is exciting. When you look at how Bob's music has kept alive and sold for the last two years of its own accord, the potential of his work if it's promoted internationally is immense. We are very pleased with the decision."

During the weeklong hearing, competition between the two contenders was intense, each attempting to outdo the other with terms more attractive to the beneficiaries. Both offered ownership shares to the Marley heirs: MCA proffered a 4% share to each of the beneficiaries, and Island Logic provided a similar option to the infant beneficiaries, to be exercised when they came of age.

Island Logic bought the Marley music assets (together with real estate in Kingston that includes Marley's Tuff Gong Studio and manufacturing facilities) for $8.2 million in 1989, but the purchase was halted midstream when the U.K. Privy Council upheld an appeal by some of the beneficiaries that alleged that the assets had been insufficiently advertised. When, after the assets were advertised internationally, MCA almost doubled the Island Logic figure, Blackwell, who had earlier said that such a high bid was suspect, joined forces with the Marley family, upped his price by $3.2 million, and changed some of the terms of the Island offer.

The terms of the revised Island Logic tender provide that the adult beneficiaries will waive their right to immediate financial benefit so that the sale proceeds can be divided equally among the five infant beneficiaries—each child to receive U.S. $1,174,000. MCA's monies would have been split among all 11 legatees, giving each one $1,234,242. However, the court stated that although the potential proceeds of MCA's offer were higher, Island Logic's figure was firm and unconditional and of more tangible benefit to the Marley heirs.

Bob Marley was a Rasta rebel who did not believe in wills, a belief that cost his heirs 10 years of courtroom drama and, in the last five years alone, more than $8 million in administrative and legal fees. With a widow, 11 children (by eight mothers), and a backing band (the Wailers) all entitled to a portion of the proceeds, acrimony and dissension have plagued the estate over the decade since Marley died of cancer in a Miami hospital, leaving what was then estimated to be $30 million.

Lawsuits Charge Fraud

Litigation filed by or against estate administrator Kingston-based Mutual Security Merchant Bank includes a lawsuit against Rita Marley (who was dismissed as co-administrator) and her U.S. attorney and accountant, David Steinberg and Marvin Zolt, respectively, for alleged fraud and withholding of funds totaling $14 million; a countersuit by Rita Marley against the administrator; an action against Marley's mother, Cedella Booker, for the recovery of $500,000; an action against the estate by Marley's backing band, the Wailers, for a 50% share of royalties; and an action against Mutual Security Merchant Bank brought by the guardians of three of the infant beneficiaries alleging mismanagement of funds. There were 10 lawsuits in all, and most remain unsettled.

The most recent controversy erupted last month when Chris Blackwell, at a London press conference, implied the administrator had misappropriated funds, an accusation that Louis Byles, the bank's executive director, called a "blatant lie." Byles added that "if Chris Blackwell said this, he should bring an action against the administrator instead of shooting off his mouth."

Asked whether he intended to carry out his threat of legal action, Blackwell explained that his threat had been made to force the administrator "to present our bid to the court. I believe if we had not had that press conference, we would not have had our day in court."

Up until Nov. 15, the administrator had not presented Island Logic's increased offer to the court. Even though the original sales price of $8.2 million had been paid by Island Logic to the administrator (and the administrator had transferred some of the assets to Island Logic before the U.K. Privy Council's surprise ruling), Mutual Security Merchant Bank had deemed Island Logic's increased tender of $ 11.5 million (first presented to the court by letter) "only a proposal." It was the MCA bid that won the endorsement of the administrator, according to Hylton.

Retorted Byles, "When I stated that the MCA offer was to be pre-ferred, I felt that this was so. After Island Logic revised their offer and made certain other concessions, their offer came very close to MCA's."

Byles added, "I have no quarrel whatsoever with the judge's deci-sion ... It was a very fair decision in view of the circumstances. The conditions of the MCA offer allowed it to pay less than $15.2 million if, after due diligence, the values on which they had based that sum were found to be different. The judge asked how could we know what they were really going to pay? This is where MCA fell down."

Island Logic will manage the estate on behalf of the adult beneficia-ries through the already formed Bob Marley Foundation. "The man-agement contract is for 10 years," said Blackwell. "There is an option to renew, but hopefully [the beneficiaries] will then take it on them-selves." Blackwell will retain 50% of Marley's publishing income.

Among the guardians of the five infant progeny, reaction to the court's ruling was said to be mixed. Anthony Levy, counsel for Cindy Breakspeare (mother of Damian), who was earlier said to favor the MCA offer, was "shocked at the decision." He believes that the infant beneficiaries "are going to be a lot worse off" than they would be if MCA had won its bid for the estate.

Let's Get Together and Deal All Right

by Kirk Semple

(Source: **Miami New Times** *[Florida], March 18, 1992)*

*A*FTER *six years of litigation and millions of dollars in legal fees, one strand of Bob Marley's tangled estate has been sorted out. Almost.*

It's early afternoon, only hours before the opening bash at the newly restored Marlin Hotel on Miami Beach, and the place is alive. The traffic outside on Twelfth Street backs up behind semi-trucks unloading sound and stage equipment, and young, suave workers from Jamaica, Britain, New York, and Miami bustle around making final arrangements for the party, securing adequate booze supplies, coordinating a guest list chock-full of Very Important People.

And everyone wants to say hello to Chris Blackwell. The founder of Island Records, director of the Island Trading Company (which owns the Marlin), international music-industry giant, has just awoken, having jetted in on the redeye from New York and partied at the Warsaw Ballroom until well after dawn. But he's already holding meetings and reveling in the festiveness of the new hotel, the first of several renovation projects he's planned for South Beach. Besides celebrating his arrival on South Beach, Blackwell also uses the occasion of an interview to declare an end to a decade of legal skirmishes that have tied up the estate of reggae great Bob Marley. "That's all gotten resolved," Blackwell remarks curtly. "That was settled last December."

It's not quite that simple, however, nor has it ever been.

When he died on May 11, 1981, Marley left behind at least eleven children by seven different women, but no will. He also left behind an extraordinary musical legacy. Roger Steffens, a reggae historian and Marley expert, says it's difficult to gauge the size of the Marley musical library because the musician scattered his work among several production deals with several different producers during his career. "Nobody really knows because it's never been under one roof," Steffens explains. "Between the uncollected singles and the unreleased materials, I would say conservatively that there's enough for at least a dozen new albums." In addition, Steffens says, many videotapes of live performances await release. There's no telling exactly how much all this is worth, although appraisers last year valued the estate between $10 million and $12 million.

With no will to divvy the assets, Marley's death provoked an endless series of claims and counterclaims for his fortune, involving feuding family members, former bandmembers, record companies, and a battalion of lawyers and accountants. In 1987 the courts ordered that the estate be sold, with proceeds to be split among the beneficiaries (who, according to Jamaican inheritance law, include the eleven children and the singer's widow, Rita Marley).

Blackwell, who signed Marley to Island Records in 1973, beginning a business relationship that lasted until Marley's death, has been intimately involved in the estate tug-of-war. In 1988 Island Logic, another of Blackwell's companies, made an $8.2 million bid for the estate, which the Jamaican courts had placed under the auspices of the Mutual Security Merchant Bank and Trust Company, Ltd. of Jamaica. With its bid, Island Logic offered to buy Marley's song catalogue, recordings, writer's royalties, record royalties, record distribution rights, and all rights to his name, likeness, and biographical materials.

A Jamaican court approved the sale, but all of Marley's beneficiaries appealed the decision. The Jamaican Court of Appeals upheld the sale with some modifications, but the beneficiaries again appealed, this time to the Privy Council in England, the final authority over Jamaican matters. Opposition to Blackwell's offer was led by Marley's mother, Dade County resident Cedella Booker, who at the time was the legal guardian of one of the Marley children. "Mrs. Booker, through her attorney, kept trying to delay the sale to Island Logic, saying she had a better offer," explains Miami attorney J. Reid Bingham, the ancillary estate administrator in the United States. "She didn't want to see the assets go out of the family." Moreover, those who opposed the sale to Blackwell thought the purchase price was too low.

In the summer of 1990, the Privy Council finally heard the case, and sent it back to the Jamaican courts with an opinion that the courts should consider soliciting new bids and reappraising the estate. The estate administrators advertised the estate and attracted a handful of new bids, all but two of which quickly dropped out. A Jamaican judge weighed those two offers—one by MCA Music Publishing, the other a joint bid by Island Logic and Marley's adult beneficiaries—last fall.

"It has always been Chris Blackwell's intention that the assets be acquired and managed in a way that would keep alive the memory of Bob Marley and which would help take care of the family members and also provide money for charitable purposes in Jamaica," says Charles Ortner, attorney in the U.S. for Island Logic. "This new structure was worked out to be sure that the assets would be controlled by the family and those closest to the family instead of allowing them to get into the hands of MCA."

The judge, Justice Clawrence Walker of the Supreme Court, ruled on December 9 in favor of the Island/beneficiaries' $11.5 million bid. Under the offer, the purchasing group reaffirms the 1988 bid, and in addition:

- Buys the estate's rights to 50 percent of royalties from Marley's songs recorded for Cayman Music, including most of the reggae star's recordings from the years prior to 1976.
- Takes over the estate's litigation against Cayman Music, which allegedly owes the estate back royalties and interest of more than two million dollars.
- Assumes defense of the action brought against the estate by several members of Marley's back-up band, the Wailers, who claim they're entitled to royalties even though they never signed any contracts with Marley.
- Buys Marley's property in Jamaica at newly appraised values.

- Waives the adult beneficiaries' rights to monetary proceeds from the sale.
- Immediately pays $995,000 in cash to each of the five minor beneficiaries and distributes to them what's left of the purchase price after all the legal bills and estate taxes are paid.

According to Walker, the Island/beneficiaries' proposal offered several advantages over the MCA offer, including a larger amount of money for the child beneficiaries; maintenance of litigation against Cayman Music; and the pre-empting of possible litigation by Island Logic (which claimed it was owed a fee for managing some of Marley's assets since his death, according to estate administrator Bingham). In addition, Walker considered what he referred to as the "minor" issue of sentimental value. "Taking the factor of sentiment into account . . . I ask the question: All other things being in their favor, who better than the widow and children of Bob Marley to own the music of Bob Marley?" wrote Walker in his decision. "It seems to me that the answer must be no one." After making his ruling, the judge sent away the lawyers for both sides to work out the details of a court order, which Walker signed December 20.

Which, as Chris Blackwell says, settled the purchase of the estate.

Wrong. Since December 20, estate administrators and attorneys for the Marley family have been locking horns over the terms of the order. "In my view, the judge's order was the end of the matter," says Michael Hylton, a Jamaican attorney representing the purchasing group in the Jamaican courts. "The administrator has taken the view that there is still scope to argue the terms of the document. There has therefore been a dispute as to whether the order can be renegotiated."

Attorneys for both sides met in Miami late last month to work out their differences, and met again in Jamaica a week ago Friday. "There are one or two outstanding issues, and I have confidence that we can resolve those quickly," Hylton says. "No, I would say I'm optimistic we can resolve them." In these protracted estate proceedings, he adds, there's little room for confidence.

Even with a final agreement on the terms of the sale, Bob Marley won't exactly be able to rest in peace. Former advisers to Marley's widow, Rita, face charges that they defrauded the estate of about $14 million in assets while Rita managed the estate from the time of Marley's death until 1986. And there's still the matter of the Wailers' claims and the lawsuit against Cayman Music. There also remain several other smaller issues, ancillary estate administrator Bingham says, including a tax claim against the IRS filed by the estate, and a tax liability issue in the United Kingdom.

But completing the sale to Blackwell's group would remove the largest obstacle to a resolution of the morass, which to date has generated millions of dollars in legal and accounting fees. Michael Hylton explains that representatives from both Island and the family will oversee the management of the estate once the sale is complete. The agreement between Blackwell and the Marley family stipulates that at the end of the century, the family take over full management of the estate, Hylton says.

It remains unclear, though, how Blackwell and the beneficiaries will exploit the vast marketing potential of the estate's artistic assets. "Until the sale is complete, we could not make any kind of statement or announcement," Hylton says. "There are a great number of projects we are looking at and a number of different people have contacted us."

Chris Blackwell also refuses to offer any details about the group's plans for the estate. "I think the main thing is to keep the spirit of what Bob Marley wants us to do while trying to maximize the income," he says, adding that Island Records and the beneficiaries have already turned down a "huge" contract from Miller Brewing Co. to use a Marley tune in a commercial. Marley's religion didn't permit him to drink alcohol. "We haven't compromised anything to do with Bob," Blackwell insists, "and we don't intend to."

Early Wailers: Fussing & Fighting; Ska Compilation Generates Intrigue

by Don Jeffrey

(Source: **Billboard,** *June 18, 1994)*

A well-known compilation of early ska singles by Bob Marley & the Wailers has become the source of problems as well as profits. The producer charges that he never received any payment for the reissue, while the presence of these seminal recordings in the market-place raises the question of who actually owns the rights to the work.

This behind-the-scenes music story is more shadowy and unsavory than most claims of unrewarded royalties, however. It involves record men with ties to mobsters, an unsolved murder, a flamboyant Jamaican producer, and a major multinational music company.

The recording in question is "The Birth Of A Legend 1963–1966," a collection of 20 singles recorded by Marley & the Wailers in a Kingston, Jamaica, studio owned and operated by the legendary reggae producer, Clement (Sir Coxsone) Dodd. The songs—in the pre-reggae style known as ska—were hit singles in the Caribbean, preparing the band for the worldwide success it later attained. These tracks sound somewhat like R&B records of the time, and, in fact, represented a merger of American black pop music and jazz with existing Jamaican styles.

The remastered album collection, released by Sony Corp's Epic Associated label, has been among the best-selling reggae reissues of all time. SoundScan says the recording has sold 118,000 copies in the U.S. from the time the market research firm began reporting retail sales in January 1991 through May of this year.

However, both Dodd and principals of the Marley estate claim that they have not received a dollar of the money made on these releases. In an interview with *Billboard*, Dodd says that he had talks with Sony (and its predecessor company, CBS Records) several years ago. "It was getting somewhere and then it went blank about three or four years ago," Dodd says.

Marley's widow, Rita Marley, told *Billboard* that she never received royalties from Dodd or Sony on any of her husband's early ska recordings. Dodd says that he "took the blame" for that situation for many years.

But that may be rectified soon, at least in Dodd's case. He says Sony has again begun talks with him and his attorney. "They promised they would try to come to a reasonable settlement," he says.

A spokesperson for Sony Music says, "Our relationship with Clement Dodd is an amicable one and we are currently in negotiations. So it is inappropriate for us to comment at this time."

Unique Climate

The story begins in 1963 when Marley, Bunny Livingston, Peter Tosh, and Beverly Kelso—the original Wailers—recorded the first of the ska singles for Dodd's Studio One label at his studio in Kingston.

At that time in Jamaica, there was no sophisticated royalty system in place. Sound recording there was unlike the situation that existed in other countries. The producer, rather than the songwriter or performer, controlled the rights to the music. Dodd said that practice was justified because in Jamaica, a producer hired musicians for a flat fee and exercised more creative control over them than was found in ordinary recording sessions. "I had, like, a stable of musicians and artists under contract," said Dodd. "I had my own studio and at the time, I was in the business. I knew how to direct the musicians."

After the singles became hits in Jamaica, Dodd says he licensed them to Chris Blackwell for distribution in the U.K. (Blackwell later signed Marley & the Wailers to his Island Records label.)

Visiting the U.S. in the mid-'70s, Dodd says he met a fellow Jamaican, Nate McCalla, who was in the music business. McCalla also was an associate of Morris Levy, the notorious record retailer, label head, and impresario whose exploits were documented in Fredric Dannen's book, *Hit Men*. Dannen wrote that McCalla—a 6-foot-tall, 250-pound ex-paratrooper, sometimes referred to as "Big Bad Leroy Brown"—was said to be Levy's "enforcer" and that his loyalty was rewarded with his own label, Calla Records.

Dodd says he cut a deal with McCalla in 1976, agreeing to "lease" but not sell the ska masters to him. Dodd says McCalla released the singles in 1976 in a two-record album set on the Calla imprint called "The Birth of a Legend." Dodd adds that McCalla gave him a check for $5,000 as an advance, but the check bounced.

Although Dodd has been publicly critical of the subtle overdubbing on Sony's masters of these Wailers ska singles, he acknowledges that he supervised the overdubbing process. He says the redubbing included the addition of more drums and other percussion to the raw tracks—for example, some high-hat cymbals to increase the "brilliance of the top end."

Although Dodd says he never got a dime from McCalla, for the past 18 years he did not file suit against him or take other measures to either recoup his masters or seek payment for their widely advertised dissemination. "Nobody knew where he was," says Dodd of McCalla. "His address was unknown for a couple of years. I couldn't find him."

According to "Hit Men," McCalla disappeared in 1977 after a concert deal involving the Genovese mob family went sour. In 1980, he "turned up in a rented house in Fort Lauderdale, dead of a gunshot wound in the back of his head, which had literally exploded," the book stated. No suspects were found.

In the years between McCalla's acquisition of the masters from Dodd and his mysterious disappearance, the rights were sold to CBS Records (now Sony Music). It is unclear who cut the deal with Sony, but some sources believe it was Levy, not McCalla. Levy died of cancer in 1990. Sony declines to make a copy of the contract available.

In May 1977, the ska singles were released by CBS as a two-album set on vinyl, titled, "The Birth of a Legend" and "Early Music." In April 1984, the songs came out on two CBS cassettes under the same titles with the band listed as Bob Marley & the Wailers featuring Peter Tosh.

In 1990, Sony's Epic Associated label decided to release the set on CD for the first time. Its master tapes were remastered by audio expert Stephen St. Croix, whose Revectoring (noise removal and stereo imaging) technique also was used by him in the restoration of the film soundtrack to "The Wizard Of Oz." Sony then reissued the fully restored set on one album, now titled "The Birth of a Legend 1963–1966," to distinguish it from the label's previous reissues of Marley's ska music using the "legend" design.

But because the original sale or lease of the masters to McCalla was executed with a check that allegedly bounced, the question has been raised whether this transaction and the subsequent sale to Sony might be illegal or invalid.

Dodd says he did not seek litigation against CBS/Sony over the years because "we figured we are a small person and we wouldn't have a chance against a big corporation."

About four or five years ago, Dodd hired a royalty-collecting company that was working toward an agreement with Sony, but the firm went out of business before a deal could be concluded. Meanwhile,

Dodd continued over the years to release the Wailers ska singles in various compilations on his own label in Jamaica and abroad, but he says sales of these were not as great as those of the Sony albums. (A compilation of the same ska singles released by Rounder/Heartbeat in 1991 and called "One Love" has sold 8,500 copies to date, according to SoundScan.)

M. William Krasilovsky, an attorney who deals with music copyright matters, says that "Jamaica was a no man's land on copyrights" for many years. Regarding the legal ownership of master tapes that may have been acquired with a bogus check, the lawyer said, "If Sony/CBS bought the rights without noticing the fraudulent transfer, they have a legal right if they can show they were a bona fide purchaser for value."

Marley Deal Prompts Lawsuit; Producer Sues Family, Universal

by Eileen Fitzpatrick
(Source: **Billboard,** *June 28, 1997)*

A Los Angeles movie producer has filed a $ 1 million lawsuit against Universal Studios Florida and several family members of the late reggae star Bob Marley, claiming he was cut out of a deal to develop a Marley-themed complex for the amusement park.

In papers filed in Los Angeles Superior Court June 9, Andrew Gaty alleges he initiated negotiations between Marley family heirs and Universal Studios Florida but had the idea taken from him without permission or compensation.

Gaty is suing for "breach of implied in fact contract," breach of confidence, misappropriation, fraud, and other charges (*Billboard Bulletin*, June 11).

Defendants listed in court papers include Marley Boys Inc.; Rita Marley, the widow of the reggae legend; Richard Booker; Cedella Marley Booker; Universal Studios Florida; and three other Universal divisions connected to the theme park.

Universal Studios Florida announced plans for a Marley entertainment complex in February 1996. The complex, to be named "Bob Marley—A Tribute To Freedom," is scheduled to open in early 1998 (Billboard, March 2, 1996).

In the lawsuit, Gaty says he approached the Marley heirs in early 1995 to discuss "ways in which the Bob Marley name and legacy could be exploited for profit."

Among the ideas discussed, according to the lawsuit, were a movie and a replica of Marley's home in Jamaica that would be the model for a restaurant, club, and retail venue. The Marley house venue would have been opened in different locations around the world.

Gaty then suggested the family take the idea to executives at Universal Studios Florida, according to court papers.

The lawsuit claims Gaty "sold" the idea of the Marley venue to Universal at a pitch meeting held in April 1995 with all parties present.

Gaty, who had no written contract with either Universal or the Marley family, says the parties accepted his idea with the "knowledge and understanding that the idea was the property of Gaty and could not be used without his knowledge or consent," according to the lawsuit.

In addition, Gaty was to receive profit participation in the Marley venue concept, the suit claims.

A spokeswoman for Universal declined to comment on the lawsuit; a representative for the Marley heirs could not be reached for comment by press time.

MUSIC GONNA TEACH
THEM A LESSON

The Meaning of Bob Marley

1

Zion Train:
Religion, Rasta, and Revelation

Marley, largely influenced by his half-brother Bunny "Wailer" Livingston and their acquaintance with Mortimo Planno, became a major proponent of Jamaica's singular religion, Rastafarianism. As such, he became a spokesman for the movement, an icon within it. Bob's relationship with Rastafarianism is certainly complex.

On the one hand, he never saw himself as anything more or less than a mouthpiece, a spokesperson for what he believed. While he mildly derided the gospel music his grandfather would listen to, he was making a kind of gospel of his own, preaching a gospel of Rastafarianism. Marley's gospel, however, had his own personal bent, one that could be traced from "Simmer Down" through "Redemption Song": "Emancipate yourself from mental slavery." His take on his religion centered on what makes it—and most other religions, properly practiced—righteous: the ability of people to better themselves.

On the other hand, the power of both his message and his faith inspired millions, not necessarily to become Rastafarians, but to respond to the heart of the message, to improve themselves and the way they interacted with their fellow man. Especially in his later music, his message had less to do with blaming Babylon and more to do with advancing the state of humanity.

With that message, he could be a modern prophet in any religion.

Bob Marley—Rastaman, Reggae Musician

by Rose Blount
(Source: **Black Book Bulletin***)*

> *Africa unite/'cause we're moving right out of Babylon*
> *and we're going to our father's land*
> *How good and how pleasant it would be*
> *before God and man*
> *to see the unification of all Africans*
> *As its been said already*
> *Let it be done right now*
> *We are the children of the Rastaman*
> *We are the children of the higher man.*

BOB MARLEY, SURVIVAL ALBUM

IN any discussion of Reggae music in general, and Bob Marley in particular, it is important to address the concept of Rastafari, since it is from this consciousness that Marley lives and creates his music. He has achieved a oneness of purpose that predominates in his existence and his art.

Reggae music had its beginnings in the 1960's in Jamaica, and incorporated American R & B sound with Jamaican rhythms. Groups such as Bob Marley and the Wailers (which included Peter Tosh), Jimmy Cliff, Toots and the Maytals, and the Mighty Diamonds became popular. Marley's early work, then as now, focused on the plight of Jamaica's poor in Trenchtown, Kingston's ghetto.

Reggae became the music of the Rastafarians, a sect founded by Marcus Garvey, which believes in the divinity of Haile Selassie I, former

Emperor of Ethiopia. Evidence of Selassie's divinity is traced through the Bible, as are many other aspects of Rasta culture and consciousness. Selassie, or God, is referred to as Jah, and his followers as Rastafarians, after Selassie's title—Ras Tafari. Asked what the movement stands for, Marley reveals that, "In 1930 when His Majesty was crowned, the movement get stronger, and it take the name Rasta. This movement deal with Christianity in reality, so this what happening in the world."

While the movement does advocate the Christian ideals of peace and love, it is also concerned with bringing about the actuality of unity among all Black people and eventual repatriation to the motherland. These are very strong themes in Marley's latest album, which features on its cover both the stowage plan of a slave ship and the flags of all African nations. The album includes such titles as "Zimbabwe," "Africa Unite," "Wake Up and Live," and "Survival."

As an indication of Marley's consciousness, he released "Wake Up and Live" as a U.S. single, and "Ambush in The Night" as the Jamaican single, because as he states, "'Ambush in the Night' is a reality in Jamaica right now. 'Wake Up and Live' is needed up here. People won't wake up and live up here."

As the vanguard of the political movement in Jamaica, the Rastafarians suffer as much political and economic oppression as U.S. Blacks. They are subject to imprisonment and unemployment; their children are denied an education because of their hair—dreadlocks—symbol of the Rastafari. But they continue to fight for freedom and dignity. Marley feels, "We grow more and more every day . . . the Rasta movement in Jamaica is the movement . . . Rasta is the only one to stand up and fight."

"The society in Jamaica is in line with any other society. Like for instance now, we as Rasta in Jamaica. The government is not Rasta government. The government different. That mean, even if you not a Rasta, you going to be an outcast . . . society is not for Rasta . . . Rasta government give people freedom. No terrorization, brutalization. I can run our own life. People in authority carry tradition of the devil. They know exactly what I'm fighting against."

Considering the vehemence with which any movement of oppressed people is undermined by the European power structure and its media, it is curious that Marley and Reggae have survived. Even more curious is the fact that Marley's audiences are predominantly white, and Reggae receives very little airtime on Black radio stations. White artists such as the Rolling Stones, Bob Dylan, Barbra Streisand, and others have experimented with Reggae sound and incorporated it into their acts, once again usurping Black creativity. Marley concedes that the majority of his audiences are white, but notes that "there's more Blacks . . . listening to the music." He has recently established his own record label, Tough Gong International, and hopefully can establish more control over the distribution of his music.

A step in that direction was achieved during his recent tour of Africa. In addition to having his music well received during his tour, Marley was able to define his own opinions of the motherland. "My general impression is that Africa need Black people, all sides of Africa, because Africa need the development that the people of the West know . . . everything we learn that is benefit of community."

"Africa is more revolutionized today than yesterday. The real thing is that Africa (doesn't) unite as Rasta. They unite as Marx and Lenin . . ." Marley notes the case of the Soviet presence in Ethiopia and their attempt to set up Soviet-style government, "they should not be there." Marley plans to move to Africa himself "as soon as our work is finished . . . what you have to understand, what's going on can't go on too long. Anyway, it just can't go on too long."

Marley tries to bring about positive growth through his music and none of his musical energy is wasted. There is a constant struggle to enlighten, to teach, to revolutionize. In describing his music during a discussion of the labels invariably placed upon that which is different, Marley comments: "You might have people who don't know—people who can't play music. And then ones who limit the inspiration of the musician . . . what I deal with, I tell the truth . . . freedom of mankind. Lyrics can be the truth. Even disco, you can sing a Rasta message. I never have anything bad to say about music, but lyrics. . . . In time, make people know the truth."

Perhaps one of Marley's biggest personal achievements was the One Love concert staged in Jamaica in April 1978. This concert was an attempt to bring together the rival youth gangs which were literally killing each other. The message was peace and unity. "It has made a change, youth and youth come together. That is the biggest change I ever make anywhere."

Bob Marley has been criticized by some for his use of ganja, or Jamaican marijuana. It is another aspect of Rasta culture, which most outsiders do not fully understand. The use of ganja is considered a sacrament, a form of meditation. "Herb is the healer of the nation. If you smoke, smoke herb. Rastaman use herb for meditation. Especially in our busy world like this, you smoke herb . . . what is going on, it still can't trouble you . . . keep your meditation."

While everyone may not agree with this statement on herb, one can't deny that Marley's potential as a moving force behind Black cultural consciousness is great. His music is popular in such diverse areas as the Caribbean, the U.S., Africa, England (especially within London's large population of Blacks), and Canada (primarily Toronto).

In any case, it is important that artists such as Bob Marley and other Rasta/Reggae musicians be supported in their struggle to continue producing "music with a message." With this in mind, representatives of the Progressive Arts Center in Chicago held a reception for Bob Marley and the Wailers in November 1979. Marley was given the Asanti name Osahane, meaning "redeemer."

In light of some of the negative statements about Marley, his music and Rasta culture put forth by the white press, he clearly deserves our support. A major Chicago music critic once said of Marley: "With foot-long dread locks flying about with every shake of his heed, and eyes that have probably been at half-mast since puberty, Marley still retains the charisma of a drug-addled tropical mystic." Such a conception merely indicates the critic's very limited understanding of Bob Marley and his music, and is, therefore, a thoroughly irresponsible review. It is this type of assessment that undermines progressive attempts by Black people to continue to struggle for survival. Marley's latest album, aptly titled, *Survival*, is a testament to both his struggle as well as ours.

Bob Marley Live: Reggae, Rasta, and Jamaica Fourteen Years after Marley's Death

by Mark Jacobson

(Source: **Natural History,** *November 1995)*

As I stand in front of Bob Marley's former home, at 56 Hope Road in Kingston, now the site of the Bob Marley Museum, watching busloads of Japanese and German tourists drive through the iron gate and park on the now blacktopped field where, twenty years ago, I saw Bob, Alan "Skill" Cole, and other Rastafarians play soccer, a perhaps appropriately cynical thought crosses my mind: well, at least the King of Reggae, the Lion of Jamaica, isn't buried in the backyard like a pet gerbil, the way Elvis is at Graceland.

Following the musician's death fourteen years ago (he would have been fifty last February) and other wrenching disasters—including the murder of Peter Tosh (one of the original members of Marley's trio, the Wailers) and the still unresolved litigation over Marley's reputed $30 million estate—the Bob Marley fan is thankful for small favors. Even as I walk past the bulbous statue of Marley done in cement, which looms, golemlike, over the front yard, and am led through the museum's somewhat meager collection of memorabilia inside the two-story, jalousied house ("Dis dere is Bob's blender, where he mix up healthy ital ['holy'] drinks. . . . Dis is de tree 'bout which Bob wrote 'Three Little Birds'. . . . Dere's Bob's rusted bicycle. . . . Dere's a buncha articles written 'bout Bob"), it is not difficult to remember another time.

This was the early fall of 1975, scant months after the fall of Saigon, when the properly stoned observer might easily have mistaken the small but culturally fecund island of Jamaica in general, and 56 Hope Road in particular, for the temporary center of the universe. Back then it seemed that no one had ever encountered anything as splendid as Robert Nesta Marley (already the most famous man in Jamaica but not yet the huge international pop star he would become), sitting on the front steps of this ramshackle great house, dreadlocks hanging over his face, strumming out a few verses of his most recent local radio smash, "Jah Live." When he sang, reedily, "fools sayin' in dere heart/Rasta yar God is dead . . . The truth is an offense but not a sin/is he laugh last, is he who win . . . Jah lives," it was enough to make me weep.

I'll never know exactly why the often irascible-with-white-folks author of "Burnin' and Lootin'" chose to favor me with this private little concert, unless it was because he'd just saved my life, more or less, by shooing away several of his former associates from Trench Town. (Wielding machetes, they had accosted me in the upstairs hallway of his house, stolen my ticket for the upcoming Wailers concert with

Stevie Wonder, and locked me in the room that now contains "The Bob Marley Library.") It was an emotional time. Haile Selassie, the emperor of Ethiopia, proclaimed Lion of Judah, alleged 225th direct descendant in a line back to King Solomon, the man worshiped by Rastafarians as Jah, or "the living God," had recently died. The brethren looked to Marley, the best-known Rastafarian in the world, to comment on this unsettling metaphysical development. "Jah Live" was his rejoinder. "Jah live because you can't kill God."

For me and other ex-hippie press junketeers, thoroughgoing secularists all, sent to Kingston's scruffy version of paradise to check out this new Big Thing, it was the defiance of Marley's reply, and its unimpeachable sincerity, that was so thrilling. To Bob, it didn't matter what the denizens of Babylon (the Rasta term for all that is not ital in the sight of Jah) said. Let them bring their dried-up rationalism, let them slice God's flesh with their sharp autopsy blades, claim to throw his so-called body in an unmarked grave, it didn't matter. The wicked cabal of back-stabbing communists, Vatican hypocrites, and corporate sons of pirate, slave-master fathers were all wrong. And Bob, along with his marijuana-smoking, wild-haired, Bible-quoting, prophecy-believing, guitar-playing crew were right: Jah live.

After all, given the steadfast free association requisite for a small bunch of people on an isolated Caribbean island to come to the fervent conclusion that the diminutive Haile Selassie—the inept and petty autocrat described in Ryszard Kapuscinski's scathing book *The Emperor*—was the living God on earth, the denial of the monarch's death was no big leap.

To gain a degree of insight into the brilliantly off-the-wall, modernist synthesis that is Rastafarianism, it is useful to know that, as recounted in any number of reggae songs, the cornerstone of the creed rests on a prophecy supposedly spoken by Marcus Garvey, the formidable Jamaican-born Pan-Africanist of the early twentieth century.

"Look to Africa for the crowning of a black king; he shall be the re-deemer," Garvey is held to have said, thereby playing the John the Baptist role in Rasta cosmology by alerting the brethren to the subsequent crowning of Selassie as the emperor of Ethiopia in 1930. But as detailed in Timothy White's definitive Marley biography, *Catch a Fire*, Marcus Garvey not only never made such a prophecy, he was actually publicly critical of Haile Selassie.

Not that this historical discrepancy would have mattered much to those Jamaicans for whom the beautiful island of the tourist ads was a Kafkaesque limbo-with-banana-trees from which they craved an exit and a solution. To them the entire slavery experience of their fore-bears was tantamount to a terrible nightmare from which they had awakened in "a strange land" as tragically misplaced, debased squatters. The prophecy led them to believe that they would be repatriated to a purified and glorious Africa. (Whether this millenarian vision was to come about through divine intervention or practical efforts was up for interpretation.)

Taking Selassie's princely name, Ras Tafari, for their own, the Rastafarians went on to find biblical justification for not cutting their hair, never eating processed food, and smoking "the herb of the land." Herb (which should never be called dope, because "no plant can be a dope") facilitated for the Rastas the proper state for much subsequent "reasoning." It didn't matter if the British-tutored, nose-to-the-grindstone Jamaican middle class berated the Rastas as skylarking layabouts whose philosophies made no sense. It certainly didn't matter if accoutrements like dread-locks scared people out of their wits.

That was the thing about Bob Marley: he was a true believer. In 1975, no less so than today, that really was a Big Thing. Plus, the music was unbeatable. The first Wailers' albums to be released world-wide, *Catch a Fire*, *Burnin'*, and the subsequent *Natty Dread* (made after the breakup of the original trio—Marley, Peter Tosh, and Bunny

Livingston), each lyrically seething with revolution, remain in the canon of the greatest pop records ever.

Best of all, from the down-home music fan's point of view, was that the Wailers didn't belch forth from the corporate vacuum. As anyone who saw the vigorous film *The Harder They Come* suspected, Jamaica was filled with Bob Marleys and Wailers and would-be Wailers. There was an entire hothouse music industry run by producers, players, and singers—seat-of-the-pants capitalists all, outfitted with healthy stacks of scratchy 45s that were peddled from shoe boxes. The special brand of "roots" reggae played by Bob Marley was only the most recent mutation of Jamaican pop, which began with the Louis Jordan/Fats Domino-influenced "blue beat" in the early 1950s. Blue beat became the miraculous "ska" (as pioneered by the invincible Skatalites), which then became the love-man, vocal-dominated "rock steady" of Ken Boothe and Alton Ellis, followed by the angelic early reggae harmonies of the magnificent Heptones, Desmond Dekker, and a hundred more.

For the continuity-minded, that was another neat thing about Bob Marley and the Wailers: they'd grown up on the indigenous Jamaican industry, played every style (check out Bob's teenage ska vocal on "One Cup of Coffee," circa 1962), scuffled and suffered like dem artists must in de ghetto. When, infused by the brimstone idiosyncrasies of Rasta, they broke "wide," they were wholly themselves. A real Big Thing.

What no one could have guessed was how big it would become. By 1981, when Marley succumbed to cancer (supposedly the result of a soccer injury to his toe, which he refused to have amputated because "Rasta don't amputate"), the Wailers were unthinkably huge, with 100,000 people in attendance at a single show in Milan. One of the most eloquent artists of social unrest in the second half of the twentieth century, Marley became an icon in what used to be called the

Third World through his exhortation to "Get Up, Stand Up" and his across-the-board condemnation of "de downpressers."

These days it is impossible to walk through any major city—from Bangkok to Bamako—without seeing teenagers wearing Bob Marley T-shirts. *Legend*, Bob's eternally selling "greatest hits" album, sells on. Tales of the Wailers' epic concert in newly independent Zimbabwe routinely include spurious details of prisoners breaking down the jail doors just to see Bob. With the passing years, the reputed number of escapees grows.

A few years ago, as we sat in a café in Lamu, on Kenya's coast, a dreaded-up Swahili guy in a Bob shirt laughed pityingly when I questioned his assertion that Marley was murdered, his cancer injected by the ruthless Mason-controlled assassins who have ruled the Vatican in the name of Satan for more than a thousand years. As it turned out, this wasn't just a lone nut spiel; a friend of mine heard a nearly identical saga in Indonesia a couple of years later. Needless to say, many in Jamaica believe the story. Marley iconography will only grow as a result of the recent publication by Marvel Comics of a graphic account of Bob's life and times (it is contained in three issues: *Iron*, *Lion*, and *Zion*).

More tangibly, there's little doubt that without the precedent of Bob Marley, the entire genre of "world beat" (contemporary music of the non-Western world) would have been far slower to succeed internationally, at least commercially. "For me, Bob Marley is very important," says Paul-Bert Rahasimanana, a.k.a. Rossy, the dreadlocked master of accordion, *valiha*, and *kabosy*, who is currently the biggest thing in the vibrant pop scene in Madagascar, home of a local industry not unlike Jamaica's in its nascent days. "When I heard Bob Marley, I understood people around the world might like my music."

This sentiment is echoed time and again by musicians coming out of local pop-oriented industries. Baaba Maal, the noted singer from Senegal, and numerous Zairian "soukous" stars have all paid tribute to Marley, the enabler. Beyond this is the explosion of Jamaican-style reggae itself in Africa. Actively modeling themselves after Marley and other Jamaican stars, people like Alpha Blondy from Ivory Coast and Lucky Dube of South Africa have made international careers playing social-activist reggae. "African reggae, it's like some 360 thing, mon," says Neville Garrick, the artist who drew several of Marley's album covers and now, with Bob's widow, Rita, administers the Bob Marley Foundation, which runs the museum.

He notes the transcontinental cross-pollination of Latin rumba, mambo, and so on, which had their beginnings in African rhythms and then returned to the Mother Continent, becoming elemental to the development of soukous and Ghanaian "high-life," among others. "The music come from there, Jamaicans mix it up, it go back," Garrick says. Then he watches another busload of tourists drive through the gate at 56 Hope Road. "You know, mon," he sighs, "if I have known all this would happen with Bob, I would have been a prophet myself."

Garrick's assessment is borne out by a series of huge murals painted on the stone fence inside the museum grounds: Bob in Trench Town with Rita and the children; Bob with fellow Wailers Peter and Bunny as young "baldhead" ska musicians dressed in Vegas garb, their true shaggy-headed Rasta personas looming overhead; Bob at the famous 1978 One Love concert, where he shamed warring political leaders Michael Manley and Edward Seaga into shaking hands; Bob in Africa—this beside a gigantic picture of a rainbow with the words "give thanks for the birth of Bob . . . February 6, 1945." All in all, there must be several hundred photographs and paintings of Marley on the museum grounds: the happy Bob, the sad Bob, the triumphant Bob, the brimstone Bob, the sensitive Bob, and the sick, soon-to-die Bob.

This is the case throughout the country. Once hounded by the island's police to throw away his "little herb stalk," Bob, recipient of the

Jamaican Order of Merit, is now an official national hero. They sell his T-shirts for $15 at the airport, feature him in the tourist literature. His picture is on telephone poles, inside restaurants, in every club. For sheer lionization, he's far surpassed the Lion of Judah, Haile Selassie himself.

"Bob was someone who came along at a certain moment. What he have to say was perfect for that moment," continues Garrick, his dreadlocks now flecked with gray. "To tell the truth, though, most of what Bob sang about, in Jamaica, things stay the same. They don't change. That's why Bob sells better today than ever. So it's wrong to say time pass Bob by . . . but it wrong too to say that time don't pass."

As one drives around Kingston these days, it seems so: some things are the same, some not. The town does appear tidier, more well-to-do. The economy, if not booming, certainly seems capable of erecting and supporting any number of shopping centers. Jamaica is not exactly mellow, but the old tension that pervaded even the smallest transaction seems to have fallen away, at least in what's called uptown and midtown.

On the other hand, downtown—Rema, Trench Town, and the rest, the corrugated-hut "concrete jungle" where Marley was raised and which was the inspiration for many of his best songs—looks as fearsome as ever. The "posse"-dominated culture of political violence in these slums that spurred the 1976 assassination attempt at 56 Hope Road (Marley was shot in the arm—the tour guides dutifully point out bullet holes left in the back wall) continues, albeit more on a siege level.

As for the local music industry, it soldiers on, pumping out the vinyl (yes, vinyl!—at least for the "domestic" market) at an unprecedented rate. What they mostly do these days is "dance hall," which any and every Jamaican will be more than happy to tell you is the "real" rap music, since rap was "invented" in Jamaica by such "dub-kings," "toasters," and "deejays" as Big Youth and U Roy. (Dem robbin' American Public Enemies, Tupacs, Snoop Doggy Doggs only stole it to mek dere lowlife tribal gangsta ting.) The justification for such a claim aside, suffice it to say that dance hall covers a sociosexual terrain similar to the harder side of the United States version, except that the Jamaicans, as usual, are more in your face. The late Peter Tosh's take on the music that has come to dominate the Jamaican market—his streetwise, Rasta take—was that it was "all slackness, talk of bumbaclaat gun play and slamming what's 'neath lady's dress, 'bout soiled underwear and whatnot."

"The youth listen to what the youth listen to, can't fight against it," Garrick says, indicating that these days, the Rasta finds himself in a "pocket," with "dread" nothing more than "a fashion, like everything else." Several of the left-leaning middle-class intellectuals who were sympathetic to the Rasta ethos have left the island in disgust at the unchanging social conditions. When some dread artists were reported to have cocaine problems, Garrick tells me, it went a long way to destroying the Rasta community "as the image of the pure Nazareth." It's a systemic problem that won't soon be fixed because according to Rastas around the island, it's easier to get crack cocaine than ganja. Coke produces a different kind of "reasoning," to be sure.

Still, Bob Marley's shadow is long, pervasive. Gussie Clarke, owner of the Anchor Recording Company, one of Kingston's most modern 24-track, 24-hour-a-day recording mills, gets a bit misty when Bob Marley's name comes up. "Bob Marley is literally the single greatest example of what this industry, what Jamaica itself, can produce. Bob, he wasn't in it for the money; it was something else to him. I don't care what these kids say now, every Jamaican who thinks of himself as an artist wants to be Bob Marley."

Not the Super Beagle, at least not anymore. "Yah, when I came up Bob was what I thought about," says the Beagle (his real name is Denzie Beagle), a sweet-looking guy in his thirties in an undershirt who wears a jewel-studded guitar charm around his exceedingly well-developed neck. "Bob can't be nothing but a hero, you know. But he pass on. . . . I got my own things to say. Today, I'm one of the biggest names on the island."

Tonight he's trying out a few new "roots" tunes at the Centerpole Club, the Super Beagle reports, so maybe I should stop by and check them out. "Sure," I say.

That night, it quickly becomes apparent that the Super Beagle is not exactly one of the biggest names of the island, and the club, rather than a straight musical venue, appears more in the go-go/barroom mode. The Beagle and his five-piece band are shoehorned into a stifling six-by-six storage room out back. "Ya, mon," the Super Beagle says. "Just doing a little practicing, you know."

If the slight misrepresentation of his position in the hierarchy of Jamaican pop stars makes the Super Beagle feel guilty, he does not show it. Nor does he seem sheepish about the fact that his repertoire, while including some of the advertised "cultural" tunes, also encompasses much dance-hall rapping, in addition to several old-style, rock-steady love ballads. As the Beagle later says, "In this day and age, good to remain flexible." Not that any of this is a problem, because the Super Beagle sounds terrific. Everyone in Jamaica seems to sing better than anyone not in Jamaica, and the Super Beagle is at least as good as most of them. Maybe it isn't Bob Marley in 1968, but it will do.

The next morning, when I go to 56 Hope Road one last time, my cab driver, a man in his fifties wiping the sweat from his face with a handkerchief, provides me with some unsolicited insights: "It's hot today. In Jamaica, it's hot every day. Each year a little hotter, with not so much rainfall. When I was a little boy, I remember there was ample rainfall. The water soaked into the ground. You could breathe then. Now there is no ample rainfall, so the earth feels like it is dying. It folds up on itself, and reaches up till it starts to tear the meat from the bodies of human beings, ripping and tearing till there's only the bones, gleaming in the sun. That's what's going to happen to me, to you, and what happen to Bob Marley."

Over at 56 Hope Road, tourists from Munich pour in; they had their choice of the Marley museum or downtown Kingston for their day's excursion in the Jamaican capital. Their tour begins with Bob's herb garden, where the lone spindly marijuana plant is described as "something that is used for smoking."

"They keep coming," says Bragga, kneeling on his haunches. "That show even if Bob in his coffin, he don't die." Anywhere from fifty to eighty. Bragga has been around for a long time. He claims to remember me from my three-day visit twenty years earlier. This is ridiculous, but who knows? He also claims to have been with Bob when he wrote his first recorded song, "Judge Not," back in the early 1960s.

"Ya mon," Bragga says, talking a little slow so I understand half of what issues from his nearly toothless mouth. "In the cemetery yard, the boys were there, and bring fruit from Coronation Market. All the boys want the biggest fruit. One take it, but the big one, it is not sweet. So Bob write 'bout the illusion of that. Judge not, before you judge yourself, judge not, if you're not ready for judgment, so why talk about me, someone else is judging you."

"There it is now," Bragga says, off-handedly. It takes a moment to realize what he is talking about. As part of the Bob Marley experience at 56 Hope Road, Bob's music plays incessantly on the sound system. Mostly it's the familiar international hits off the later albums, tunes like "Is This Love," "Jammin'," the new version of "One Love." It doesn't matter that these often weary-sounding songs, many made when Bob was already dying, cannot compare with the classic political tunes, stepping razors like "Concrete Jungle," "Mr. Brown," and "Small Axe."

Yet there it is, coming out of the loudspeaker. "Judge Not": the seventeen-year-old Bob, his voice up a couple of registers from where it would settle, innocent and brand-new.

2

Babylon System: Politics in Jamaica and Beyond

During a particularly brutal period in Jamaican politics, when former record salesman Edward Seaga and People's National Party candidate Michael Manley fought for control of the island's political future, the people engaged in gang warfare in the streets of Kingston. By this time, Marley was both revered and feared. On December 3, 1976, at the height of the bitter campaign, several gunmen broke into the Marley compound on Hope Road in Kingston, shot Bob in the arm, his wife Rita in the head, and manager Don Taylor five times. A year later, during the massive One Love Peace Concert in Jamaica, Marley brought both Seaga and Manley on stage during the Wailer's set and joined their hands together, an act which earned him the United Nations Third World Peace Medal. Though the symbolic gesture's measurable effects were ultimately fleeting, no other artist could have done this, and no other artist would have dared.

Marley was unlike other musical stars from developing nations. Fela Anikulapo Kuti maintained that he could say he wanted to be president and be carried into office by acclamation. Ruben Blades frequently talks of a possible future in public service in Panama; he also could be carried into office by acclamation. But Bob Marley had a major aversion to "politricks." He saw himself as a singer. When politicians wooed his support, especially after the attempt on his life, he would have none of it.

Yet that didn't stop him from being politically relevant, both at home and in Africa. While he never set out to be an icon, with songs espousing freedom, justice, and standing up for your rights, with songs that pointed out that a small axe could fell a big tree (actually a reference to the three big record companies in Jamaica), he was, as he would have said, *woooo*—dangerous.

Reggae and the Revolutionary Faith . . . The Role of Bob Marley

by Michael Manley

(Source: **The Rising Sun** *[People's National Party newspaper], May 1982)*

ROOTS—'UP ROOTED'

Within the Third World there is a unique social phenomenon. It was created by one of the terrible diaspora of history. The slave trade, stretching in the main from the 17th to the 18th Centuries, uprooted millions of Black Africans, depositing them throughout the Caribbean, the United States and the more northerly regions of Latin America. There our ancestors were subjected to the most systematic and sustained act of deculturization in modern history. Here was no oppression of a people on their native soil. The slave had no familiar ancestral earth into which to plant his feet and dig his toes while waiting for the tide of oppression to recede or the opportunity for rebellion to present itself. The slaves were uprooted, detribalized, denamed, de-humanized. The only thing the oppressor could not take away was their humanity.

Through it all, music was one of the means through which the slave held on to the past and endured the present. Any discussion of the BLUES, the CALYPSO, the REGGAE begins at this point. Like all folk music, it is all essentially commentary; but what is unique about this commentary is it reflects in every thought, in every musical pulse, something to do with survival and accommodation. The children of the diaspora struggle for a place in society to this day. Worse, they struggle for their identities, mislaid as the slave ships made their way to the New World through the MIDDLE PASSAGE. Therefore, their commentaries must deal with these realities.

CALYPSO

THE CALYPSO, exclusively Trinidadian, is cynical, satirical, amoral and often savage. The Trinidadian masses survived at least until the 1960's by a collective disregard of both the laws and the values of the oppressor. The individual spirit endured its degradation and transcended its hopelessness by laughing at everything including itself. But this was not the laughter of gentle good nature, illuminating a comfortable companionship. This was laughter like a weapon, like a rapier or a razor honed in centuries of surviving.

BLUES

THE BLUES have some of this but are more reflective of the consciousness of oppression. Perhaps, the American black has always known his situation to be closer to the hopeless.

REVOLUTIONARY POSSIBILITY

Of them all, the REGGAE is the most explicitly revolutionary. It is commentary; satirical at times; often cruel; but its troubadours are not afraid to speak of love, of loyalty, of hope, of ideals, of justice, of new things and new forms. It is this assertion of revolutionary possibility that sets reggae apart. It has evolved from the original folk form of the MENTO. From this there sprang SKA, which began a sort of marriage between American Rhythm and Blues, Gospel and the indigenous mento form. The mento itself often was driven on the strong beat of the digging song, which helped the workers to survive the monotony of long hours with the pickaxe. It was unlikely, therefore, that the beat of Jamaican music would be more than influenced by Rhythm and Blues and would certainly never entirely succumb to it. In due course, SKA yielded to ROCK STEADY, the entire period of transition providing its heroes like the late great trombonist DON DRUMMOND. But we were still in transition. Then it all came together with REGGAE.

When one listens to everything from mento to reggae, one sees in instant reflection the dilemma of identity. The strong African root is there, particularly in the rhythm and the use of drums. But so great was the act of cultural destruction that all of the infinite subtlety and sophistication, which sets African drumming apart, is missing. I can remember the first time I heard an authentic African drummer, I was astonished and for a while had difficulty in understanding what was going on, so intricate were the variations, so complex the rhythmic embroidery around the central driving beat. In Jamaica, only the central beat has survived. EVEN THIS SURVIVAL IS A MIRACLE IN THE CIRCUMSTANCES.

The most fundamental question that arises about reggae is: how did it become so explicitly and positively political? The greatest of the calypsonians, the MIGHTY SPARROW has journeyed into political commentary; but even he, quintessentially a part of the Trinidadian environment, although born in Grenada, has stopped short of the assertion of rights, has not essayed a positively revolutionary call. BY CONTRAST, THE GREATER PART OF BOB MARLEY IS THE LANGUAGE OF REVOLUTION.

CLAIMING A FUTURE

Middle class intellectuals had claimed a future for the Caribbean. But this was not reflected in the spontaneous music of the ghetto.

WHAT GAVE MARLEY THE COURAGE TO GO BEYOND MOCKERY TO HOPE: TO TRANSCEND COMMENT AND ASSERT RIGHT? TO FIND THE ANSWER TO THIS YOU MUST ENQUIRE: DID BOB MARLEY REDEEM HIS IDENTITY BY RE-CROSSING THE MIDDLE PASSAGE AND REENTERING THE KINGDOM OF HIS PAST? HE WHO KNOWS HIS PAST CAN BELIEVE THAT THE FUTURE IS THE TERRITORY OF HOPE. HE WHO KNOWS NOT HIS PAST FINDS THAT IN SPITE OF HIMSELF, HIS FUTURE IS, IN HIS MIND, A BURIAL GROUND. FAITH BEGINS WITH AN ACCEPTANCE OF THE POSSIBILITY OF CONTINUITY. IF YOU CANNOT SURVEY A CONTINUITY INTO YOUR OWN PAST, YOU CANNOT BELIEVE IN A CONTINUITY INTO YOUR OWN FUTURE. MARLEY HAD THAT FAITH.

RASTA—THE FAITH

How did Bob Marley successfully undertake this journey into his past, which released him to a belief in his people's future? The answer is: Rastafarianism. I enter into no controversy about people and their faith. To each his own. But it is inextricably a part of the psychodrama in which the black of the diaspora are enmeshed that their traditional, Christian faith is visualized in white terms. Inevitably and obviously, a religion that was spawned at the very centre of white civilization expresses its faith through familiar symbols. If the servants and children of God are white, they will think of both God and Christ in terms of self-image. Therefore, the God that emerges will be imagined to be white. Every church has its sculpture and its painting expressed in white terms. So the children of the slaves begin with a visual contradiction. To compound the problem, the particular expression of Christianity was first the creature of the oppressor. Yet, the children of the slaves need faith and have faith. They are sure there is a God and they are sure that somewhere that God is their God rooted in the land of the past and visualized in terms of their self-image.

Rastafarianism is a true faith in the sense that its believers have taken that step beyond mere rationality into the acceptance of a view of the unknown, unknowable and improvable which is faith. To them Haile Selassie is the symbol of God on earth and God himself is as revealed in the Holy Scriptures. The true Rastafarian, therefore, has traced his identity beyond mere history and geography to the ultimate source of all things, for the believer, the Creator himself. BUT HE HAS ARRIVED AT HIS CREATOR THROUGH THE IMAGES AND THE SOIL OF AFRICA. BY THAT ACT HE HAS RE-DISCOVERED THE SELF THAT WAS MISLAID IN THE MIDDLE PASSAGE.

ROBERT NESTA MARLEY, O.M.

ROBERT NESTA MARLEY, Order of Merit (O.M.), super star, father and definitive exponent of reggae, was a Rastafarian. He had taken that journey. By that act he had solved his identity crisis. He had become a complete human being. In his completeness he could sing songs of compassion: "No Woman, No Cry"; he could spit revolutionary defiance: "War"; he could embrace proletarian internationalism: "Zimbabwe"—AND HE COULD DO IT ALL WITH AN UNSELFCONSCIOUS CONVICTION THAT MADE HIM A KIND OF SPONTANEOUS, UNCOMPROMISING REVOLUTIONARY, UNTOUCHED BY WEALTH, UNFAILINGLY GENEROUS, ETERNALLY UNSPOILT.

I AND I

I first knew Bob Marley in 1971, in the days of "Trench Town Rock". At this stage his music was still like visceral protest carried on the wings of a relatively uncomplicated commentary on the ghetto. Throughout that year, he used to perform as part of a group of artists who traveled all over Jamaica with me as the Party which I led prepared for the General Elections of 1972. Until that time, my own political perceptions had reflected a mutually reinforcing marriage. On the one hand, there was the political theory, which I had absorbed from my Father as a youth and had developed into explicit Socialist doctrine as a student in University. On the other hand was some twenty years as an organizer and negotiator with the Jamaican Trade Union Movement. To this was now added a vital and new ingredient. I could never pretend that the lyrics of the protest music, which were the driving motivations of reggae, taught me things that I did not know. From an intellectual point of view, they were confirmatory of all that I believed as a Socialist, and have struggled against as a Trade Unionist. But I had not myself been born in the ghetto and was not personally a part of that experience. Reggae music influenced me profoundly by deepening the element of emotional comprehension.

STRUGGLE FOR CHANGE

I suppose a rough equivalent might be sought by a consideration of the influence of a writer like Dickens upon the sensibilities of English readers in the Nineteenth Century. In highly literate societies, the pen is a mighty instrument. It cannot change the structure of classes, nor the relations between classes, because it cannot, of itself, change the nature and organization of production. But it can pry loose from traditional class attitudes those extraordinary individuals who become a part of the process of political change in a society.

Jamaica had produced a handful of great writers like GEORGE CAMPBELL, ROGER MAIS and VIC REID who had spoken to the issues of suffering and oppression. Their works helped create an awareness of the imperatives of change. But how many people read them? Everybody listened to Marley and his school of reggae protestors. Certainly, I listened and was reinforced in the conviction that we had to STRUGGLE FOR CHANGE.

REGGAE GONE INTERNATIONAL

The invention of the gramophone, the radio and television has created a mass market for contemporary music. Where the symphony orchestra became the principal instrument for the dissemination of the great music of the classical European tradition, simpler forms of music would now have international currency. Technology brought into the market the broad masses of the people virtually everywhere on the globe. So there is no mystery about the means by which Bob Marley's music, and reggae along with it, have become familiar to the peoples of Europe, Africa and the Americas.

The real issue to be examined however is why has reggae established an audience for itself among the myriad of competing musical forms, which jostle for space in the communication apparatus? Pride of place is held by synthetic, escape music. With its bromides and anodynes it is there to pour balm on the souls that are either damaged by the failure to beat the economic system or bored because they have.

At the other end of the spectrum is the biting but parochial satire of the calypso, which makes no impression on the international system whatsoever. Blues hold a significant place because sadness is a recognizable part of the human condition. In any case, America has produced most of the greatest technical virtuosos who have come out of the non-classical tradition. Clearly, reggae cannot, and is not going to compete with the escape music; but unlike the calypso, it has already carved a significant niche for itself. I can only hazard a guess that this owes much to two factors. Firstly, there is Marley himself: an authentic innovator, a genuine original in the sense that is true, say, of a STEVIE WONDER. Reggae has "gone international", therefore partly on the back of Marley's gifts. But it must also be true that the protest of reggae, the positive assertion of moral categories goes beyond parochial boundaries. AMONG OTHER THINGS REGGAE IS THE SPONTANEOUS SOUND OF A LOCAL REVOLUTIONARY IMPULSE. BUT REVOLUTION ITSELF IS A UNIVERSAL CATEGORY. IT IS THIS, POSSIBLY, WHICH SETS IT APART EVEN TO THE INTERNATIONAL EAR.

Bob Marley in Zimbabwe: The Untold Story

Adapted by Ree Ngwenya from *Bob Marley: Songs of Freedom* by Adrian Boot and Chris Salewicz

(Source: Zimbabwe Standard/African News Service, June 12, 2001)

IT was April 1980, the end of a hard week, around 4 pm, on a Friday afternoon. Mick Carter was in his office, thinking about maybe leaving early for the weekend. Then the phone rang.

Bob Marley was calling from the Tuff Gong International offices in Kingston. Could Mick organize a crew and all the necessary equipment and fly to Salisbury in Rhodesia over the weekend? On Tuesday, 18 April, the country was changing its name to Zimbabwe, and the city would be renamed Harare.

Bob had two officials from Zimbabwe's government in his office with him, and they had asked him to perform at the independence ceremonies. Cost was to be no barrier: Bob, whose tune "Zimbabwe" had proved inspirational to the ZANLA freedom fighters, was paying for it all out of his pocket. He would be playing amidst the ruins of Great Zimbabwe.

At the Islands Record offices in West London, Denise Mills received a similar call: "Bob said he was flying into London over the weekend and wanted to continue straight on to Africa. Could we arrange it?"

Within two hours, Carter had booked his crew and PA equipment. More importantly, he had also chartered a 707 waiting on the tarmac at Gatwick airport.

The next day the plane took off at Gatwick, carrying the agent, the lighting, the soundmen and the sound equipment.

The advance party for this Bob Marley expedition to Africa caused much bewilderment when it arrived at Salisbury airport, as it was then still known.

"The import people hadn't a clue what to do, how to deal with us," Carter said.

"What got us and everyone through was a huge bag of Bob Marley T-shirts that I had sensibly persuaded Island to give me before I left. These were liberally dispensed all around. And it also helped enormously that I was wearing an Exodus tour jacket, which was my passport to everything."

The only contact Carter had been given was an address in Harare—Job's Nite Spot, a club run by one Job Kadengu, a second-hand car dealer who worked for Zanu PF, who had somehow become the promoter.

Kadengu passed Carter to a certain Edgar Tekere, the minister for planning and development. At 3:30 am, on Sunday morning, Carter was driven in a taxi to Tekere's bungalow to wake him up and receive instructions.

A bleary-eyed Tekere directed Carter to the Rufaro Stadium on the edge of Harare where the independence ceremony was to be held. When he and his crew arrived there, a team of night watchmen loomed out of the darkness, trying to chase them off.

Within hours, Carter had secured the services of a squad of soldiers and a scaffolding company to build the stage.

"But the wood we were given was green and came from a damp warehouse. As the sun came and dried it, the planks turned rotten. We laid down tarpaulin, but we kept having to make chalk-marks where the holes were. I saw two wooden gates, and had them taken down and they became the PA stage."

But there was still no electrical power and there seemed little hope of the promised generator arriving to provide it.

"However," Carter remembers, "we found a cable running underneath the pitch. It provided electricity to a nearby village (township). So this guy jumped in and cut it for us to tap into it and as he did so, you could see the lights go out in the village."

There were no hotels booked for the Marley party. Everywhere was full, booked up weeks before, to accommodate visiting dignitaries who were coming from all over the world for the independence ceremony. Although he temporarily managed to secure a hotel room, Carter was kicked out of it at gunpoint by several soldiers.

Bob and the Wailers were taken to a guest-house 20 miles out of town; even so, there were not enough rooms for the group and Bob shared his room with Neville Garrick, Family Man, Gillie and Dennis Thomson, the engineer.

Bob took a commercial flight to Nairobi. As he waited in the transit lounge for his plane, he received an unexpected message from a royal equerry: Prince Charles was waiting in the VIP suite; would Bob care to come and join him and pay his respects?

If Prince Charles wanted to meet him, he should come out there and check him with all the people. Needless to say, Bob's invitation was not accepted.

Some time later, as Bob and the Wailers sat by the window of the departure lounge, they saw the royal party crossing the tarmac in the direction of the royal jet. When Prince Charles had walked only a few yards, however, he turned and looked up at the window where Bob was sitting. Looking directly into Bob Marley's eyes, Prince Charles smiled broadly. Then he continued on his way.

Bob and his party flew into Harare in the early evening of Sunday, 16 April.

With him were Denise Mills, Robert Partridge, and Phil Cooper, respectively the heads of press and international affairs at Island Records in London.

"The most amazing thing," Denise remembers, "was the arrival at the airport.

"Joshua Nkomo, who was minister of home affairs in Robert Mugabe's new government, and various cabinet officials had to line up and shake our hands. I couldn't believe it: there were about 26 of us and I'm sure none of the people had a clue who we were.

"When we went to tea at the palace with these drunken soldiers and the president, it was so English and colonial: cucumber sandwiches and lemonade—all considered a bit off by the Wailers.

"However, Bob sang 'No Woman No Cry' at the piano for the president's family."

What no one had thought to inform Bob and his team was the precise nature of the first show they would be playing: it was scheduled for the slot immediately following the ceremony in which Zimbabwe would receive its independence and was to be performed in front of only the assembled dignitaries and the media as well as the party faithful, the international luminaries included Britain's Prince Charles and India's Indira Gandhi.

Such a scheduling implied that the events would have an exact order. But instead, Carter said: "It was complete anarchy. Bob went on immediately after the flag-raising ceremony. We had arrived at 8:30 in the evening, and were leisurely getting ready. We hadn't realized just how suddenly they expected us on stage. When they announced us, we weren't ready at all."

In fact, the first official words uttered in Zimbabwe, following the raising of the new flag, were: "Ladies and gentlemen, Bob Marley and the Wailers."

Twenty minutes later, Bob and The Wailers started their set. As soon as the first notes rang out, pandemonium broke loose in the enormous crowd gathered by the entrance to the sports stadium: the gates shook and began to break apart as the crush increased, the citizens of Harare, both excited and angry at being excluded from seeing these inspirational musicians.

As clouds of teargas drifted almost immediately into the stadium itself, the audience on the pitch fell on their feet in an attempt to protect themselves. The group members tasted their first whiffs of the gas and left the stage. "All of a sudden," said Judy Mowatt, "you smell this thing taking over your whole body, going in your throat until you want to choke, burning your eyes. I looked at Rita (Marley) and Marcia and they were feeling the same thing."

"I feel my eyes and nose," remembered Family Man, "and think, from when I was born, I have to come all the way to Africa to experience teargas."

Bob, however, seemed to have moved to a transcendent state. His eyes were shut, and for a while the gas didn't seem to have an effect at all. Then he opened his eyes and left the stage.

Backstage, the group had taken refuge in a truck. Outside they could see small children fainting and women collapsing. It looked like death personified to Mowatt, who briefly wondered whether they had been brought to Zimbabwe to meet their ends.

She persuaded someone to drive her and the other I-Threes back to the hotel, only to discover on the television that the show had resumed. After about half an hour Bob and the Wailers had gone back on stage. They ended their set with "Zimbabwe," a song Bob had worked on during his pilgrimage to Ethiopia late in 1978, and which became arguably his most important single composition.

Bob was just coming offstage as Mowatt and her fellow women singers returned to the stadium. "Hah," he looked at them with a half-grin, "now I know who the real revolutionaries are."

It was decided that the group would play another concert the following day, to give the ordinary people of Zimbabwe an opportunity to see Bob Marley.

Over 100,000 people—an audience that was almost entirely black—watched this show by Bob Marley and the Wailers. The group performed for an hour and a half, the musicians fired up to a point of ecstasy. But Bob, who uncharacteristically hadn't bothered to turn up for the sound check, was strangely lackluster in his performance; a mood of disillusionment had set in around him following the tear-gassing the previous day.

After the day's performance, the Bob Marley team was invited to spend the evening at the home of Tekere. This was not the most re-laxed of social occasions.

As the henchmen strutted around with their Kalashnikovs, Mills was informed by Tekere that he wanted Bob to stay in Zimbabwe and tour the country. "Bob told me to say he wasn't going to, but the guy didn't want to hear me."

While Bob remained in the house, Rob Partridge and Phil Cooper sat out in the garden. "I could hear," said Cooper, head of interna-tional affairs, "Tekere saying to Bob, 'I want this man Cooper. He's been going around putting your image everywhere. He's trying to portray you as a bigger man than our President.' I could hear all this.

"Then Bob came out and said to us, in hushed, perfect Queen's English; 'I think it's a good idea for you to leave.'

"Partridge and I went and packed, and took the first international flight out, which was to Nairobi. About five months later Tekere was arrested and put in jail; he had been involved in the murder of some white settler."

The next day Carter found himself being cajoled in the way Mills had been.

"Job Kadengu told me that there was a show in Bulawayo we had to do. But I was signing for trucks on behalf of the minister of devel-opment, Tekere, in other words. So we drove out to the airport with all the gear, loaded up the plane we'd chartered and left the country."

3

Children Playing in the Street: Bob Marley, Family Man

Bob Marley had 11 children (that he acknowledged). He performed and recorded with his wife, Rita, and she also had a solo career before they met, during their marriage, and after Bob passed on. Needless to say, their children are also extremely talented. Ziggy Marley and the Melody Makers—featuring Ziggy's older sisters Cedella and Sharon and his brother Stephen—have made inroads into the mainstream that eluded their father (several pop hits, the theme song to a TV show). Damian "Jr. Gong" Marley, Stephen Marley, and several other of his children also have developed fairly substantial recording careers.

But there are other routes to creativity. In addition to singing, Cedella has made her bones in fashion design with a line called Tuff Gong clothing.

Beyond that, one of the underplayed points about Bob Marley the man was that he was an accomplished athlete. In his youth, he might have dreamed of becoming a world-class soccer player instead of a world-class musician, and he was a committed, often daily player throughout his life. But at a shade over 5-foot-4, professional sports were not in his future.

However, his son Rohan became a football star in college, helping to lead the University of Miami Hurricanes to a college championship in 1991. Despite his size (5'7"), he played briefly for the Ottawa Rough Riders in the Canadian Football League. Rohan also had the good taste to sire several children with multiple Grammy–winner Lauryn Hill.

Marley Boys Set to Popularize Reggae

by Anya McCoy
(Source: Variety, June 8, 1998)

WELCOME to Jamaica North.

Bob Marley himself could not have predicted the new popularity of reggae, nor its move into big business, with Miami as its base. Long after his death, members of his family and other South Florida artists are leading reggae into the mainstream.

The last few years have seen a flurry of activity, as local bands have evolved their music with new multi-genre sounds and taken greater commercial control of their product.

While such bands are cutting Grammy-winning albums, they also are producing songs for soundtracks, leasing others for commercials and even getting into the restaurant biz.

Reggae's close association with Miami dates back to 1977, when Marley purchased a home here. Since then, practically the whole Marley clan has come to be based in South Florida, and in the 1990s several dozen more top reggae artists have relocated to Jamaica.

Family affair

Last year, Bob's brother Richard Marley Booker, and Bob's sons Ziggy, Stephen, Rohan, Robbie, Julian and Damian formed the promotion company Marley Boys Inc., with the idea of taking reggae mainstream. Hence Ziggy Marley and the Melody Makers—the most successful of the second-generation Marley bands—are featured in television ads for Cover Girl cosmetics.

From Miami, Booker heads up Nine Miles Inc., overseeing the Visitors Center in Jamaica, where tourists go to make pilgrimages to Bob's birthplace. Booker also is exec producer of Miami's Bob Marley Caribbean Festival each February.

The Marleys will swim further into the mainstream in late 1998 when they open the flagship of a planned chain of reggae cafes, similar to House of Blues, at Universal Studios in Orlando. More film and music deals are in the works.

Circle rounds up hits

After the Marleys, one of the earliest major bands to migrate to Miami was easy-listening reggae outfit Inner Circle. Two years ago, this self-managed outfit built a large, Mediterranean-style recording studio in North Miami, which also hosts IC's in-house label, SoundBwoy Entertainment.

Miami's indigenous reggae label, Shang Records in South Beach, is helmed by Clifton "Specialist" Dillon, who has his eye on the big prizes—film soundtracks, world tours, signing or creating big names in reggae.

Dillon has guided the recent career of Ky-mani Marley, snagging him spots on three soundtracks, "Money Talks," "Senseless," and

"Movin on Up." He also has Patra and Shabba Ranks (both new Miami residents), plus M.K. Shine and Mad Cobra on the Shang roster.

Only Natural: the Marleys Carry on Their Father's Mission—As They See It

by Celeste Fraser Delgado

(Source: **Miami New Times** *[Florida], May 2, 2002)*

SOMETIME past midnight a heavily tinted black Mercedes pulls up to the gate of Circle House, the posh private North Miami recording facility owned by reggae veterans Inner Circle. The driver cracks the window and extends an arm to activate the intercom, his long dreads brushing across his dark skin as the gate swings open. This is Stephen Marley, second son to Robert Nesta and Rita Marley, who inherited from his father not only a harrowing wail but also his less-celebrated-but-no-less-keen sense for the business of music, making him a sought-after producer by both reggae and hip-hop artists. Beside Stephen sits little brother Damian, son of Bob and Cindy Breakspeare (Jamaica's former Miss World); he has inherited his father's nickname "Gong" (Jr. in his case) and his mother's long limbs, light complexion, and gorgeous face. Together the two Marleys recently scored the family's fourth Grammy, taking the reggae award for Halfway Tree, a star-studded multi-artist collaboration held together by Damian's pretty pout and Stephen's savvy production.

As a Melody Maker back in the day with big brother Ziggy and sisters Cedella and Sharon, Stephen also had a share in winning three Grammys in 1988, 1989, and 1997. Their father himself never won one, dying three years before that category was added to the awards in 1984. Indeed the Grammys' recognition of reggae is owed in large part to Bob's lifework; winning seems almost an extension of their birthright. But if so many things come naturally to the Marley brood, it is Stephen who has taken charge of putting nature to good use. His is rarely the picture on the record or the name on the marquee, but like his father's spirit, he is always present, even when his influence is unseen: coordinating the long list of guest artists and beatmakers; divvying up duties on every track; conjuring the actual sound in the studio.

Tonight the brothers are groggy. They've just awakened after spending all of the night and most of the day before in the studio, laying tracks with family friend Lauryn Hill. Slowly, slowly they are getting ready to do the same thing all over again. Stephen pulls a black equipment case out of the Mercedes trunk and hauls it into the studio. Damian lights a spliff, then wanders around the Circle House patio. He is shy and standoffish, huddled into the hood of his sweatshirt, even though he is ostensibly the Grammy winner, the star. Only when Stephen bounds back onto the patio does the interview begin as big brother tells how it is decided who will record what, when.

"Nature," says Stephen, sifting a handful of herb in his palm. "You have to understand we are blood. We don't have to say, 'Jr. Gong, six o'clock tomorrow.' It's our nature. We don't force."

"It was my time," Jr. Gong pipes in from his slouch on the opposite couch.

"Julian is the next project," announces Stephen, nodding his head toward yet another brother who has recently arrived. And for Damian and Stephen personally, what's next? "For us personally," repeats Stephen. "Our personal end is Julian's record. Same thing."

Bob Marley's twelve children grew up together with a shared sense of mission and religious fervor passed on by their various mothers. "It's plain," says Stephen, after taking a long toke, "My father being an icon, women a vehicle for bringing forth the seed. Them do their duty." So there was never any friction among the households? "Woman a woman," sighs Stephen, "have jealousy, but never animosity. When you see the seed, you see Bob. Women respect that."

Is there a lot of pressure in living life as Bob Marley's seed? "We are Rasta," says Stephen through a cloud of smoke. "It's very clear what we have to do on earth. Jah send a soldier to deal with the music for the revolution." Passionate now, he rises to his feet. "We have been chosen as an instrument, a tool, to bring people together. One aim, one destiny, one heart." He pauses, then walks toward a table laden with freshly delivered pizza. "No pressure in that."

Cedella Marley Launches a Distinctive Line of Customized Denim and Leather Reminiscent of Her Father's Rude Boy Style

(Source: Tuff Gong press release, 2001)

A PIECE of new, a piece of old, Cedella Marley has taken pieces seen before and combined them with contemporary urban style to create a medley of then and now. Her premier line, Catch A Fire, introduces patchwork denim and leather to help every woman express her frivolously casual side.

Reared in an era that is already enjoying a revival, Cedella took fashion cues from all that surrounded her growing up. "My aunt used to take one of my mom's dresses and make two tiny ones for me and Sharon," said Cedella. "She taught me how to sew and I've loved it ever since." The Catch A Fire line pays homage to the legendary I-Threes and to her stylish father, the natty dresser Bob Marley, Cedella's biggest fashion influence. Adopting the name of his first album as dub for pieces he influenced, Marley's lyrics brand belt buckles and t-shirts, while his rude boy style leaves its mark throughout.

Giving rebirth to retired wear is what Cedella's clothing is about. With a refreshing combination of vintage styles and today's urban trends, the line offers something for every independent woman. Without a doubt, Catch A Fire shows the unique perspective of a creator loyal to the classic '70s look but who integrates her personal vision into every creation. "I couldn't find anything out there that I really liked for myself," Cedella explains, "so I started making these clothes for myself and it just took off from there." Customizing denim for her family and celebrities such as Lil' Kim, Sarah Jessica Parker, Amanda Lewis, Destiny's Child, and Eve, Cedella recently decided to share her passion and past with the general public.

Catch A Fire offers everything from jeans to jackets, belts to bags. Full-length dresses and wrap-around skins are seductive. Patterned patches of leather or studded accents personalize each piece, all with a weathered look of comfort. Leather flower pins are the perfect accessory. Asymmetrical tees add flair and a line of under-tanks and briefs are shyly sexy.

For the woman who is confident about her sexuality but wants to keep it relaxed and understated, Catch A Fire is now available at themarleystore.com and select stores throughout the country.

Cedella Marley's life has always been rooted in music and culture. Growing up in the hills of Jamaica, and touring the world as a Melody Maker, Cedella has had the best of both worlds. A little bit country, and a little bit rock 'n' roll. As the first child of the legendary Reggae singer Bob Marley, Cedella has witnessed history in the making and she has not for one moment stopped to let anything pass her by. She has taken her vast influences of people and places, culture and sounds, and put them all to work.

Currently living in Miami, Cedella balances her life as performer and one of four Melody Makers with the considerable demands of being CEO of Tuff Gong International and a full-time mom of two. With her group she has eight acclaimed albums and two Grammy awards under her belt, has toured internationally and performed on numerous TV shows. As head of the record label formed by her father, Cedella has developed razor sharp business skills. She is a natural performer and has received critical acclaim for her on-screen work with Gina Gershon in *Joey Breaker*. It is in every aspect of her life, be it performing, administering, or at home, that Cedella has actively safeguarded and developed her father's great legacy and style. It is a challenge she has always met with determination, self-confidence and energy. It is now that Cedella has harnessed her creative energy and put it towards developing a line of customized women's clothing, appropriately named Catch A Fire, the title of her father's first album. Through this project, Cedella once again intends to keep her father's memory and message alive while sharing with the world her own distinct sensibility.

4

So Much Trouble in the World Today: "Third World" Hero

Bob Marley's image is ubiquitous. His face adorns posters, T-shirts, and jackets. It adorns walls in thousands of different renderings. Throughout Africa and the Caribbean, Marley has become an object of near deification, a star with a following of Elvis-like proportions, perhaps even bigger and stronger. In many countries, his image evokes the dreams of freedom that he sang of, redemption songs in reality. He inspired freedom fighters in Zimbabwe and gave hope to the down-pressed everywhere. His face has become the emblem of the quest for freedom, both politically and spiritually.

He has also become symbolic of sympathy for the African diaspora. In a way no other artist of African extraction has, Marley has reached people of all races and given them a taste, through his music, through his life and celebrity, of what it means to be poor, what it means to be part of a hungry mob looking at people with dem belly full.

The place of his birth (wherein his tomb also resides) has become a tourist mecca, despite its relative isolation. Indeed, the village is called Nine Miles because it was nine miles away from any other outpost of humanity back when Marley was a boy. His Hope Road home in the "good" area of Kingston has become a museum with guided tours. He has been celebrated in literature and panel graphics and even at theme parks. If ever there were an icon for the rise and need of developing nations of the world, Bob Marley has become that icon.

Redemption Day

by Alice Walker

(Source: **Mother Jones,** *December 1986)*

B Y five o'clock we were awake, listening to the soothing slapping of the surf and watching the sky redden over the ocean. By six we were dressed and knocking on my daughter's door. She and her friend Kevin were going with us (Robert and me) to visit Nine Miles, the birthplace of someone we all loved, Bob Marley. It was Christmas day, bright, sunny, and very warm, and the traditional day of thanksgiving for the birth of someone sacred.

I missed Bob Marley when his body was alive, and I have often wondered how that could possibly be. It happened, though, because when he was singing all over the world, I was living in Mississippi being political, digging into my own his/herstory, writing books, having a baby—and listening to local music, B. B. King and the Beatles. I liked dreadlocks, but only because I am an Aquarian; I was unwilling to look beyond the sexism of Rastafarianism. The music stayed outside my consciousness. It didn't help either that the most political and spiritual of reggae music was suppressed in the United States, so that "Stir It Up" and not "Natty Dread" or "Lively Up Yourself" or "Exodus" was what one heard. And then, of course, there was disco, a music so blatantly soulless as to be frightening, and impossible to do anything to but exercise.

I first really heard Bob Marley when I was writing a draft of the screenplay for *The Color Purple*. Each Monday I drove up to my studio in the country, a taxing three-hour drive, worked steadily until

Friday, drove back to the city, and tried to be two parents to my daughter on weekends. We kept in touch by phone during the week, and I had the impression that she was late for school every day and living on chocolates.

My friends Jan and Chris, a white couple nearby, seeing my stress, offered their help, which I accepted in the form of dinner at their house every night after a day's work on the script. One night, after yet another sumptuous meal, we pushed back the table and, in our frustration at the pain that rides on the seat next to joy in life (cancer, pollution, invasions, the bomb, etc.), began dancing to reggae records: UB–40, Black Uhuru . . . Bob Marley. I was transfixed. It was hard to believe the beauty of the soul I heard in "No Woman No Cry," "Coming In from the Cold," "Could You Be Loved," "Three Little Birds," and "Redemption Song." Here was a man who loved his roots (even after he'd been nearly assassinated in his own country) and knew they extended to the ends of the earth. Here was a soul who loved Jamaica and loved Jamaicans and loved being a Jamaican (nobody got more pleasure out of the history, myths, traditions, and language of Jamaica than Bob Marley), but who knew it was not meant to limit itself (or even could) to an island of any sort.

Here was the radical peasant-class, working-class consciousness that fearlessly denounced the *wasichu* (the greedy and destructive) and did it with such grace you could dance to it. Here was a man of extraordinary sensitivity, political acumen, spiritual power and sexual wildness; a free spirit if ever there was one. Here, I felt, was my brother. It was as if there had been a great and gorgeous light on all over the world, and somehow I'd missed it. Every night for the next two months I listened to Bob Marley. I danced with his spirit—so much more alive still than many people walking around. I felt my own dreadlocks begin to grow.

Over time, the draft of the script I was writing was finished. My evenings with my friends came to an end. My love of Marley spread easily over my family, and it was as neophyte Rastas (having decided that *Rasta* for us meant a commitment to a religion of attentiveness and joy) that we appeared when we visited Jamaica in 1984.

What we saw was a ravaged land, a place where people, often Rastas, eat out of garbage cans and where, one afternoon in a beach café during a rainstorm, I overheard a 13-year-old boy offer his 11-year-old sister (whose grown-up earrings looked larger, almost, than her face) to a large hirsute American white man (who blushingly declined) along with some Jamaican pot.

The car we rented (from a harried, hostile dealer who didn't even seem to want to tell us where to buy gas) had already had two flats. On the way to Nine Miles it had three more. Eventually, however, after an agonizing seven hours from Negril, where we were staying, blessing the car at every bump in the road to encourage it to live through the trip, we arrived.

Nine Miles (because it is nine miles from the nearest village of any size) is one of the most still and isolated spots on the face of the earth. It is only several houses, spread out around the top of a hill. There are small, poor farms, with bananas appearing to be the predominant crop.

Several men and many children come down the hill to meet our car. They know we've come to visit Bob. They walk with us up the hill where Bob Marley's body is entombed in a small mausoleum with stained-glass windows: the nicest building in Nine Miles. Next to it is a small one-room house where Bob and his wife, Rita, lived briefly during their marriage. I think of how much energy Bob Marley had to generate to project himself into the world beyond this materially impoverished place; and of how exhausted, in so many of his later

photographs, he looked. On the other hand, it is easy to understand—
listening to the deep stillness that makes a jet soaring overhead sound
like the buzzing of a fly—why he wanted to be brought back to his
home village, back to Nine Miles, to rest. We see the tomb from a
distance of about 50 feet, because we cannot pass through (or climb
over) an immense chain link fence that has recently been erected to
keep the too eager (and apparently destructive and kleptomaniacal)
tourists at bay. One thing that I like very much: built into the hill fac-
ing Bob's tomb is a permanent stage. On his birthday, February 6,
someone tells us, people from all over the world come to Nine Miles
to sing to him.

The villagers around us are obviously sorry about the fence. (Perhaps we were not the ones intended to be kept out?) Their faces seem
to say as much. They are all men and boys. No women or girls among
them. On a front porch below the hill I see some women and girls,
studiously avoiding us.

One young man, the caretaker, tells us that though we can't
come in there is a way we can get closer to Bob. (I almost tell him
I could hardly be any closer to Bob and still be alive, but I don't
want to try to explain.) He points out a path that climbs the side of
the hill and we—assisted by half a dozen of the more agile villagers—
take it. It passes through bananas and weeds, flowers, past goats
tethered out of the sun, past chickens. Past the lair, one says, of Bob
Marley's cousin, a broken but gallant-looking man in his 50s, nearly
toothless, with a gentle and generous smile. He sits in his tiny,
nearly bare house and watches us, his face radiant with the pride of
relationship.

From within the compound now we hear singing. Bob's songs
come from the lips of the caretaker, who says he and Bob were
friends. That he loved Bob. Loved his music. He sings terribly. But

perhaps this is only because he is, though about the age Bob would have been now, early 40s, lacking his front teeth. He is very dark and quite handsome, teeth or no. And it is his humble, terrible singing—as he moves proprietarily about the yard where his friend is enshrined—that makes him so. It is as if he sings Bob's songs for Bob, in an attempt to animate the tomb. The little children are all about us, nearly underfoot. Beautiful children. One little boy is right beside me. He is about six, of browner skin than the rest—who are nearer to black—with curlier hair. He looks like Bob.

I ask his name. He tells me. I have since forgotten it. As we linger by the fence, our fingers touch. For a while we hold hands. I notice that over the door to the tomb someone has plastered a bumper sticker with the name of Rita Marley's latest album. It reads: "Good Girl's Culture." I am offended by it; there are so many possible meanings. For a moment I try to imagine the sticker plastered across Bob's forehead. It drops off immediately, washed away by his sweat (as he sings and dances in the shamanistic trance I so love) and his spirit's inability to be possessed by anyone other than itself (and Jah). The caretaker says Rita erected the fence. I understand the necessity.

Soon it is time to go. We clamber back down the hill to the car. On the way down the little boy who looks like Bob asks for money. Thinking of our hands together and how he is so like Bob must have been at his age, I don't want to give him money. But what else can I give him, I wonder.

I consult "the elders," the little band of adults who've gathered about us.

"The children are asking for money," I say. "What should we do?"

"You should give it," is the prompt reply. So swift and unstudied is the answer, in fact, that suddenly the question seems absurd.

"They ask because they have none. There is nothing here."

"Would Bob approve?" I ask. Then I think, "Probably. The man has had himself planted here to feed the village."

"Yes," is the reply. "Because he would understand."

Starting with the children, but by no means stopping there (because the grown-ups look as expectant as they), we part with some of our "tourist" dollars, realizing that tourism is a dead thing, a thing of the past; that no one can be a tourist anymore, and that, like Bob, all of us can find our deepest rest and most meaningful service at home.

It is a long hot anxious drive that we have ahead of us. We make our usual supplications to our little tin car and its four shiny tires. But even when we have another flat, bringing us to our fourth for the trip, it hardly touches us. Jamaica is a poor country reduced to selling its living and its dead while much of the world thinks of it as "real estate" and a great place to lie in the sun; but Jamaicans as a people have been seen in all their imperfections and beauty by one of their own, and fiercely sung, even from the grave, and loved. There is no poverty, only richness in this. We sing "Redemption Song" as we change the tire; feeling very Jamaica, very Bob, very Rasta, very *no woman no cry*.

Marley: Tale of the Tuff Gong (excerpt)

Written by Charles Hall (from a treatment by Mort Todd); Pencils by Gene Colan, paint by Tennyson Smith, lettering by John Costanza

(Source: Marvel Comics, September 1994)

5

Work:
Recording Bob Marley

Bob Marley only had six years at the top of his game as a touring artist. As such, the majority of people who are familiar with Marley's music know it through his later studio recordings.

Legend, the posthumous best-of compilation put out by Island, has become one of those essential records, one of the albums that no collection is complete without. It mostly captures his recordings from those last six years, his days on Island that produced all those global hits.

What Island brought to the party was something that the Jamaican music industry lacked: international distribution and marketing. Island was not only equipped to offer both, it was in fact initially set up to bring reggae to the world, from the days of "My Boy Lollipop" until Chris Blackwell finally sold the company for hundreds of millions of dollars. He continued to bring the best of global sounds to a worldwide audience with his Palm Pictures records, exposing artists like venerable Jamaican guitarist Ernest Ranglin and renowned vocalist Baaba Maal to an enormous range of listeners.

But Marley had been recording for over 10 years before his career caught fire on a global scale. As both Rita Marley and Coxsone Dodd said in the first section of this book, there was a time when Bob lived in the recording studio. It became an environment in which he learned to thrive.

Bob Marley: In the Studio with the Wailers

by Richard Williams

(Source: **Melody Maker,** *June 23, 1973)*

THE Rolling Stones are upstairs in Studio 1, where they've been for the past five weeks. Jagger strolls around the foyer, looking for something to do, all neat in white blouson jacket and fawn velvet jeans. But that, you may be surprised to hear, is not where the real action is at this night in Island Studios, Notting Hill.

Not, at any rate, if you're a Wailers fan. On this occasion, even the Stones' long-delayed newie comes second to Bob Marley and his brothers from the shanty-towns of Kingston, Jamaica.

The Wailers have been in Britain for some weeks now, playing various kinds of gigs, and generally doing very well. There have been problems: Bunny Livingston never wanted to come in the first place. He's happy being poor in Jamaica, he says, and he'd rather not witness the fleshy delights of a European metropolis. The temptation might be too great. Nevertheless, he's here.

There's a problem, too, with food. Being Rastafarians, they don't eat meat at all, or fish with scales. So cartons of vegetables and plaice have been delivered most days to their communal house on the Kings Road, and on the road they've eaten mostly out of fish 'n' chip shops.

"Huh," says Bunny, stuffing most of a battered plaice-and-six into his face, "London's national dish." No salt, though—that's also forbidden by the Rasta creed.

In general, they're delighted with the response they've received over here. Only one thing puzzles Marley: when they've played at black clubs, the audiences don't applaud. But the white college audiences have applauded each number loudly.

"Before they came here," confides an Island person, "they'd never heard of doing encores. So the first night, when they left the stage and the audience carried on cheering, they thought maybe something was wrong. We had to persuade them that it was actually good, and push them back on stage."

Tonight, anyway, the Wailers are in Studio 2, the smaller one, working on their follow-up to the brilliant *Catch a Fire* album. They laid the rhythm tracks down at Harry J's studio in Kingston, as is their custom, and have already overdubbed voice parts plus extra guitars and keyboards.

Island boss Chris Blackwell is back from a millionaire-style excursion down the Colorado River, on a 20-foot rubber raft, to supervise the mixing process. He picked up the Wailers for Island in the first place, and is closely involved in their success for various reasons. It's he who decided that *Catch a Fire* should be packaged as if it were a major rock album, and projected at a whole new market.

Amusingly enough, someone is showing round the original copies of two 1966 Wailers records, "Put it On" and "Who Feels It Knows It," which came out here on Island. It's ironical because they were, for all intents and purposes, "pirate" records. Bunny sniffs when he sees them, and goes into a long discussion on the iniquities of the Jamaican record scene.

The session starts with a quick run-through of the rough mixes, which Blackwell is hearing for the first time. As the eight or nine songs glide by, his expression remains on the brighter side of contentment. The raw material is—how shall we put it?—magnificent.

The mixing proper begins with a Marley song called "I Shot The Sheriff," a sort of humorous musical version of the plot from *The Harder They Come* (which you should have seen by now, or heaven help you). Marley's role as lead singer is similar to that of the outlaw character, Ivan, played by Jimmy Cliff in the movie. The high falsetto chorus, delivered by uncharacteristically strained voices, adds to the comic quality.

However, it's the music that carries this track. Listening to Blackwell and his engineer bringing separate instrument tracks up and down, hearing either the bass or the drums in isolation, one begins to grasp the mastery of these men. There are, for example, two rhythm guitars here, chopping through and around each other as if by telepathy. Beneath them runs the suavest, lithest, most inventive bass line, courtesy of Aston "Family Man" Barrett, meshing in perfect sympathy with his brother Carly's drumming.

Ah, the drumming. Had you noticed that these guys play the bass-drum on 2 and 4, the off-beats? Maybe you remember the fuss when Jo Jones transferred the beat-carrying role from the bass-drum to the hi-hat, with Count Basie's band in the thirties. Isn't there just a chance that what the Reggae drummers are doing is equally revolutionary, and might have a similar effect? If that were all they did, it would be noteworthy enough, but when the musicologists start taking this stuff seriously (in, say, ten years' time), they're going to find enough material to last them through years of research and analysis.

It's a bit early in the session to get involved with a masterpiece, but that's what comes up next. Whatever you thought was the best track on *Catch a Fire*, its equivalent on the new album will be a thing called "Duppy Conqueror". The song will be familiar to most stone Reggae fans because Bob wrote and cut it a couple of years ago.

The song is reminiscent of both "Put It On" and "Stir It Up" in that it's built on the familiar "La Bamba" pyramid chord changes, and it resembles "Stir It Up" most of all because the rhythm is a swaying slow-medium. Mostly it's call-and-response between Bob and the other voices, his nasal asides and interjections growing out of the chorus.

"Yes me friend (me good friend) they say we free again . . . The bars could not hold me (whoo-hoo), force could not control me now. They try to put me down, but Jah put I around now. I been accused (whoo hoo) and wrongly abused now. . . ."

The engineer silences all the tracks except the voices, and suddenly the truly sublime quality of the Wailers' harmonies is brought home with a vengeance. Have they ever recorded anything a cappella, without instruments? No, says Peter Tosh. You should, says Blackwell. They should indeed.

Music like this is Bob Marley's forte; soft, supremely sensual, and making its point through understatement. It doesn't shout at you; rather it insinuates, suffusing the brain like a heady wine. Unfortunately, some otherwise intelligent people have missed the point, and expect him to come on like Toots Hibbert or Desmond Dekker, shouting and bashing. That attitude is so patronizing as to be beneath contempt. Does Wilson Pickett invalidate Smokey Robinson? Of course not. At this point, Jagger walks in. "You've met Bob?" says Blackwell. "Uh . . . hi," says Mick, extending a hand.

The album the Stones are mixing was, of course, recorded in Jamaica, where Jagger met many Reggae musicians until, he says, he got a bit bored with it. He must be getting pretty bored with his own album, too: it's months since they began it, although he maintains that only seven weeks' hard work have been put in so far.

Jagger has come to enlist Blackwell's aid. It seems that Keith Richard's old lady, Anita, has been staying in Kingston with a Rasta band which Keith plans to produce. Their house was raided, Anita was busted, and she can't get bail. Blackwell, being rich and of Jamaican descent, might have some pull. "I don't really have any," he says, and asks Tosh: "What are the police like with Rastas now? Are they specially hard on them?"

"Depends," Tosh replies. "Depends on the Rasta, and depends on if he knows the right policeman."

"Duppy Conqueror" goes round and round, played at least two dozen times, and it could go on for ever. Nobody here would mind. Make a 40-minute tape-loop of it, someone suggests, and there's your album.

But, of course, there are other songs. "Get up, Stand Up", "Reincarnated Soul" (out on the B-side of the new single, "Concrete Jungle"), the fabulous "Rastafarian Chant", Bunny's "Oppressor Song", and a beauty from Marley called "Burnin' And Lootin'", with another incredible lyric: "Give me the food and let me grow/Let the roots-man take a blow now/All them drugs gon' make you slow now/it's not the music of the ghetto . . . "

The "roots-man" is the man who boils plant roots, distilling a drinkable substance of allegedly spiritual properties. It also makes you high. Nothing one hears suggests that this will be anything less than a worthy successor to the last album, and in "Duppy Conqueror" it will contain a true classic.

Chris Blackwell: An Interview with the Founding Father of the Reggae Music Industry

by Timothy White

(Source: **Billboard,** *July 13, 1991)*

ISLAND Records was founded at 13 Connaught Square in London on May 8, 1962, by Christopher Blackwell, scion of an old Anglo-Jamaican trading family. Young Christopher had been an aide-de-camp to the Governor General of Jamaica, a club owner, professional gambler, manager of 63 rural Jamaican jukeboxes, a motor scooter and water-skiing concessionaire before delving into the Jamaican record business on the production end while also licensing native ska hits for the British market. From the instant he stepped into the Kingston recording arena, Blackwell pioneered virtually every sophisticated modern distribution, production and marketing technique for the reggae industry, as well as rescuing it from the ghetto chaos and sordid technique business practices that commercially had held back the music and the artists.

"Island make a big difference," declared Bob Marley in 1975. "No cheatin', no robbin'. Before I sign with Island, I had three albums that I didn't even know about."

Not only was Island Records the first company to apply the same artistic standards to reggae as had been customary for rock, but it was also the first label to lavish care on the manufacture and promotion of the recording output of the Caribbean and the rest of the Third World. Whether it was the quality of the vinyl and the pressings, the technical levels of studio craft, the often-pathbreaking design concepts for packaging, the distinctly stylish retail drives, the comprehensive radio initiatives, or the dignified and culturally aware press campaigns, Island always found an ingenious way to reinvent the notion of popular music. Without Island, there might never have been a global reggae enterprise of a pan-cultural concept like world music.

Lastly, while it was Bob Marley who inspired the world with his remarkable music and socio-cultural vision, it was Island Records that worked tirelessly during Marley's lifetime to make this outreach possible, and the label's dignified stewardship of the Marley catalog demonstrates the durability of that commitment. From the start, Blackwell's involvement in Jamaican popular music has plainly been a labor of love.

TIM WHITE: Describe what the West Indian record business was like in the U.K. and The States before Island Records.

CHRIS BLACKWELL: I don't know much about The States. I think there was little or no record business in The States other than people importing—wholesalers in Brooklyn or such that would import in the early '60s. Calypso from Trinidad, which was mostly represented on a label called Cook—used to sell much more than music from Jamaica. The biggest record Cook had, I think, was the first by the Antigua Steel Band.

Now in England, before Island started, there was a label called Esquire Records, which was a jazz label, and they had a sub-label called Starlite on which they put Jamaican music. And the other Jamaican music label in England was called Melodisc. Melodisc was also a jazz label, and then it started a label called BlueBeat—and BlueBeat put out Prince Busters' records, and also they put out the very earliest Jamaican records. The first one was probably "O Carolina"—I always consider "O Carolina" to be the first Jamaican record.

So what happened was that from Jamaica, I licensed my records to Starlite in England; and Esquire, I don't think, had any other Jamaican product except from me. Melodisc, however, dealt with lots of different people. When I started Island in England in 1962, I found myself in the same situation, I guess, as someone starting to sell vacuum cleaners and they were up against Hoover, where it became virtually a generic, because in England it was called bluebeat music!

That's why I really pushed the name ska, to try and get across the fact that this music is not bluebeat music—it's Jamaican music, it's ska music. We really pushed that name. The first record I made was a big hit, "Little Sheila," by Laurel Aitken. The other side was called "Boogie In My Bones." So we recorded those at a JBC radio station. At the session we had the mixture of a couple of musicians who were Australian, who were living in Jamaica, and the rest were Jamaican. Then

I just put it out in Jamaica, took it down to Federal Records, which was owned by Ken Khourie, and then manufactured them there and I had a tiny office on Orange Street. Coxsone's shop was there, Leslie Kong, Prince Buster were there—all the producers.

WHITE: Orange Street was like Kingston's Music Row?

BLACKWELL: Yeah, and when you drive up there you'd get sound systems blasting out all the time. But you see, the root of the business in Jamaica was the sound systems. That's how it all started—because the radio would never play the music. Even today you don't hear a lot of reggae in Jamaica.

The people who had money in Jamaica would consider this "trash" music; they wouldn't be interested. And when I left Jamaica in 1962, the biggest record that had ever been in Jamaican was the soundtrack of "The Student Prince." That gives you some idea of where it was at!

I decided that I would start out with records in England because it had become very competitive in Jamaica and I was starting to sell or license a lot of records in England. So I went to see all of my Jamaican competitors which were Duke Reid, Leslie Kong, Coxsone Dodd, Prince Buster. And with all of them—with the exception of Buster—I made a deal that when I went to England, they'd give me their records. So I came to England and I told these people at Starlite I was going to start my own label. They were kinda upset about it.

I bought from them, for about 50 pounds, a list of all the stores in England who they dealt with. Stores in London, Nottingham, Birmingham, Coventry, Bristol, Liverpool. I manufactured my first Island single and I went around to these stores and I sold it to them.

WHITE: Where'd you manufacture it?

BLACKWELL: At a little company called British Homophone, which is a pressing plant [in Dagenham, Essex]. "Darling Patricia" by

Owen Grey, with "Twist Baby" on the flip side, was the first record we put out. "Independent Jamaica" was the second one, by Kentrick "Lord Creator" Patrick.

When I started Island, I raised some money in Jamaica; I put up what money I had at the time, which was money I made off working on the first James Bond picture, "Doctor No." I had scouted location, I picked hotels for them, I got the transportation, that kind of thing. They looked after me very well. They offered me a piece of the film, you know 1% of the film. And I said, no, I prefer the thousand pounds!

So that money I put into Island in England, and the other investors were basically Leslie Kong and his family—they were the other share holders, so that I would get product from them. Because he was good, Leslie; great records used to come out of his place. So that's really how we got Bob Marley's records—because Bob, through Jimmy Cliff's introduction to Leslie, recorded with Leslie.

WHITE: Do you have any vivid memories of listening to those early Bob singles like "Judge Not"?

BLACKWELL: No, I wish I could tell you I did. When we first got it I even spelled his name wrong on the label! It was just another record that came from Leslie and we put it out.

WHITE: Did you have a role model for the kind of record person you wanted to be—a certain record label, leader, producer?

BLACKWELL: Yes, my favorite labels—there were two: Blue Note Records because that was a jazz label, and I love jazz, and Atlantic Records. Before I started producing records, I used to come up to New York. They used to have a tremendous amount of second-hand record stores on Sixth Ave. here. I used to buy 78s, mainly R & B records. I'd bring them back to Jamaica, having crossed off the labels to frustrate my competitors. What they were for were to sell to the sound systems. Because, you see, the sound system was the engine room of the whole thing, like traveling discotheques. And they were all owned by people who sold liquor. The sound system guy would promote his own event. And at that gig you would sell all the food and all the liquor, etc., etc. So there was tremendous competition to have the hottest sound system, not only by having the most tweaked-up amps and speakers, but also by the records. So I would go up and buy these records for 63 cents each, cross out the labels so nobody knew what it was, and I'd take them there and sell them for 20 pounds each.

How ska emerged, was through the Jamaican attempt to play the grooves of New Orleans R & B, like Fats Domino or Smiley Lewis. King Records, Imperial Records and Atlantic Records—those were the three labels that were really popular in Jamaica. So the Jamaicans were trying to play these records, and their rhythm kinda turned around a little bit; it became more exaggerated and ska really emerged from that. But there was no deliberate attempt to change the beat—it just kinda happened.

One of the records from Coxsone Dodd—it must have been pretty early because it was the fifth record we put out in England—was a record called "We'll Meet" by Roy and Millie. Roy Shirley sang the first verse and chorus. And then when Millie Small came in, she sounded so quirky and so funny that people would say, "Yeah, give me the record."

I went down to Jamaica and met her and she had a great personality—vivacious, bubbly. She lived in the country, in Clarendon, which is a sort of semi-desert part of Jamaica. And I don't know how she found her way into Kingston—I think she had a boyfriend who was a policeman and he gave her 10 shillings to go into Kingston. Anyhow, I'd decided to bring her over to England.

On one of the records that I had imported long ago and scratched off the label of was a song called "My Boy Lollipop," which I had Millie re-record. I changed it into a ska beat—a "pop" ska. When it was finished I felt so sure that this was a hit that I didn't put it on Island—I decided to license it to a label which I felt could really handle a pop hit—Fontana, a big label in the U.K. This record became huge, and suddenly I was in the pop business, the mainstream record business.

I still kept my hand in Jamaica—because I used to go back lots. In fact, on one of the trips back there, coming out of one of the Orange Street sound systems, I heard this incredible record, a record called "Mockingbird" by Inez and Charlie Foxx. I went to New York to see the person who owned the record so I could make a deal—and that was a person named Juggy Murray from Sue Records. That's how Sue Records started in England!

Then there was a whole period from about 1966 onward when I had very peripheral knowledge of what was going on in Jamaica—I wasn't directly involved at all. I got pulled back in around 1969 with Jimmy Cliff, because we sent him in 1968 to Brazil to a Brazilian song festival and he won it. After Brazil he came back to Jamaica, and with Leslie Kong he produced this song called "Wonderful World, Beautiful People." So it was at that time that I became involved in reggae again, but only with Jimmy Cliff. Then it was around 1972 that the Wailers walked in off the street in England and asked me to sign them!

WHITE: Had you been following the Wailers' rocksteady and early reggae recordings back in Jamaica?

BLACKWELL: A little bit. "Put It On" was one of my favorite songs. At that time we had a pretty amazing array of artists—King Crimson, Traffic, Emerson Lake & Palmer—a huge amount of acts. The fact that I made a deal with Bob Marley in England, and I gave him this money—everybody said it was a dumb thing to do: "Why give him the money? These guys are bad guys, everybody knows they're bad guys, nobody wants to deal with them." I said to Bob: "O.K., I'm going to trust you. Here it is—go ahead and do it."

The deal was for 4,000 pounds but the guy who introduced us and effected that meeting took 25%, so that took it down to 3,000 pounds that I gave them to make their first album for me. After a month or so I sent a message to the Wailers that I was coming to Kingston and that I was staying at such and such a hotel—so they came to pick me up, to take me to Harry J's studio to hear it. I was thrilled about it—because they at least had recorded something; so already all the nay-saying motherfuckers were wrong, you know. So I went in the studio and they played me all the tracks and I was just totally blown away by the musical quality of "Slave Driver" and "Concrete Jungle." You know, "Concrete Jungle" was just so far ahead of anything that had ever been made in Jamaica before—that one particular track, the structure of it, the whole thing. It was just unbelievable. This LP, *Catch A Fire*, was the first reggae record conceived as an album. Leslie Kong had previously put out that so-called "Best Of The Wailers," which was drawn from a series of late rock steady sessions that took place in a concentrated period of time. But *Catch A Fire* was conceived by the group as a cohesive project, and they went ahead and executed it.

It was unprecedented in reggae—and also, you have to remember that around 1967 was the first time that even rock records or "pop" records were being conceived as albums. Albums would be collections of various attempts at singles and B sides.

So, when I heard *Catch A Fire*, it was a justification for putting the faith in them and also a justification of how to establish a relationship with somebody who is a natural rebel, a natural revolutionary. I felt the only way to do it was to say, "It's up to you—go ahead and do it."

Reggae at that time didn't have any respect for musicians. It was music that there would be big hits with, but they were novelty hits—there was no artist behind them. When I heard the Wailers' music and I heard the complicated musicianship in it, I knew I had to try to work them as a reggae band.

When we first worked together, it was Bob Marley & The Wailers; that's how some of the records came out before I signed them. And that was, like, a '50s name. So I changed it to The Wailers. It's also true that I changed it back to Bob Marley & The Wailers later.

And I wish I could tell you that *Catch A Fire* was a huge hit, that the record came out and was a success, but it wasn't. After the first year that it had been out, I think it only sold 14,000—24,000, something like that. But the fancy cigarette lighter packaging and the music itself sparked a big word-of-mouth campaign, which *Burnin'*" and "Natty Dread" increased, and radio people in San Francisco and Boston were supportive. Commercially, the *Rastaman Vibration* album in 1976 was the big breakthrough.

WHITE: Describe Bob's approach with that record.

BLACKWELL: Well, I guess that record was more R & B-ish; I think that was more Bob being influenced by the R & B side. He was really keen to try to sell records to black America. With the *Live!* record, he had really cracked Europe and become very hot there, but black America became the next goal. *Rastaman Vibration* was a conscious attempt to break into that market. So at this time we started to go back and try to establish the cultural roots in the mass audience's mind. After that came the period when Bob was shot [on Dec. 3, 1976] in Jamaica. He left the country after that, and he went to England, where he recorded *Exodus* and much of *Kaya*. Both of those albums represented where this person's head was at that time. They were unique records musically, but they were also personal milestones, diaries about his thinking spiritually, as well as his role leading this band of reggae messengers, if you will.

WHITE: Those records pulled people deeper into Rasta and into the future of that faith. *Exodus* is an album about Rasta's destiny.

BLACKWELL: That's right. *Exodus* was designed to be a much more conscious record than any previous one, much more prophetic. It's a great record, *Exodus,* but the one that gets missed a lot and is not considered great is still my favorite record, which is *Kaya.* Everyone said, "Well, *Kaya,* it's soft." The irony is that *Kaya* was composed largely in support of the Jamaican peace movement amongst the rival political gangs, thus being Bob's riskiest record image-wise. He was a Tuff Gong who was now showing his tender side in order to help establish this ghetto truce.

WHITE: "Is This Love" was meant as a sign of strength, not weakness.

BLACKWELL: Exactly. That's what I felt, and that's why I always defended that record. But often when people list all of Bob's records, they mistakenly diss that one, but I love it. What's also interesting is the evolution of a rock sound in Bob's albums. I consider the first record, *Catch A Fire,* to be the least reggae-like, because it had overdubs from a rock guitarist I was working with named Wayne Perkins, and I edited the backing tracks in order to double the length of the songs and create space for solos, which reggae never had much of. These ideas were unique for reggae, yet these techniques later influenced Bob and the band's thinking when they recorded *Rastaman Vibration* and *Exodus,* and you can also hear the rock-inclined performances on the *Babylon By Bus* live collection. Bob combined R & B and rock and reggae in a way never done before.

However, once Bob had experimented with these things, he turned inward again and concentrated on developing new avenues for reggae—with "One Drop" on "Survival" for instance. So that the last normal studio effort, *Uprising,* was the least rock-influenced of his albums. He'd come full circle, but was an innovator every step of the way.

WHITE: There's always been Bob Marley's music, and then there's been reggae. The former proved so original, it became a genre apart from the latter music, influencing it while continuing to pioneer on its own terms. Where is reggae now? What comes after dancehall and modern conscious reggae?

BLACKWELL: You know, there's two acts I've got in Jamaica now that I can't get to square one with, yet I think they're both fantastic because of their soulfulness. One is a guy called Donovan, and the other is a group called Foundation. Theirs is a country, rural sound, and if I had to predict a worthwhile trend in reggae, I would call it rural soul. These guys have great harmonies, soulful songs, and simple lyrics that are a kind of naive art. This stuff is the best thing I've heard since the early Wailers. But all anyone wants to know about in reggae now is dancehall. There's a great excitement to dancehall, it's like the Wild West, but I don't know that it's very lasting or very rich musically. This rural soul stuff is rich. Dancehall music tends to eat its young; it feeds on itself to a negative extent.

That's one of the problems, you see. When ska and reggae started, people in Jamaica would be listening to Miami and Jamaica radio stations which were playing American R & B, and all these outside influences would come in considerably more than today and have their nurturing effect. Now, since Bob died, people are trying to copy Bob or recycle some old rhythms and lyrics in attempts to emulate or imitate the past in a different way. As you say, the whole Jamaica scene has fed on itself. When there's a hit, everybody wonders what it was that made it a hit and copies it exactly or samples it.

WHITE: Dancehall is stimulating but not creatively important.

BLACKWELL: But you have to remember that Jamaica has a population of only two and a quarter million people, and it's almost astounding how the music from there has expanded to reach the world.

These days, there's almost more reggae being played live now in clubs than rock. I was in Miami recently and every single band along the oceanside club strip was playing reggae! Island is planning this autumn to put out a boxed set of Bob's best singles over the decades, including those never released in America, like "Screw Face," "Craven Choke Puppy," and Bob's version of "Guava Jelly."

WHITE: Artistically and philosophically, what do you hope to cement in peoples' minds through the new boxed set?

BLACKWELL: The idea with that is to put together a really good document of the different recordings to reflect what was going on with Bob at each personal stage, and back it up with a kind of storyline of what was going on in Jamaica during each period. Bob worked with a lot of people in Jamaica; he worked with Leslie Kong, with Coxsone, with Lee Perry, and all these different people also had an influence on him. I think it's time to show how his music and his reputation were formed. In this boxed set we want to get across what caused all this to emerge, and all of Bob's travels, including the thing of him going to America to live [in Delaware] and then coming back—all those different elements played a part.

WHITE: In other words, how his life and his art were all of a piece?

BLACKWELL: Yes! It's an audio-biography. Bob has taken on such huge proportions that it's important to do something of real value in terms of showing where he came from and where he got to as a man and as a musician. Also, next year we're planning on releasing a boxed set of 30 years of Jamaican music to coincide with the thirtieth anniversary of Jamaican independence. First we're celebrating Bob Marley, and then we're celebrating the land he came from. That sequence seems appropriate, really, 'cause Bob has always been ahead of his time.

6

Wailing: The Musicians He Left Behind

I s it some sort of curse on the remaining Wailers, or is it just the prevailing atmosphere in Kingston that has seen three of the former members of the band—Peter Tosh, Carlton Barrett, and Junior Brathwaite—gunned down? Or both Marley and his manager dying relatively young of natural causes?

For those who survive—his children, his wife, his former bandmates—Bob Marley has become a cottage industry, perhaps the greatest Jamaican export outside of bauxite and tourism (and depending on the prevailing social conditions, the latter is iffy).

The Wailers continue to tour with most of the original musicians—New Jersey native Al Anderson, Earl Lindo, "Family Man" Barrett, Junior Marvin, and Secco Patterson (as Coxsone Dodd points out, the guy who started it all). They also continue to record, albeit with no original Wailers. They are something of a duppy band, with the ghosts of Marley, Junior Braithwaite, Carlton Barrett, and Peter Tosh lingering nearby.

Then there are artists like noted sideman Dean Fraser, whose *Dean Plays Bob* may be his most successful solo album. Or the I-Threes—Marcia Griffiths, Judy Mowatt, and, of course, Rita Marley—all of whom have moved on to relatively successful solo careers, and all of whom continue to sing Bob Marley songs.

Even the rogue Wailer, Bunny, will sing a Marley song every now and again when he can be brought out of the bush to tour. He's even recorded several tributes to his fallen bandmate and entire albums of Bob Marley songs. And his music has remained remarkably vital, as has Rita's, Griffiths's, Mowatt's, and even the Wailers'. It happens when you're touched by magic.

A Good Smoke with Peter Tosh

by Stephen Davis
(Source: **Oui,** *1979)*

JAMAICANS look to Peter Tosh for uncompromising Rastafarian preaching and for moral authority undented by the lead-tipped clubs of the police. Wherever he goes in this world, Tosh brings that righteous aura along with him. At some concerts, steel manacles hang from Peter's left wrist, symbolic of the social chains that bind a suffering people back home. In Toronto, a reviewer said that watching a Peter Tosh show was like staring the entire black race dead in the face.

After leaving the Wailers in 1974, Tosh recorded the pro-ganja anthem "Legalize It" and the anti-cop polemic "Mark of the Beast," as well as *Legalize It* and *Equal Rights*, two crucial albums in the development of reggae from local ricky-tick into a planetary sound. But the turning point in Tosh's career was the so-called "Peace Concert" held in Kingston in 1978, at which Jamaica's top reggae groups agreed to perform.

Among those attending the show were members of Jamaica's political elite: Prime Minister Michael Manley and his cabinet, the
opposition leaders, and most of Jamaica's parliament and judiciary.
Tosh sauntered onstage with a ganja cigar in his beak and pro-
ceeded to lecture his captive audience for 45 minutes on the evils of
oppression, neocolonialism, and the "shitstem." Pointing a long
black finger at Manley, Tosh harangued the prime minister on the
sufferings of a poor people deprived of human rights and legal marijuana. The crowd of ordinary Jamaicans in the audience, assembled in the bleachers, cheered themselves hoarse. Tosh and the
band then lit into a stinging set that ended pointedly with "Legalize It."

Mick Jagger of the Rolling Stones, who had just signed Tosh to the
band's vanity label, Rolling Stones Records, was at the Peace Concert.
He witnessed Tosh's brilliant folk essay on the Jamaican political
economy and the spellbinding music that Tosh and his band, Word
Sound & Power (propelled by Sly Dunbar on drums and Robbie
Shakespeare on bass) put forth afterward. "I don't want no *peace*,"
Tosh sang. "I want *equal rights and justice!*" Perhaps Jagger also got
that eerie, impossible-to-resist feeling of staring the entire black race
dead in the face while listening to Peter Tosh.

Peter Tosh, Sly and Robbie recorded three important albums for
the Stones' label (*Bush Doctor, Mystic Man, Wanted Dread or Alive*) that
showcased updated versions of Tosh classics ("Soon Come," "I'm the
Toughest") and new avant-garde reggae ideas like "Buck-in-Hamm
Palace" and "Oh Bumba Klaat." With the Stones' support, Peter
Tosh retained his place through the early 1980s as one of the premier
reggae singers of his generation.

This interview took place at the Howard Johnson Motor Inn on
Memorial Drive in Cambridge, Mass., during the first Word Sound &
Power tour in 1979. In the corner of the room, Tosh's omnipresent

"Inicycle" leaned against the wall. Tosh rides the tall unicycle every-where—backstage, while visiting radio stations, down long hotel cor-ridors at four in the morning. The Inicycle has been all over the world with Tosh and seems emblematic of its owner's stance in a dangerous world: precarious yet balanced, eccentric, uniquely upright. During the interview, Winston Hubert MacIntosh manhandled and drew upon an impressive cone-shaped spliff. *SSSSwwwwwfffffittttttt*!!!!

Stephen Davis

❁ ❁ ❁

STEPHEN DAVIS: It must be difficult for a touring reggae band to maintain its herb supply.
TOSH: Well, herb is all over America, mon. You don't have to bring no herb here no more. Ssssswwwwwffftttt. Ahhh.

DAVIS: Is it as good as what you find in Jamaica?
TOSH: No way. Psychologically, you just have to pretend that it is good—pretend that you smoking the best draw—till you reach home, where the best is.

DAVIS: As a connoisseur of herb, what do you prefer?
TOSH: Well, Thai stick not bad. And the Colombian now, the qual-ity varies, but the other day I get a draw of Colombian in Milwaukee. *Exclusive!!* [Ssssswwwwwffftttt.]

DAVIS: In many of your songs, you call for legalizing marijuana. But there's a theory that if Jamaica legalized ganja, the country would be transformed into an outlaw agronomy operating under United Na-tions sanctions . . .

TOSH: Bullshit! (He kisses his teeth bitterly.) Nine out of ten people in Jamaica smoke herb. Everyone an outlaw!

DAVIS: No, I mean the United Nations has these anti-dope statutes . . .

TOSH [FURIOUS]: United Nations *bullshit!* Me nuh wan' hear that argument—dem. Who are them who take counsel against I&I, to see that I&I are separated from I&I culture? He who created the earth created herb for the use of man, seen? If herb was growing in the blood-clot United Nations, you think Jamaica could go tell United Nations what to do? So how come the *bumba ras clot* United Nations dare to come and tell us what to do? Fuck the United Nations! My Father grow herb, and if my Father know what is right, He would have made herb growing in the United blood-clot Nations, not just in Jamaica for I&I who praise him continually.

DAVIS: Why do Jamaican politicians pay so much attention to the music?

TOSH: Well, dem have to listen to what the people say, to know the people's view. Reggae is telling them what's on the people's mind, seen? Because the singers and players of instruments are the prophets of the earth in this time. It was written: Jah say, "*I call upon the singers and players of instruments to tell the word and wake up the slumbering mentality of the people.*" Seen?

DAVIS: What about your political speech at the [1978] Peace Concert?

TOSH: I devoted my time and my energy to making a speech, because sitting before me I saw the prime minister and the whole establishment approximately. So it seemed the right time to say what I had to say as a representative of the people, because irrespective of the

way I would like to live, I still must live within the "shitstem." I've become a victim of the shitstem so many times.

DAVIS: What happened to you after the speech?

TOSH: Three months later, yes, yes, yes! I was waiting for a re-
hearsal outside Aquarius Studio in Half Way Tree [a main Kingston
avenue], waiting for two of my musicians, and I had a little piece of
roach in my hand. A guy come up to me in plain clothes, and grab the
roach out of my hand. So I say him, "Wha' happen?" He didn't say
nothing, so I grab the roach back from him and he start to punch me
up. I say again, "Wha' happen?" and he say I must go *dung-so* ["downtown" in police jargon]. I say, dung-so? Which way you call dung-so?
That's when I realized this was a police attitude, so I opened the roach
and blew out the contents. Well, him didn't like that and start to grab
at me aggressively now—my waist, my shoulder, grabbing me and
tearing off my clothes and t'ing. Then other police come, and push
their guns in my face, and use brute force on me.

DAVIS: Did they know who you were?

TOSH: No. Well, I don't know. But you don't have to know a man
to treat him the way he should be treated. But, because I am humble, and don't wear a jacket and tie, and drive a big Lincoln Conti-
nental or Mercedes-Benz, I don't look exclusively different from the
rest. I look like the *people*, seen? To dem police, here's just another
Rasta to kill. Now, eight-to-ten guys *gang my head*, with batons and
weapons of destruction. Dem close the door, chase away the people,
and gang my head with batons for an hour and a half, until my hand
break trying to fend off the blows. I run to the window, and dem
beat me back with blows. I run to the door, and dem beat me back
with blows. Later, I found out these guys' intention was to *kill me*,

right? What I had to do was, play dead by just lying low. Passive resistance! And I hear dem say, 'Yes, him dead.' But I survived dem, by *intellect*. Yes I.

DAVIS: Why did they pick on you?

TOSH: It was because of my militant act within the society, because I speak out against repression and the shitstem, seen? Yes mon! I know it is a *direct connection*. I have been threatened before in Kingston; the superintendent of customs *drew his gun*, and said he had wanted to kill me for *years*.

DAVIS: Why are militant artists such a threat to Jamaica?

TOSH: Because their works are corruption, and where there's corruption, there must be an eruption. Yu nuh see? *Politricks!* The politician been promising the most good, but dem doing the most dangerous evil. And all the people get is . . . *promises*. A generation come, and a generation go, and *nothing* is accomplished.

DAVIS: What about your relationship with the Rolling Stones?

TOSH: Well, even their name alone is a great input. I see it as a blessing, seen? One of my Father's blessings, because I determination to spread the word. Finding Mick [Jagger] and Keith [Richards] to spread the word, and deal with the music—knowing they not only are *interested* in the music, but love and respect the music—is a great, great blessing.

DAVIS: Is there an affinity between reggae's outlaw roots and the Stones' outlaw image?

TOSH: Well, I see it, and *know* it, so because I see and I know—*who feels it knows it*. Yeah, mon!

DAVIS: Why did you and Mick choose to showcase an old Motown song ("Don't Look Back") on your *Bush Doctor* album, instead of one of your more militant songs?

TOSH: Well, that is a psychological procedure, because I am a scientist, seen? 'Cause I am a man who has studied human psychology, and knows what *two-thirds of the world* loves, seen? If you are trying to get across to two-thirds of the world, you proceed—psychologically—by giving them what they want. After they dance to what they want, they must listen to what you got next, seen? And also, I like the title—"Don't Look Back"—because I don't intend to.

DAVIS: Why does preaching play such a strong role in reggae, especially in your music?

TOSH: Well, mon, that is coming from my Father's message chamber, seen? I preach, yes mon, but I do not judge. No man is here to look upon what another man is doing. "Judge not, lest ye be judged." I say, make sure your doings are right, so that when the payday comes around, what you get in your envelope will be satisfactory. You nuh seen?

DAVIS: Why have so many cultural explosions—reggae, Rastas, ganja—come from Jamaica?

TOSH: Because we are the prophets of this Earth. We are they who were executed by Alexander the blood-clot Great and those great pirates who used to go round and chop off the saints' heads. All these things are revealed between the lines, through the Third Eye. I&I see ourselves as the reincarnated souls of those carried off into slavery.

DAVIS: Are you suprised by the dramatic acceptance of reggae over the last few years?

TOSH: It was prophesied, my brother. Only fools are surprised at the manifestations of prophecy. Seen? Only those who cannot see between the lines will be surprised.

DAVIS: What about the future of reggae?

TOSH: Yes mon. Fifteen years from now, there will be a different dispensation of time. The shitstem will no longer be. All the places that are built upon corruption shall be torn down and shall be no more upon the face of creation. Yes mon! Five years from now will be a different age! Five years from blood clot now—will be *totally different*. No wicked left on the Earth. By 1983, Africa will be free!

Bunny Wailer, Reggae Survivor: Last of Wailers Returns to Reggae Road

by Mitch Potter

(Source: **The Toronto Star,** *August 24, 1990)*

HE is the last living Wailer and, to hear Neville O'Riley Livingstone tell it, he always expected fate would treat him so.

For Livingstone—better known for the last two decades as Bunny Wailer—there is something almost prophetic about having outlasted Bob Marley and Peter Tosh, the vocal partners with whom he rode reggae music from the government yards of Trenchtown, Jamaica, to international stardom in the early 1970s.

Now 43, the diminutive singer has passed a full 17 years since taking his leave from those original Wailers for largely unexplained reasons, at a critical moment when Marley and band were in the process of becoming World Music's first serious incursion into the realm of Western pop.

Time has been kinder to Marley, whose legend as a musical flashpoint against global oppression has grown exponentially since he died of melanomic cancer in 1981.

Tosh, too, aggressively sought and achieved solo fame with his own strident reggae spin before being gunned down by a gang of motorcycle bandits at his Kingston, Jamaica, home in 1987.

But if Wailer's ensuing work has amounted to something of a footnote to that of his more celebrated colleagues, it is a footnote of considerable and consistent influence.

Named one of the three most important musicians in the Third World by *Newsweek* magazine shortly after Marley's death (Brazil's Milton Nascimento and Nigeria's King Sunny Ade shared the honors), Wailer's post-Marley music, if sporadic, has held firmly to the same moral high ground from whence the socially conscious group came.

Interestingly, Bunny Wailer's own songs of freedom are ringing loudly these days; louder, some would argue, than the music's heir-apparent Ziggy Marley, the eldest of Marley's sons, who has himself been groomed by Virgin Records to resuscitate reggae's waning influence over Western pop.

Last year—following a stunning headline set at Jamaica's 1987 Reggae Sunsplash festival that by all accounts stole much of Ziggy's thunder—the reclusive Wailer galvanized his audience with a new album, *Liberation*.

The release was hailed as an uncompromising return to roots-conscious reggae, anchored by lyrics that foretold eerily of such events as the tumbling Berlin Wall and the release of jailed African National Congress leader Nelson Mandela.

A rare live airing of the singer's music will be available tomorrow night at Toronto's Varsity Arena, as Wailer delivers his first-ever concert in Canada, complete with a 22-piece "Reggaestra".

During a press conference this week at the Bam Boo club and earlier, in a telephone interview from Jamaica, Wailer reaffirmed a pledge to make his "long overdue" Canadian debut "something greater than tongue can tell."

All of Wailer's words, it should be noted, come couched in the rhetoric of Rastafari, the Jamaican movement that recognizes the late Ethiopian emperor Haile Selassie as the black messiah, but delivers its Word in elliptical patois that will regularly confound the linear Western mind.

Asked if he lives in Kingston, for example, Wailer responds with booming portent, "I live inside of myself . . . anywhere."

Asked if he has ever been to Africa, his answer is an elusive "I am Africa."

Wailer speaks more directly to the reasons for his renewed interest in performance, after so many years of hermitic living.

"I believe that the one who lives longest will see the most, and tell the most, and now is my time.

"I see that every nation is struggling for liberation of some sort.

"We saw the wall of Berlin fall, we saw Mandela freed, we see apartheid being dismantled, we see ladies struggling for liberation from abortion, from the instruments of destruction that take away their purpose for being here.

"There is an international liberation going on, and we've come too far to turn back now."

Born in the country village of Nine Miles, St. Ann's Parish (province), Wailer and Bob Marley were casual pals almost from the time they could walk.

Their friendship flourished—and took on a musical dimension—in the early '60s when the pair moved with their parents to the impoverished government housing project Trenchtown, a squatter settlement on the western outskirts of Kingston.

By 1964, as Jamaican pop music was slowing down from the clipped rhythms of ska to rock-steady (straight 4/4 time, with percussive emphasis on the second and fourth beats), Wailer and Marley had taken to harmonizing versions of early American R & B hits by groups such as the Drifters, the Moonglows and the Impressions, accompanying themselves on a homemade acoustic guitar.

A lanky third from the Trenchtown yard, Peter Tosh, soon joined the jams, reportedly by virtue of owning a real guitar.

The Wailing Wailers were born, and that year launched the ska single "Simmer Down" as the first in a string of successful but financially unrewarding recordings cut at nearby Studio One, under the tutelage of popular Jamaican deejay Clement "Sir Coxsone" Dodd.

They were a menacing trio, crowned with knit wool tams and fast adapting to the rebellious "rude boy" culture that was sweeping the yard's downtrodden youth population. Three years and one hiatus later (Marley worked briefly on an assembly line in Wilmington, Delaware; Wailer was jailed for possession of marijuana under Jamaica's strict narcotics laws), the group reformed with a new-found interest in Rastafari.

The era gave rise to classic Wailer/Marley collaborations such as "One Love" and "Who Feels It Knows It", while Wailer himself branched out to sing lead on his own songs—"Dreamland", "Dancing Shoes" and even a cover of Bob Dylan's "Like A Rolling Stone".

Today, Wailer will recall only positive vibrations, including the group's standard-setting recordings with producer Lee "Scratch" Perry at the turn of the '70s.

But he bristles at the mention of Island Records' owner Chris Blackwell, with whom the Wailers signed in 1972, setting the stage for the groundbreaking *Catch A Fire* and *Burnin'* albums.

Those records contained such politically charged classics as "Get Up, Stand Up" and "I Shot The Sheriff" (soon to become a world-wide smash via the bluesifying hands of Eric Clapton), paving the way for Marley's pending superstardom.

"I saw destruction ahead," Wailer says tersely, when asked of those troubled days.

"I saw hurt for a lot of people, because the plan was wrong. The direction Blackwell was setting was like taking a fish and putting him in the goddamn oven to survive.

"I was too conscious and aware for that. I was way ahead of their plan.

"A lot of things could have been avoided. If Bob and Peter had taken my direction and gone back home, they'd be here today. Alive.

"The fact that I am here and they are not is proof enough for me. I miss them, but that is what we have today."

When pressed, Wailer won't put specifics to his bizarre innuendo; in any event, the departure of Wailer and Tosh in 1974—they were supplanted by the introduction of the I-Threes (Judy Mowatt, Marcia Griffiths and Marley's wife, Rita) as Marley's new harmony squad—is regarded by many as the end of the Wailers' truest fire.

Says Toronto broadcaster/commentator Milton Blake, host of the weekly Musical Triangle on Toronto campus station CKLN-FM (88.1): "Ultimately, Bunny's reasons for leaving are something only he can explain, but you have to respect the fact that he turned his back on certain fame to stand for his principles."

But Blake, a former radio host with the Jamaican Broadcasting System in the early to mid-'70s, says Wailer's prolonged absence from the spotlight may in itself point to a simpler explanation.

"It's particularly interesting that Bunny has waited so long to return. The fact is that the mystique of the Wailers has long outlived the group itself and, because of it, he could've translated that into megabucks a long time ago.

"Maybe he just wanted to stay in Jamaica."

If it was homesickness that took Wailer home in 1973, he has clearly overcome the sensation in 1990.

The latter-day Wailer, trumped up with confidence, sounds virtually bursting to snatch the grail of reggae he so handily passed on a generation ago.

"It is dangerous to think that reggae is the responsibility of one individual. I don't see it that way. I am just a part of the shoulder that the music rests upon.

"But, as an artist who deals with the prophesies and links with history, I see these things and I have a need to tell them.

"I'm not saying it's supernatural—anyone who follows the same route will arrive at the same conclusion.

"Even Nostradamus didn't prophesize events, he just happened to be paying attention to the signs of his times and he related to it. If you're alert and you study, you will find it."

Wailer's message for now—and the next few years—calls for a continuation of world liberation, where eventually "people will embrace each other for what they are.

"We went through a time of building walls, we went to the limits of hating and destroying each other, so where else can we go but to a point where mankind will be born anew.

"We will tear down and embrace each other for what we are."

Wailer has finished work on two separate album projects, both slated for release on New Jersey-based Shanachie Records. One, *Just Be Nice*, is Wailer's gesture to youth, incorporating hip-hop, R & B/disco, and technology-driven dance patterns.

The other, *Gumption*, he describes as a continuation of the lyrically low-cal dancehall experiments he dabbled in at the turn of the '80s with his *Rock 'N' Groove* LP.

"You can't give children an adult's food—it will hurt them—so instead you must give them lollipops and candy. *Just Be Nice* is very childish, but very educational, and is meant to depict the new generation and what they're into.

"'Gumption,'" Wailer continues, "deals with dance hall because that situation needs direction right now. The reggae dance hall children are in confusion at this time, they don't know where they want to go.

"You have to use their language, but if you do, you can get beyond the formulas and give them something that says more than, 'I love you, baby,' and, 'Darlin' I need you'.

"In this world of market and commerce, it doesn't pay to have one kind of stock. You'll stagnate and be run out of the market.

"On top of reggae music being the Bible of our times, the direction of our times, it has different ranges, different levels. You could go on playing reggae music for years and years and just play hard messages, and then you could play reggae music for another decade and do just lover's rock. Then another decade of hard-core dance hall stuff.

"But in the end, the source is Jah."

Still Wailing; Aston "Family Man" Barrett of the Wailers Is Keeping a Reggae Tradition Alive

by Joshua Green

(Source: Denver Westword, February 19, 1998)

IT'S no exaggeration to say that behind every great reggae band is a great bass player—and the bass player who's been behind more great

reggae bands than practically anyone else is Aston "Family Man" Barrett. His work with the Skatalites, Lee Perry and the Upsetters, Bob
Marley and the Wailers and countless other acts in this bass-driven
genre clearly establishes him as one of reggae's most influential instru-
mentalists. Moreover, the history of his career is in many ways the history of the music. Barrett has been at the heart of everything from the
development of ska to the most recent performances of the Wailers,
which he helped revive a little over a decade ago.

Of course, Barrett is primarily known for the years he spent with
Bob Marley, and that's as it should be; practically no one outside of
Kingston, Jamaica, had heard Marley's name until his vocal trio (fea-
turing Bunny "Wailer" Livingstone and Peter Tosh) hooked up with
Barrett's band. But Barrett claims that this famous team might never
have come together had he been blessed with better pipes.

"That was my first general approach to music—I wanted to
sing," Barrett reveals from his Jamaican home. But his voice,
which, as he laughingly demonstrates, resembles the squawk of a
tortured parrot, was not up to the challenge. "I guess I find that
area of the music taken care of, you know?" he says. "So I take a
different curve."

Before long, Barrett gravitated toward the bass guitar. He taught
himself to play as a child, and by immersing himself in soul, funk
and jazz, he learned how to convey subtle nuances on his ax of
choice. He subsequently formed a makeshift band with his brother
Carlton and friend Max Romeo, who went on to fame as a singer.
"We were just flexin' as youths, just playin' music," he recalls. The
group was so informal, in fact, that it didn't even have a name when
the players were discovered. "There was a manager for a hotel
called the Flamingo that was looking for a resident band to play
there in the times that they got tourists in and things like that,"

Barrett explains. "Someone who worked there was passing by and heard us rehearsing and come in and look at us and say, 'Look dem youth. Dem look like musicians, not bad boys. Just different; down to earth.' He liked the way we sound. He say we sound the way we look."

This talent scout arranged an audition, and for the tryout, the three nascent performers chose to play the ska music that was then all the rage. Their efforts went so well that they were hired immediately—as long as they came up with a suitable moniker, that is. Fortunately, the hotel manager came to the rescue. "The manager see how we look and hear us play and she say, 'You guys remind me of the hippies.' So we ended up being the Hippie Boys."

The appellation wasn't chosen at random. Since most of the tourists who vacationed in Jamaica during the early Sixties were from the United States, the musicians who played the circuit did whatever they could to Americanize themselves. Ska helped them do so: it was derived from the so-called Jamaican boogie of the late Fifties, but it caught on with U.S. visitors because of its kinship with jazz and swing music.

Unfortunately for the Hippie Boys, Jamaica's tourist industry began to dry up after the country won its independence, in 1962. But around the same time, an indigenous recording industry sprang up to provide other employment opportunities. Barrett and company quickly became session men working under some of the island's premier producers.

"We do a lot of session gigs in the studio for Lee Perry, who was another kind of revolutionary-type people, and him love the sound that he hear from us," Barrett notes. "We work with Bruce Ruffing, Derrick Morgan, Burning Spear, Justin Hines, Delroy Wilson, John Holt, Slim Smith of the Uniques, and many, many others."

In those days, producers tried to set themselves apart from their competitors via studio bands that worked for them exclusively. Barrett, however, didn't want to limit himself to performing for only one label, so he came up with a plan to rechristen his combo for every new producer who hired it. "For Perry, we called ourselves the Upsetters," he says. "For Joe Gibbs, we added a singer and called ourselves the Reggae Boys. The last name that we work under before we join with the Wailers was called Youths Professional, because I figured that is what we are. So we had some distinguished names, I tell you."

Barrett's scheme came to an end—not because he ran out of good handles, but because the band landed a gig so good that it didn't need any others. Perry, whose relatively diminutive stature stood in direct contrast to his power as a star maker, paired his foremost vocal group, the Wailers, with the Upsetters, and the combination became an immediate smash. After scoring with blockbusters like "The Return of Django," Barrett says, "we decided to swing with the small guy."

The unprecedented global success of the Wailers/Upsetters teaming had a lot to do with Marley's obvious, well-documented talents, but Perry's foresight and Barrett's bass prowess should not be overlooked. Because Perry recognized that Marley, Livingstone, and Tosh would need a self-contained band in order to court success abroad, he encouraged the Upsetters to become full-fledged Wailers. In addition, he recognized that reggae's sound was mutating in the face of influences such as Rastafarianism—and thanks to Barrett, he found a sound that symbolized this seismic shift. The bass hadn't been an important part of the Jamaican sound, but Perry boldly axed the horns and pianos that dominated ska and moved Barrett's sinister playing to the forefront. The result was spectacular and lastingly influential. To this day, ominous bass lines are reggae's hallmark—and Barrett's were the first and the finest. Barrett puts it simply: "Everything started out right at Lee Perry's table."

But if Perry, a recent Westword profile subject ("Learning From Scratch," November 6, 1997), deserves much of the credit for the bass-heavy revamping that marks classic Wailers albums like African Herbsman and Soul Rebels, Barrett confirms that the driving force behind them was Marley. He portrays Marley, now thought of as a musical deity, in very human terms. "He was a regular, ordinary guy doing some extraordinary work," he says. But even Barrett admits to being awed by the man. "You can feel a vibration with him, feel it coming out. You can see how the people are reacting in the audience. Like in the early years in London, they write upon us and said our first number cause a spell, and then after that it was like magic. I tell you, that was the best way you could express it. I never forget that because it's true."

Tosh and Livingstone left the Wailers to pursue solo careers in 1974, but Barrett stuck with Marley. It turned out to be a good move: The outfit, dubbed Bob Marley and the Wailers, became more popular than ever upon the release of several platters that Barrett refers to as "the international series": *Natty Dread*, *Exodus*, *Uprising* and *Kaya*. With the support of a new label, Island Records, the Wailers introduced reggae to the world.

Recording and touring with Marley filled most of Barrett's days, but he still managed to appear on many of the era's biggest reggae hits by other artists. "In my spare time, I managed to do a couple things, like Bunny Wailer's first, *Blackheart Man*," he says. "Also Peter Tosh's first album, *Legalize It*. And I support Burning Spear on *Social Living*." Barrett appeared on countless lesser albums, too—so many that even he can't remember them all.

Things changed for the worse in 1981, when Marley died of cancer. A creative vacuum followed: Without Marley to lead the way, reggae lacked a clear direction. Today Barrett puts a positive spin on this difficult period. "A good thing doesn't last forever," he philosophizes. "But within the work, there's a message, a consciousness, that we can still bring forth."

Five years later, Barrett realized that the best way to keep Marley's flame burning was to reform the Wailers, with keyboardist Junior Marvin as the new frontman. The idea, he insists, was Marley's own: "He tell us to do it. And that's what I am gifted for; that's what I am destined for. Him say, 'When one door is closed, many more is opened.'" Money was also a factor, he acknowledges. "It's business, too. After Bob pass, everybody was doing their little different shows. I was moving around with some of the local groups. So we discuss and say, 'Why don't we take a vacation, play some music with all expenses taken care of, and have a pack of money and get ourselves back together?'"

The group toured quite happily until two years ago when, Barrett says, "Junior Marvin got carried away with certain business aspects and run off to Brazil." On the surface, Marvin's replacement—a 23-year-old Israeli-born UCLA student named Elan—seems unlikely, but Barrett thinks otherwise. He calls Elan "spiritual—like a Sabbath man," adding, "Some people listen and them say, 'Are you sure he's not one of Bob's kids you didn't know about?'

"Jah Rastafari is one person; same person, different name," he continues. "Him move in a mysterious form. Even Bob's father was a white man. So you see the lineage Bob came through and you know Jah work in a mysterious way."

But without Marley, can the Wailers still be regarded as reggae's top act? Barrett puts forth a convincing argument in favor of this viewpoint. "Every reggae band out there has to play Bob Marley and the Wailers' songs, you know?" he says. "Even just one. And no one plays them like the Wailers does, 'cause we're the ones who create and inspire them. They're the only thing that lasts forever."

The Wailers' Al Anderson

by Klaus Ludes

(Source: **Classical Reggae Interviews,** *May 29, 1998)*

How Could This Music Grow So Big?

KLAUS LUDES: The music of Bob Marley and the Wailers is well-known all over the world. What is the reason for that?

AL ANDERSON: Bob! You know, Bob. It was his plan, you know. He basically wanted to take it away from just Jamaica and to pass it to other places where people could accept the music that he was representing.

LUDES: In a documentary film we hear him say: "I DON'T COME TO BOW I COME TO CONQUER. . . "

ANDERSON: Yeah, yeah, that was like a lot of people wanted to take his songs and they wanted him to be a pop star and they wanted him to be what he didn't want to be as an artist and he stuck to his guns and did it his way, you know.

He was always talking about wailing and that meant the suffering. He made a point that he was still a sufferer although he was financially a lot better conditioned than others. He was still a subject of prejudice and tyranny of the government!

Bob Marley As a Politician?

LUDES: I remember the One Love Peace Concert in 1978.

ANDERSON: Oh yeah, it was great. (. . .) It was cool.

LUDES: I have it on video.

ANDERSON: Really!?

LUDES: It was strong, strong. What did you feel when Bob Marley took Prime Minister Manley and the other opposition leader together on stage and made them shake hands . . .

ANDERSON: I thought he was really brave. Yeah, it was a very honorable thing he did. Because maybe they'd never even touched hands for maybe years, you know!

It was a real tough time for politics then and Bob was trying to change order. I think that if he'd had enough time that he could have run for an office and held a respectable place in politics in Jamaica, which would have been great for the government, because then Rasta would have had, like, a representative. They could see their views and understand them and change the laws of, like, maybe, legalization of herb or decriminalizing it. There's a lot of things that he could have been responsible for if he had just a little bit more time.

War and Composing

LUDES: Ras Tafari delivered a speech at the United Nations Organization in 1968 in California. This speech was put into the song "War." ("Until the philosophy which holds one race superior and another inferior . . . ")

ANDERSON: I think it was a great idea that Skill brought to Bob's attention that the lyrical content was so powerful that it could be put into a song and he did. He just arranged it the way he wanted to have it heard.

LUDES: So the chords of the song were made by Bob Marley?

ANDERSON: It was made by the band, pretty much, yeah, and Bob, with Bob's direction, yeah.

LUDES: Most of the songs were composed by Bob Marley?

ANDERSON: Let's say like 70% of it was. Bob would write the songs and the band would write the music. A lot of times we would change chords and play other rhythms that he wasn't aware of, that was gonna be in the song.

He had the song idea and we would hear the song collectively and change it and make it as best as it could possibly be and he was with the best.

Redemption Song

LUDES: Can you remember the time when Bob Marley composed "Redemption Song"?

ANDERSON: We were touring a lot in California these days. I think Wia Lindo had a lot to do with that song, you know. He wrote a lot of lyrics to give Bob the completion of that song.

And he also composed with him the several live segments you can see on tapes where Wia is with him playing guitar, you know. Bob was very accepting of anything that sounded outstanding, lyrically, you know. And he would incorporate it into his own song writing and songs.

LUDES: Do you know why Bunny Wailer (Bunny Livingstone) and Peter Tosh left the band?

ANDERSON: I think they just wanted to have an opportunity to see how far they would go by themselves. But Bob's records are still selling more so than Peter's and Bunny's are, you know. Unfortunately I mean, but this is the way it is.

The first two records that they all did as solo records were classics! All of them, you know! And so together they are great songwriters apart they are still great songwriters and musicians.

They just needed to take a break from each other, I think, musically. I think they were all gonna come back together eventually. It's just one of those things that goes around, you know, like you leave off and then you come back.

The Wailers' Earl "Wia" Lindo

by Klaus Ludes

(Source: Classical Reggae Interviews, May 29, 1998)

Bob Has Gone on Higher

KLAUS LUDES: It's still hard for you that Bob Marley is not with the band . . .

EARL "WIA" LINDO: Yeah, that he has passed and GONE ON HIGHER, *(laughing very seriously)* that's the way I think of it, you know.

Myself and Tyrone, I think, Tyrone and myself, we were very deeply afflicted by everything, the whole karma of everything. It's a very traumatic thing, because it seems just in the prime of our youth when we were looking to take over the world, you know. We were on the edge of taking over the world like we were going into a new dimension.

But spiritually I know that we would not be shaken from our spiritual position with God, with Rastafari.

The Father knows who are the Chosen Ones and who he has chosen to be with him and to be on his right hand side of God, you know. So no event on earth can shake us from that!

How Bob Composed

LUDES: What's the reason why the Bob Marley and the Wailers music is so impressive?

LINDO: Because when we write we write from a kind of high universal kind of plain of ideas, you know. From a high platonic plain of ideas.

We are like—we can feel—you know, you get that universal consciousness, you can feel the whole world in your consciousness, mind.

I think, Bob is very gifted that way, you know what I mean. Even when we feel like we are equally as high as he is it's like, you know, *(looking down on the ground)* it's like he is just looking down here like that, still!

It seems I'm always there when the ideas, when Bob has his ideas, you know when, *(getting excited)* like a brainstorm, when he gets that brainstorm idea: BOOM!!! Like that, you know. I always happen to be there.

LUDES: Where did Bob compose? In the studio or at home . . . ?

LINDO: On the road. On the road a lot. A lot of compositions, like: *men see their dreams and aspirations crumble in front of their face and all their wicked intentions to destroy the human race* (from "Chant down Babylon"). You know them kind of lyrics. I heard him compose that in Brussels!

Redemption Song

LUDES: The last song that Bob Marley composed was 'Redemption Song'. Redemption Song does not have roots reggae rhythm. But to me it is the most impressive song. How could he write such powerful lyrics and music?

LINDO: There's ideas in our minds, you know, like the magnetism in the atmosphere. We had that and it was going on and it was very strong.

LUDES: And did he compose it in the studio . . . ?

LINDO: No, when we were on the road.

LUDES: Really!?

LINDO: Yes. I think it was in Stuttgart. One Love Peace Concert in 1978.

LUDES: When you watch the video of the One Love Peace Concert in 1978 you see many performances of many musicians, but the performance of Bob Marley and the Wailers was outstanding, historical.

LINDO: We wanted to prove we are harder than that! Like we are trying to prove that we are harder than that! We are just a harder thing than just making commercial success, you know what I mean!? We can chart nyabinghi, you know!

No other group could do that, I don't think. They couldn't do that. Because they were too materially focused. They didn't . . . their perception of the mind was limited. So, that's why that was such—how you call it—"historical."

Wailers Keep Spreading Marley's Message

by Craig MacInnes

(Source: Toronto Star, February 20, 1987)

THE date is permanently etched on Junior Marvin's mind.

"Jan. 14, 1977—that was the day I joined The Wailers. I'll never forget it, what it meant to me to be playing with Bob Marley."

The late reggae giant, who died of brain cancer in 1981, remains a national hero in his native Jamaica. Internationally, his records still sell in the hundreds of thousands, and his songs of rebellion and faith are regarded as anthems of the genre.

And though reggae music has soldiered on since his death, no single performer has emerged to carry on Marley's visionary quest.

And so it is left to Marvin and other veteran Wailers (drummer Carlton Barrett, bassist Aston Barrett, percussionist "Secco" Patterson, keyboardist "Wia" Lindo, guitarist Al Anderson and new rhythm guitarist Owen Reid) to continue the cause.

Marvin, who sings and plays lead guitar, is the first to admit the impossibility of living up to his former leader's reputation.

"There's no one who could ever fill Bob's shoes," he says. "But for me, it's done out of respect and love for Bob, which is something I felt before I even joined the band."

Originally from Jamaica, Marvin was educated in England and later went to the States, where he joined bluesman T-Bone Walker's group. He also did session work with Billy Preston and Ike & Tina Turner.

"When I finally met Bob, he was looking for someone with different styles of music who could help reggae develop and reach more people. He thought there were touches of Hendrix in my playing."

Marley's missionary zeal in promoting reggae to new audiences is still being felt on this tour, says Marvin.

"Marley and the Wailers went to New Zealand in 1979 and planted a few seeds. Now, his music has laid down roots there with young people who never saw him but found out about his music from others.

"The crowds were huge."

The current Wailers devote more than half their 90-minute show to Marley standards, mainly culled from his late '70s albums, *Exodus* and *Rastaman Vibration*.

"We helped him write a lot of those songs, so we feel almost a part of them," says Marvin.

For years, the Wailers' recording rights and royalty claims were tied up in litigation as claimants to the Marley legacy fought bitterly over control.

"We stayed together even though a lot of people tried to tear us apart," says Marvin. "The lawyers wanted us to just be a backing band for (Marley's wife and reggae singer) Rita Marley. I guess she was influenced a lot by her lawyers and a lot of bad moves were made."

The Wailers have won the right to tour again and record under their own name, with an album tentatively set for release this spring. Some of the tracks will be recorded when the group is in Toronto next week.

Marvin says the band has also launched an $11-million suit for lost royalties.

"But the money isn't the big issue. Whether we're making money or not, we just want to be back on the road and keep the musical foundation as strong as Bob left it."

CREDITS

"Remembering Bob Marley" by Rita Marley. Copyright © 1995 Rita Marley; "Cedella Marley Launches a Distinctive Line of Customized Denim and Leather Reminiscent of Her Father's Rude Boy Style." Copyright © 2001 Catch A Fire; "Marley: Tale of the Tuff Gong (excerpt)" by Charles Hall, Mort Todd, Gene Colan, Tennyson Smith, and John Costanza. Copyright © 1994 Bob Marley Music. All reprinted by permission of Bob Marley Music/M+ Management.

"Bob Marley: The Story Behind *Chances Are*." Reprinted courtesy of Atlantic Records.

"I Was a Wailers" by Lee Jaffe. Copyright © 2002 Lee Jaffe. Reprinted by permission of the author.

"Bob Marley Is the Jagger of Reggae" by Patrick Carr. Copyright © 1975 Patrick Carr. Reprinted by permission of the author.

"Musicmakers: Bob Marley and the Wailers," by Vernon Gibbs. Copyright © 1976.

"Innocents in Babylon: A Search for Jamaica Featuring Bob Marley and a Cast of Thousands" by Lester Bangs. From CREEM July 1976. Used with permission of CREEM Media, Inc. Copyright 1976/2004. CREEMMagazine.com

"The Rasta Prophet of Reggae Music Speaks" by Thomas Terrell. Copyright © 2000 Thomas Terrell. Reprinted by permission of the author.

INDEX

Ace, Johnny, 91
Ade, King Sunny, 280
Aerosmith, xii
Africa
  tour of, 203
"Africa Unite," 125–126, 202
African Herbsman, 167
Aftermath (the Rolling Stones), 70
Aitken, Laurel, 261
Allman, Duane, 81
Alpha Blondy, 211
Alphonso, Roland, 8, 9
"Ambush in The Night," 202
Anchor Recording Company, 213
"And I Love Her," 118
Anderson, Al, 35, 169, 271, 297
  on politics, 291–292
  on "Redemption Song," 293–294
  on reggae, 291
  on war, 292–293
Anderson, Esther, 19, 27–28
Anderson, Rita. *See* Marley, Rita
Antigua Steel Band, 261
Apollo Theatre, 144
  gigs at, 126
Aquarius Records, 54
Aquarius Studio, 276
Armstrong, Louis, xvi
Atlantic Records, 263, 264

Babylon By Bus, 268
"Babylon System," 152
Bacharach, Burt, 70
Back-O-Wall, 148
Back to Africa movement, 47
Bacon, William, 175

Baez, Joan, 81
Bam Boo Club, 281
Bangs, Lester
  Blackwell, Chris, and, 69–70, 73
  at Harry J's Studio, 86–87
  Perry, Lee "Scratch," and, 71
Barrett, Aston. *See* Family Man
Barrett, Carly, 167, 271, 286, 297
Basie, Count, 257
Bauxite, 45
BBC. *See* British Broadcasting Company
The Beatles, 240
"Bend Down Low," 15, 166
Bertolucci, Bernardo, 29
Best of The Wailers, 266
"Better Must Come," 99
Beverleys, 13
Bible, 64, 104–105, 127, 135, 153
  Marley, Bob, on, 109
Big Youth, 55, 70
  innovations of, 212
Bingham, J. Reid, 189
"Bionic Dread" (Dillinger), 121
Birth, 13, 101, 164
The Birth Of A Legend 1963–1966
  legal issues surrounding, 193–197
Bishop, Maurice
  on destabilization, 171–172
Black Music Association, 127
Black Uhuru, 139, 241
Black Woman (Judy Mowatt), 130
Blackheart Man (Bunny Wailer), 289
Blackwell, Chris, 20, 50, 60–61, 103,
  106–107, 180
  background of, 103
  Bangs, Lester, and, 69–70, 73

on "Buffalo Soldier," 140
Byles, Louis, and, 186
as engineer, 257
on estate affairs, 184–185, 188, 191
founding Island Records, 259–260
on legal struggles, 182–183
Livingston, Bunny, on, 283
on Marley, Bob, 140
in music business, 56
parents of, 65
role of, 91, 168
on Stateside music industry, 261
the Wailers and, 266
Blades, Ruben, 216
Blake, Milton, 283
Blue beat, 261
  origins of, 209
Blue Note Records, 263
Blues, 218
  defining, 218
BMW, 62–63
Bob Marley Museum, 205
Bogle, Paul, 142
Bongiovi, Tony, 9
Bongo
  on Marley's death, 143
Bongo-U
  on political systems, 153
  on Rastafarianism, 146
  on violence, 147–148
"Boogie In My Bones," 261
Booker, Cedella (mother), 3, 14, 142
  in estate affairs, 189
  lawsuits against, 198
  on Marley's death, 155
Booker, Richard, 233
  lawsuits against, 198
Booker T. and the MG's, 165
Boot, Adrian, 14
Boothe, Ken, 209
Bossa nova, 100
Boyne, Ian, 178
Bragga
  on tourism, 215
Braithwaite, Junior, 165–166
Brando, Marlon, 29
Brathwaite, Junior, 7, 13, 271
Breakspeare, Cindy, 234
Breakspeare, Damian, 187
  work of, 235–236
Brigadier Jerry, 139

British Broadcasting Company (BBC), 177
British Homophone, 262–263
Brown, James, 41, 164
"Buck-in-Hamm Palace" (Peter Tosh), 273
"Buffalo Soldier"
  Blackwell, Chris, on, 140
Burnin', 103, 168, 208, 282
"Burnin' and Lootin' ," 99, 206, 259
Burning Spear, 65, 66, 74, 76, 78, 83, 287
Bush Doctor (Peter Tosh), 273, 278
Buster, Prince, 261, 262
Butler, Michael, 73
Byles, Louis J., 181, 182–183
  Blackwell, Chris, and, 186
  on MCA, 186–187

Calla Records, 195
Calypso, 101
  defining, 218
  sales of, 261
Campbell, George, 223
Campbell, Mickey, 117
Cancer, 141, 175
Capaldi, Jim, 19–20
Capitalism, 100
Carib Theatre
  gigs at, 34–35
Cars, 62–63
Carter, Mick, 225
  on Rufaro Stadium, 227
Castro, Fidel, 52
  Manley, Michael, and, 100
Catch a Fire, 18, 20, 31, 103, 168, 208, 256,
    282
  sales of, 267
Catch A Fire (clothing company), 236–238
Cater, Mick, 111
Cayman Music, 190
  the Wailers and, 192
CBS International, 15, 16, 196
  reggae and, 61
Central Park
  gigs in, 37–38
Chances Are, 13, 14, 15–16
"Chances Are," 17
Chant Down Babylon, 177
Charles, Prince, 228
CIA, 106, 136–137, 141
  files of, 173
  machinations of, 172
Clapton, Eric, 19, 67, 283

"I Shot the Sheriff" covered by, 38, 103–104, 145
Clarke, Gussie, 213
Cliff, Jimmy, 13, 19, 41, 44, 92, 176, 201, 257, 265
  stage show of, 37
Cocaine
  marijuana and, 213
Colby, Carl, 174
Colby, William, 174
Cole, Alan "Skill," 205
Cole, Nat King, 101
Cole, Skill, 35
Columbia Records, 31, 32
Columbus, Christopher, 48
Comic books, 246–253
"Comin' In From the Cold," 126, 162, 241
"Comma, Comma," 15
Communism, 203
Conally, Michael, 175
"Concrete Jungle," 99, 215, 266
Confrontation, 139, 140
Conquering Lion (the Prophets), 69
Cook Records, 261
Cooke, Sam, 41
Cooper, Phil, 227
Cortillion Records, 13
"Could You Be Loved," 16, 241
Country Man, 65
"Craven Choke Puppy," 270
"Crazy Baldhead," 140
  lyrics of, 146
Cross of Fire, 31

"Dance Do The Reggae," 17
Dance hall, 212
  Blackwell, Chris, on, 269–270
  Livingston, Bunny, on, 285
"Dancing Shoes," 282
Dannen, Fredric, 195
"Darling Patricia" (Owen Grey), 263
Davis, Stephen, 57, 59, 78, 84–85, 162–163
Dean Plays Bob (Dean Fraser), 271
Death, 141
  conspiracy and, 141, 143
  Dodd, Coxsone, on, 11–12
Dekker, Desmond, 13, 50, 209, 258
Delaware
  Marley, Rita, in, 4
Denny, Martin, 67

Destiny's Child, 237
Diamond, Neil, 52
Diddley, Bo, 164
Dillon, Clifton "Specialist," 233
Discos
  in Jamaica, 74–75
"Do the Reggay" (Toots and the Maytalls), 103
Doctor No (movie), 263
Dodd, Coxsone, 3, 118, 165, 254, 262, 264, 270, 282
  on death, 11–12
  on guitars, 8
  on marriage, 11
  McCalla, Nate, and, 195
  production of, 193
  at Studio One, 194–195
  Studio One and, 6–7
Domino, Fats, 101, 209, 264
Donovan, 269
"Don't Look Back," 278
Downie, Tyrone, 92
  on America, 108–109
Dread in a Babylon (U Roy), 70
Dreadlocks
  Marley, Bob, on, 133–134
"Dreamland," 282
The Drifters, 31, 91, 101
Drummond, Don, 8, 219
Dub, 55, 70–71
Dubois, W.E.B., 124–125
Dunbar, Sly, 273
"Duppy Conqueror," 150, 257, 259
Dylan, Bob, xvi, 31, 47, 61, 203

Eek-A-Mouse, 139
Ellis, Alton, 209
Embalming
  of Marley, Bob, 155
Emerson Lake & Palmer, 265
EMI, 130
The Emperor (Kapuscinski), 207
Equal Rights (Peter Tosh), 272
Esquire Records, 261
Estate affairs
  on Blackwell, Chris, 184–185, 188, 191
  Booker, Cedella, in, 189
  Hylton, Michael, in, 191, 192
  Island Logic in, 185
  Marley, Rita, in, 184–185
  Marley, Ziggy, in, 183

Ortner, Charles, in, 190
  Security Merchant Bank in, 186
  U.K. Privy Council in, 185, 189–190
  Walker, Clawrence, in, 190–191
Eve, 237
Exodus, 97, 118, 169, 297
  as Album of the Century, 177
  goals of, 268
  recording of, 267
"Exodus," xix, 240
  mixing, 122
  Rastafarians on, 108

Family Man (Aston Barrett), 92, 110, 119,
    227, 271, 297
  on Africa, 229
  on bass guitar, 286–287
  bass playing of, 257
  name of, 120
  Perry, Lee "Scratch," and, 287–288
  in the Wailers, 290
Federal Records, 8, 262
Fergusson, Isaac, 176
Flavin, Dan, 31
Foundation, 269
Fraser, Dean, 271

Gad, Vernon Carrington
  on Twelve Tribes organization, 149
Gandhi, Indira, 228
Ganette Mander Restaurant, 131
Ganja. *See* Marijuana
Garcia, Jerry, 81
Garrick, Neville, 112, 114, 173, 227
  artwork of, 211
  on Marley, Bob, 212
Garvey, Marcus, 47, 94, 123, 146
  Marley, Bob, on, 133
  philosophy of, 104, 124
  Rastafarianism and, 201–202
  on Selassie, Haile, 207–208
Gaty, Andrew
  lawsuits filed by, 197
Gaye, Angus, 121
Gaye, Marvin, 139
  concert with, 33–36
"Get Up. Stand Up.", 38, 259, 283
Gibbs, Joe, 288
Gilly, 112
"Give Thanks," 139

Glasspole, Florizel
  at Marley's funeral, 158
The Gleaner, 2
"Glory Dawn" (Ras Michael), 80
Goldman, Vivien, 14
The Good, the Bad and the Ugly
  theme song of, 102
Grammys
  reggae in, 235
Great Depression, 124
Greene Street Recording Studios, 20
Grey, Owen, 262–263
Griffiths, Marcia, 271, 283
  in Bob Marley and the Wailers, 89
  on Marley's death, 142
  touring with, 113
Grounations, 75–76
  Hayes, Tom, at, 82–83
  Simon, Peter, at, 81, 84
"Guava Jelly," 15, 103, 145, 167, 270
Gumption (Bunny Wailer), 284
Gun Court
  of Manley regime, 87

Hair (musical), 73
Halfway Tree, 234
Hammond, John, 31
Hansa, 130
Harambe (Rita Marley), 142
The Harder They Come, 20, 58, 92, 209,
    256–257
  impact of, 49–50
"The Harder They Come," 19
Harry J's studio, 69, 85–86, 266
  Bangs, Lester, at, 86–87
Harvard Stadium
  gigs at, 152
Harvey, Bernard "Touter," 169
Hayes, Tom, 76, 78
  at Grounation, 82–83
Healey, Jack, xvi
"Heathen," 117
Hendrix, Jimi, 20
Henzell, Perry, 49–50
The Heptones, 86, 209
Herb. *See* Marijuana
"Hey Jude," 52
Hibbert, Toots, 103, 258
Higgs, Joe, 91
Hill, Lauryn, 232, 233

Hines, Delroy, 66
Hines, Justin, 287
Hip-hop, 20
Hippie Boys, 287
Hit Men (Dannen), 195
Holloway, Danny, 87–88
Holt, John, 287
Hooliganism, 2
House of Blues, 233
Hylton, Michael, 184, 186, 191
  in estate affairs, 191, 192
Hynde, Chrissie, 130

I-One, 156
I Roy, 55, 56
"I Shot the Sheriff," 19, 43, 99, 113, 256, 283
  Clapton, Eric, covering, 38, 103, 145
  writing of, 30
I Threes, 11, 37–38, 97, 130, 142, 271, 283
  formation of, 168
  touring with, 113
"If The Cap Fits," 139
"(I'm) Hurting Inside," 17
"I'm Still Waiting," 13
"I'm the Toughest," 149, 273
Imperial Records, 264
"In Zion" (Ras Michael), 80
"Independent Jamaica" (Kentrick "Lord Creator Patrick), 263
Inez, 112
Inner Circle, 233, 234
Irish Moss, 116
"Is This Love," 95, 215, 268
Isaacs, Gregory, 139
Island Logic, 184, 190
  in estate affairs, 185, 189
Island Records, 2, 11, 18, 20, 48, 50, 60–61, 76–77, 100, 166, 254
  founding of, 259–260
  heads of, 227
  Marley, Bob, on, 260
  in music business, 56
  reggae and, 260
  signing to, 103, 189
  Tuff Gong Records International and, 138
Island Studios, 255
Isolation, 94
Israel
  twelve tribes of, 60, 63–64, 106

"Israelites," 19
Issel, Joseph, 155
"It Hurts to Be Alone," 10

Jackson, Al, 165
Jackson, Chuck, 90
Jackson, Michael, xvi
Jackson, Vivian "Yabby," 69
JAD Records, 15, 16
Jaffe, Lee
  in the Wailers, 33–36
Jagger, Mick, 41, 70, 162, 258, 273, 277
"Jah Lives," 105, 106, 206
Jamaica
  boxing in, 71
  discos in, 74–75
  elections in, 222
  government of, 45, 60, 93–94, 99–100
  gun laws in, 87–88
  marijuana in, 52–53
  militant artists in, 277
  music of, 212–213, 282
  music volume in, 54–55
  police in, 84
  population of, 48–49
  poverty in, 46
  Rastafarians in, 105–106
  R&B in, 90–91
  record sales in, 54
  session fees in, 56
  sound systems in, 262
  tourism in, 100
  unemployment in, 99–100
Jamaica Labor Party, 150–151
  of Seaga, Edward, 106
Jamaican Court of Appeals, 189
Jamaican Trade Union Movement, 222
"Jamming," 118, 215
  message of, 123
Jazz, 263
Jefferson Airplane, 37
Jehovah's Witnesses, 47
Job's Nite Spot, 226
Jobson, Diane, 130–131
  on Rastafarianism, 132
Jobson, Dickie, 20
Johnson, Harry, 85–86
Johnson, Robert, 51
Jones, Elvin, 80
Jones, Jo, 257

Jordan, Louis, 209
"Judge Not," 13, 165, 215, 263
  release of, 102, 144
"Jump Nyabingi," 139
Just Be Nice (Bunny Wailer), 284

Kadengu, Job, 226, 230–231
Kapuscinski, Ryszard, 207
Kaya, 89
  goals of, 268
  recording of, 267
"Kaya," 118
Kelso, Beverly, 7, 118, 165–166
Kennedy, Clive, 177
Khouri, Paul, 15
Khouri, Robert, 177
Khourie, Ken, 262
King, B.B., 240
King, Ben E., 90
King Crimson, 265
King Records, 264
King Tubby. *See* Pablo, Augustus
King Tubby Vs. The Upsetter, 71–72
Kingston
  poverty in, 45, 46
  violence in, 75
Kingston Max Field Park Ethiopian Church,
  157–158
"Kinky Reggae," 38
Kirk, Roland, 111
Kong, Leslie, 262, 265, 266, 270
Krasilovsky, M. William, 197
Ku Klux Klan, 127
Kuti, Fela, 216

"La Bamba," 257
Last Tango in Paris, 29
"Legalize It (And I'll Advertise It)" (Peter
  Tosh), 56, 272, 273
Legalize It (Peter Tosh), 272, 289
Legend, 137, 181–182, 254
Lennon, John, xvi
Leslie, Alec, 111, 113
Levy, Anthony, 187
Levy, Morris, 195
Lew-Lee, Lee
  on Marley's death, 174, 175
Lewis, Amanda, 237
Lewis, Smiley, 264
Lil' Kim, 237

Lindo, Earl "Wire," 169, 271
  on composition, 295
  on death, 294
  on "Redemption Song," 295–296
"Little Sheila" (Laurel Aitken), 261
Live!, 267
"Lively Up Yourself," 113, 240
Livingston, Bunny, 7–8, 13–14, 34, 37, 118,
  255–256, 272, 279
  arrest of, 18
  on Blackwell, Chris, 283
  compositions of, 282
  on dance hall, 285
  on death, 156
  on fame, 283
  leaving the Wailers, 89, 289
  on Mandela, Nelson, 281
  on reggae, 284, 285
  session gigs of, 287–288
  songs of, 280
Lloyd, Jah, 142
Lucky Dube, 211

Maal, Baaba, 210, 254
Mad Cobra, 234
Madison Square Garden, 5, 161
  gigs at, 154
Madonna, xvi
Mais, Roger, 223
Makonnen, Lij Ras Tafari. *See* Selassie,
  Haile
Malcolm, Omeriah, 164
"Mama Say" (the Heptones), 86
Mambo, 211
"Man From Wareika" (Rico), 121
Mandela, Nelson, 280
  Livingston, Bunny, on, 281
Manhattan Center
  gigs at, 42
Manley, Michael, 49, 61, 99, 171, 292
  campaign slogans of, 108
  Castro, Fidel, and, 100
  at concerts, 107
  Gun Court of, 87
  on Jamaican music, 218
  on Marley, Bob, 150
  at Marley's funeral, 158
  People's National Party of, 106
  politics of, 94
  on protest music, 222–223

on Rastafarianism, 220–221
on revolution, 219–220
Seaga, Edward, and, 211
Tosh, Peter, and, 273
Marcus Garvey (Burning Spear), 66
Marijuana, 18, 21–24, 40–41, 105, 156,
    181
cocaine and, 213
in Jamaica, 52–53
Marley, Bob, on, 108, 134, 204
Tosh, Peter, on, 274
"Mark of the Beast" (Peter Tosh), 272
Marley, Bob
on Africa, 132
on Bible, 108
birth of, 13, 101, 164
Blackwell, Chris, on, 140
cancer and, 153
on capitalism, 100–101
on childbirth, 183
comics on, 246–253
death conspiracy of, 141, 143
death of, 139, 141, 155
on dreadlocks, 133–134
embalming of, 155
estate of, 181–183
family life of, 101–102
funeral of, 157–160, 178
Garrick, Neville, on, 212
on Garvey, Marcus, 133
on home life, 98
image of, 239
on Island Records, 260
on isolation, 94
on life, 115–116
on lyrics, 203–204
Manley, Michael, on, 150
on marijuana, 108, 134, 204
marriage of, 10–11, 137
popularity of, 177
on race, 151
on reggae, 162–163
shooting of, 216
as songwriter, 145
Marley, Cedella (daughter)
birth of, 4–5
design company of, 236–238
talents of, 231
Marley, Damien "Jr. Gong" (son), 233
talents of, 231

Marley, Julian (son), 233
    Marley, Stephen, on, 235
Marley, Ky-mani (son), 233–234
Marley, Norval Sinclair (father), 164
Marley, Rita (wife), 13, 97, 154–155, 181,
    254, 271, 283
in Bob Marley and the Wailers, 89
charges against, 192
on childbearing, 5
in Delaware, 4
distribution deals of, 130
on estate affairs, 184–185
lawsuits against, 198
marriage of, 10–11, 137
on royalties, 194
shooting of, 172, 216
in the Soulettes, 10–11
touring with, 113
in The Wailers, 3
Marley, Robbie (son), 233
Marley, Rohan (son), 231–232, 233
Marley, Sharon (daughter)
talents of, 231
Marley, Stephen (son), 6, 233
    on Marley, Julien, 235
    as producer, 234–235
    on Rastafarianism, 236
    talents of, 231
Marley, Steven (son)
talents of, 231
Marley, Ziggy (son), 142, 233, 280
birth of, 4–5
childhood of, 5–6
on estate affairs, 183
talents of, 231
Marley and Me (Taylor), 174
Marley Boys Inc.
formation of, 233
lawsuits against, 198
Marriage, 137–138
    Dodd, Coxsone, on, 10–11
Martyn, John, 65–68, 74
Marvel Comics, 210
Marvin, Junior, 169, 271, 296–298
Marxism, 152–153
Matta-Clarke, Gordon, 20
Max's Kansas City, 31
Mayfield, Curtis, 101
MCA, 184
bids by, on estate, 189–190

Byles, Louis, on, 186–187
ownership shares offered by, 185
McCalla, Nate
    Dodd, Coxsone, and, 195
McCook, Tommy, 8
McGregor, Freddie, 130
McIntosh, Peter. *See* Tosh, Peter
McPhatter, Clyde, 41
Melodisc, 261
Melody Maker, 73
The Melody Makers, 6, 142, 238
    lineup of, 231
Menstruation, 77
Mento, 219
Meringue, 101
Micron Records, 69–70
Middle passage, 218
The Mighty Mighty Bosstones, xii
Miller Brewing Co., 192–193
Mills, Denise, 225, 227
M.K. Shine, 234
"Mockingbird" (Inez and Charlie Foxx), 265
Money Talks (film), 233–234
Monk, Thelonius, 80
Morgan, Derrick, 287
Moriah, Abraham
    at Marley's funeral, 160
Motown
    Tuff Gong and, 130
MOVE trials, 127
Movin' on Up (film), 233–234
Mowatt, Judy, 130, 154–155, 271, 283
    in Bob Marley and the Wailers, 89
    on culture, 151
    on teargas, 229
    touring with, 113
"Mr. Brown," 215
Murray, Juggy, 265
"My Boy Lollipop" (Millie Small), 19, 254,
    264–265
Mystic Man (Peter Tosh), 273

NAACP, 124, 125
Nascimento, Milton, 280
Nash, Johnny, 14, 18, 103, 145, 167
    on tour, 15
National Arena
    gigs at, 106
Natty Dread, 11, 103, 143, 169, 208–209
    reviews of, 123

"Natty Dread," 240
Nelson, Ricky, 101
New Jewel Party, 171
The New York Dolls, 42
"Nice Time," 15
Nine Miles Inc., 233
Niyabingi, 147–148, 156
    on death, 156
Nkomo, Joshua, 228
Nkrumah, Kwame, 125
No Doubt, xii
"No Woman No Cry," xix, 38, 138, 222, 228,
    241
"None a Jah Jah Children No Cry" (Ras
    Michael), 80, 86
Norman, Jimmy, 15

"O Carolina," 261
"Oh Bumba Klaat" (Peter Tosh), 273
Oja
    on reggae, 151
Olatunji
    at Marley's funeral, 159–160
"One Cup of Coffee," 209
"One Drop," 8, 268
"One Love," xix, 12, 118, 215, 282
One Love concert, 178, 211, 216
One Vibe, 130
Operation Friendship, 90
"Oppressor Song," 259
Order of Merit, 221–222
Ortner, Charles
    on estate affairs, 190

Pablo, Augustus, 55
    studio of, 69
Paladium
    gigs at, 96
Parker, Sarah Jessica, 237
Partridge, Robert, 227
Patra, 234
Patrick, Kentrick "Lord Creator," 263
Patterson, Secco, 7, 102, 114, 172, 271,
    297
    on Selassie, Haile, 105
Peace Concert, 272, 273
    Tosh, Peter, at, 275–276
People's National Party, 172
    of Manley, Michael, 106
Perkins, Wayne, 268

Perry, Lee "Scratch," 11, 18, 55, 167, 270, 282, 287
  Bangs, Lester, and, 71–72
  Family Man and, 287–288
  role of, 91
  studio of, 53–54, 69
Phillips, Minion, 153
Picket, Wilson, 90, 258
The Pioneers, 50
Planno, Mortimo, 13, 14, 16
  influence of, 149, 200
The Platters, 91
Port Royal, 26
Power Station, 9
Presley, Elvis, xvi, xviii, 101–102
Professor Longhair, 164
The Prophets, 69
Public Enemy, xii
"Put It On," 13, 256, 257, 265
Pyfrom, Al, 15

Race
  Marley, Bob on, 151
Rahasimanana, Paul-Bert, 210
Rainbow Theatre
  gigs at, 96
Ramdeem, 149–150
Randy's Record Shop, 66
Randy's Studios, 66
Ranglin, Ernest, 254
Rap, 212
Ras Joe
on death, 156
Ras Michael and the Sons of Negus, 79, 80–81, 86
  Simon, Peter, and, 82
"Rastafarian Chant," 259
Rastafarianism, xii, 6, 13, 21, 39, 93, 170, 200
  Bongo-U on, 146
  celebrations of, 75–76
  dialect of, 147
  diet of, 147
  on "Exodus," 108
  Garvey, Marcus, and, 201–202
  on hair, 44–45, 148
  in Jamaica, 105–106
  Jobson, Diane, on, 132
  Manley, Michael, on, 220–221
  Marley, Stephen, on, 236
  music and, 204

  philosophy of, 37, 43, 47, 59, 104–105, 111–112, 152
  on revolution, 60
  rituals of, 146–147
  Selassie, Haile, and, 208
  sexuality of, 77
  training for, 128–129
  view of women, 129–130
Rastaman Vibrations, 103, 139, 145, 169, 297
  success of, 267
R&B
  in Jamaica, 90–91
"Rebel Music," 38, 99
Red Stripe, 138
Redding, Otis, 41, 52, 101
Reddy, Helen, 52
"Redemption Song," xix, 149–150, 200, 241, 245
  Anderson, Al, on, 293–294
  Lindo, Earl "Wire," on, 295–296
Reed, Lou, 32
Reggae, xii, 93, 218
  bass in, 285–286
  CBS Records and, 61
  current state of, 269
  deejay stars in, 55
  derivations of, 103
  direction of, 203
  drummers in, 257
  exposure of, 15, 61
  globalization of, 223–224
  goals of, 123
  in Grammys, 233
  Island Records and, 260
  Livingston, Bunny, on, 284, 285
  Marley, Bob, on, 162–163
  in Miami, 232–233
  musicianship in, 266
  Oja on, 151
  origins of, 44, 201–202
  politicians and, 275
  popularity of, 96, 232
  qualities of, 37
  revolutionary nature of, 219, 224
  "roots," 209
  royalties and, 50
  Tosh, Peter, on, 279
  Turner, Teresa, on, 152–153
Reggae Boys, 288
"Reggae On Broadway," 17

Reggae Sunsplash festival, 280
Reid, Duke, 262
Reid, Owen, 297
Reid, Vic, 223
"Reincarnated Soul," 259
Revectoring, 196
Richards, Keith, 81, 258, 277
"Road Block," 33
Robinson, Smokey, 258
Rock & Roll Hall of Fame, 162–163
Rock 'N' Groove (Bunny Wailer), 284
Rock steady, 19, 55
  defining, 219
  ska and, 282
Rodney, Winston, 66
Rolling Stone (magazine), 53, 73, 144
The Rolling Stones, 41, 42, 203, 273, 277
  in Studio One, 255
Romeo, Max, 71, 286
Roots, 75
Roy and Millie, 264
Royalties
  in reggae, 50
  of the Wailers, 8
Ruby, Jack, 66
  on recording, 67
"Rude Boy," 13, 149
Rude boys, 51
Rufaro Stadium, 226
  Carter, Mick, on, 227
Ruffing, Bruce, 287
"Rule Them Rudie," 13, 149
Rumba, 211
"Runaway Girl" (U Roy), 70
Rundgren, Todd, 32
"Running Away," 156
Ruskin, Mickey, 31

Santana, Carlos, xvii
Savane, Vernal, 156
Schomburg, Arthur A., 124
Schomburg Research Study Center, 124
School, 90
"Screw Face," 270
Seaga, Edward
  Jamaica Labor Party of, 106
  Manley, Michael, and, 211
  at Marley's funeral, 158, 159
Security Merchant Bank
  in estate affairs, 186

Selassie, Haile, 47, 49, 94, 116, 141, 143,
    147, 201–202, 207, 212, 281
  Garvey, Marcus, on, 208
  Patterson, Secco, on, 105
  philosophy of, 105
  Rastafarianism and, 208
  speeches of, 97
"Selassie I Is the Temple," 150
Senagalese Delegation, 152
Sense less (film), 233–234
"Sexual Healing" (Marvin Gaye), 139
Shabba Ranks, 234
Shakespeare, Robbie, 273
Shanachie Records, 284
Shang Records, 233–234
Sharpe, Sam, 141
Shearer, Hugh, 150–151
Shirley, Roy, 264
"Simmer Down," 2, 13, 200, 282
  success of, 10
Simon, Kate, 111, 113
Simon, Peter, 76, 78, 79, 81
  at Grounation, 81, 84
Simpson, Nicole, 174
Simpson, O.J., 174
Sims, Danny, 14, 17
Sinclair, John, 47
Sister Nancy, 139
Ska, 102, 193–194, 269
  defining, 219
  emergence of, 264
  origins of, 209
  rock steady and, 282
The Skatalites, 8, 209, 286
"Slave Driver," 266
Slave trade, 217–218
Small, Millie, 2, 19, 91–92
  voice of, 264
"Small Ax," 150
"Smile Jamaica," 107
Smile Jamaica concert, 172, 178
  Green, Cherry, 3, 7
Smith, Patti, 32
Smith, Slim, 287
Soccer, 231
Songs of Freedom, 166
Songwriting, 92
Sony Corp.
  legal dealings with, 193–197
"Soon Come" (Peter Tosh), 273

Soukous, 211

"Soul Rebel," 17

Soul Rebels, 167

The Soulettes, 3

 Marley, Rita, in, 10–11

Sound systems

 in Jamaica, 262

Sounds (magazine), 117

Spencer, Neil, 126

Springsteen, Bruce

 gigs with, 31–32

St. Croix, Stephen, 196

Starlite, 261

"Starvation on the Land" (Nadine
 Sutherland), 130

Stax Records, 165

Steel band, 101

Steffens, Roger, xix–xx, 188

Steinberg, David, 186

"Stepping Razor," 149

Stevens, Cat, 22, 168

"Stir It Up," 18, 103, 145, 167, 240,
 257

Streisand, Barbra, 103, 203

Studio One, 13, 282

 Dodd, Coxsone, at, 194–195

 recording with, 6–12

 Rolling Stones in, 255

Studio One Records

 Dodd, Coxsone, at, 6–7

Studio Two

 the Wailers in, 256

Sue Records, 265

Super Beagle

 on Jamaican music, 213–214

"Superstition," 43

Survival, 95, 139

"Survival," 162, 202

Sutherland, Nadine, 130

Swank (magazine), 53

SWAPO, 152

Taj Mahal, 103

Taylor, Don, 106, 107, 116

 on Marley's death, 141, 174–175

 shooting of, 172, 216

"Teenager In Love," 9

The Teenagers, 7

Tekere, Edgar, 226, 230

"Thank You Lord," 166

"The Aggrovators Meet the Revolutionaries"
 (The Meditations, Culture), 121

"Them Belly Full," 99

Third World, 93

 social phenomenon in, 217–218

Third World Peace Medal, 152, 216

Thomas, Lowell, 76

Thomson, Dennis, 227

"Three Little Birds," 206, 241

Toots and the Maytalls, 73, 103, 201

Tosh, Peter, 3, 8, 13–14, 34, 37, 56, 118, 139,
 166, 258, 288

 on death, 156

 on Jamaican music, 213

 leaving the Wailers, 89, 289

 Manley, Michael, and, 273

 on marijuana

 murder of, 206

 on reggae, 279

 signature of, 57

 on United Nations, 275

Tourism, 215

Traffic, 19, 22, 168, 265

"Trenchtown Rock," 25, 36, 150, 155

 lyrics of, 162

 protest elements of, 222

The Trip (Melody Makers), 142

Trojan, 50, 61

Tuff Gong Records International, 127–128,
 142, 203, 238

 Island Records and, 138

 Motown and, 130

 motto of, 138–139

 studio of, 129

"Turn The Light Down Low," 118

Turner, Teresa

 on reggae, 152–153

Twelve Tribes organization, 129

 Gad, Vernon Carrington, on, 149

"Twist Baby" (Owen Grey), 263

U Roy, 70

 innovations of, 212

UB–40, 241

U.K. Privy Council, 186

 in estate affairs, 185, 189–190

United Nations

 Tosh, Peter, on, 275

Universal Negro Improvement Association,
 104, 124

Universal Studios Florida
    lawsuits against, 197–198
Uprising, 135, 139, 145
    influences of, 268
The Upsetter. *See* Perry, Lee "Scratch"

The Village Voice, 74
Vinyl, 212
Virgin Records, 70, 280

Wail 'M' Soul 'M,' 166
Wailer, Bunny. *See* Livingston, Bunny
The Wailers, 25
    Blackwell, Chris, and, 266–267
    Cayman Music and, 192
    in Central Park, 37
    current lineup of, 297
    diet of, 112
    disbanding of, 89
    early recordings of, 194–195
    early repertoire of, 9
    European tour of, 96
    Family Man in, 290
    formation of, 13–14, 102–103
    free concerts of, 106
    Gaye, Marvin, and, 33–36
    Griffiths, Marcia, in, 89
    instrumental backing of, 142
    interviewing, 39–41
    lineup of, 14
    Livingston, Bunny, in, 288
    Livingston, Bunny, leaving, 89
    at Manhattan Center, 42
    Marley, Rita, in, 3, 89
    media response to, 2
    Mowatt, Judy, in, 89
    musical development of, 10
    royalties of, 8–9
    signing, 20
    in Studio 2, 256
    Tosh, Peter, leaving, 89
    touring with, 111
    vocal stylings of, 166
Wailin' Soul, 102
The Wailing Rudeboys, 7
The Wailing Wailers. *See* The Wailers
"Waiting In Vain," 120
"Wake Up and Live," 202

Walker, Clawrence
    in estate affairs, 190–191
Walker, Jeff, 173
Walker, T-Bone, 297
Walters, Ricky, 142
Wanted Dead or Alive (Peter Tosh), 273
"War," 97, 151–152, 222
"War in Babylon" (Max Romeo), 71
Warhol, Andy, 31
WEA International, 13
"We'll Meet" (Roy and Millie), 264
"What A Plot" (Melody Makers), 142
"What Am I Living For?", 41
What's Goin' On, 33
White, Timothy, 172, 208
    on West Indian record business, 261
"Who Feels It Knows It," 256
Williams, Clinton, 71, 74
Willington, Rupert, 66
Willoughby, Neville, 14
Wills, 185–186
Wilson, Delroy, 287
Wilson's Heartbeat Records, 9
Winecarnes, 72
Wonder, Stevie, 43, 224
"Wonderful World, Beautiful People" (Leslie
    Kong), 265
Word Sound & Power, 273
    on tour, 273–274
"Work," 126
Worldwide Church of God, 178

Yellowman, 139
Yesehey, Abouna, 157
"You Poured Sugar On Me," 15
Youths Professional, 288

ZANLA, 225
ZANU, 152
Zimbabwe
    concert in, 210, 228–229
    freedom of, 170
    teargas in, 229
    turmoil in, 225
"Zimbabwe," 162, 202, 222
    impact of, 152
"Zion Train," 126
Zolt, Marvin, 186